IDIOT'S GUIDES.

AS EASY AS IT GETS!

Options Trading

by Ann Logue

ALPHA

A member of Penguin Random House LLC

Publisher: Mike Sanders
Associate Publisher: Billy Fields
Senior Acquisitions Editor: Brook Farling
Development Editor: Rick Kughen
Cover Designer: Lindsay Dobbs
Book Designer: William Thomas
Compositor: Ayanna Lacey
Proofreader: Amy Borrelli
Indexer: Tonya Heard

As always, to Rik and Drew.

First American Edition, 2016
Published in the United States by DK Publishing
6081 E. 82nd Street, Indianapolis, Indiana 46250

Copyright © 2016 Dorling Kindersley Limited
A Penguin Random House Company
16 17 18 19   10 9 8 7 6 5 4 3 2 1
001-285168-SEPTEMBER2016

Published in the United States by Dorling Kindersley Limited.

IDIOT'S GUIDES and Design are trademarks of Penguin Random House LLC

ISBN: 9781615648627
Library of Congress Catalog Card Number: 2015948635

Note: This publication contains the opinions and ideas of its author(s). It is intended to provide helpful and informative material on the subject matter covered. It is sold with the understanding that the author(s) and publisher are not engaged in rendering professional services in the book. If the reader requires personal assistance or advice, a competent professional should be consulted. The author(s) and publisher specifically disclaim any responsibility for any liability, loss, or risk, personal or otherwise, which is incurred as a consequence, directly or indirectly, of the use and application of any of the contents of this book.

Trademarks: All terms mentioned in this book that are known to be or are suspected of being trademarks or service marks have been appropriately capitalized. Alpha Books, DK, and Penguin Random House LLC cannot attest to the accuracy of this information. Use of a term in this book should not be regarded as affecting the validity of any trademark or service mark.

DK books are available at special discounts when purchased in bulk for sales promotions, premiums, fund-raising, or educational use. For details, contact: DK Publishing Special Markets, 345 Hudson Street, New York, New York 10014 or SpecialSales@dk.com.

Printed and bound in the United States of America

idiotsguides.com

Contents

Appendixes

Introduction

Options are powerful tools for managing financial assets. They can be used to manage risk, generate income, and make money. They're also complicated. Let's get that upfront. As a result, too many investors shy away from options because they confuse "complication" with "risk." Others are led astray by advisers who take advantage of the complication to recommend high-commission, low-return strategies. It's unfortunate, but it happens.

Because options are complicated, though, they are an ideal topic for a book like this. Here, I break down the terminology and function of options to help you understand how you can use them to manage risk and to make money.

An option is a contract that gives you the right to buy or sell something at a predetermined price on a predetermined future date. You are not obligated to exercise the contract, so you won't unless it is to your advantage to do so. Most options are not exercised.

It sounds like a goofy thing, doesn't it? It sounds like something that's not quite real, not quite practical, and possibly sketchy, doesn't it? Perhaps it sounds like something that's used by financial people just to confuse the rest of us. However, options have real value.

Suppose you think about an option in another way: as insurance. Your car insurance policy gives you the right, but not the obligation, to file an accident claim up to the amount of value of the car while the policy is in force. You don't have to file a claim, and it might not be worth your while to even file it if you do have a minor accident that will cost less to repair than to cover your deductible. And yet, that policy has real value to you even if it expires unused.

An option is a form of insurance. It is written on the value of an underlying asset, such as a share of stock, a market index, or a foreign currency. Some people buy options to insure against an unfavorable price change.

Some people sell options to bet that the price change won't be favorable. They are not bad people. Instead, they are providing the insurance. In a same way, your car insurance company is betting that you won't get into an accident so that it can keep the premiums you pay each month.

The more likely you are to get into an accident, the higher car insurance costs. Parents of newly licensed teenage drivers know this well! And the more likely an option is to be exercised, the higher its cost will be.

Traders who buy options for their insurance value are known as hedgers. Those who provide the insurance are known as speculators who are looking to profit from price changes in the options.

Speculators aren't bad folks because they want to profit. The presence of speculators ensures that there's a healthy market for options. That, in turn, ensures that prices are fair. All this trading gives everyone—inside and outside of the market—important information about the value of underlying assets, the amount of volatility in the market, and the outlook for prices over different time periods.

Your interest in options might be to hedge, to speculate, or to understand the price-discovery function. This book will give you information and ideas so that you can use the options market to fit your needs.

How This Book Is Organized

I've divided the book into a few parts:

Part 1, Introduction to Options Trading, covers basic terminology and operations of options. This segment of the financial market has its own language, borrowed heavily from calculus and Greek. It's not difficult, just different; the material here will give you a great basis to begin a trading plan that suits your needs.

Part 2, Options Valuation and Trading Strategies, reviews the factors that affect the price of an option and introduces the basic uses of puts and calls for both the hedger and the speculator. Armed with this knowledge, you'll know how to use puts and calls to benefit your portfolio.

Part 3, Advanced and Synthetic Strategies, goes into detail on some of the ways that options can be used to hedge certain types of positions, make complicated speculative bets, and mimic the performance of other financial assets. You might never use this material, or you might find it unbelievably useful as you design your trading plan.

Part 4, The Business of Trading, discusses research, taxes, and trade planning from the perspective of an options trader. Whether you use options a little or a lot, this information can help you improve your overall approach to the financial markets so that you are better able to reach your goals, whatever they may be.

At the back of the book I've shared a glossary of common terms and an appendix of resources for further study.

Extras

Throughout the book, you'll find these types of sidebars:

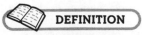 **DEFINITION**

These sidebars contain explanations of words and phrases commonly used in options trading.

DID YOU KNOW?

This is a bit of trivia or background information that may help you understand the information in the chapter better.

MARKET MAXIM

These sidebars contain helpful words of wisdom about the financial markets as well as refreshers of key points.

TRADING TIP

Here's a little extra, but handy, bit of advice for applying the information just covered.

WARNING

Take heed. The information here might save you a lot of time, money, and headache. And that's good, yes?

Acknowledgments

There are so many people I need to thank for their help. Linda Brink, Rik Lantz, and Baptiste Lecomte assisted in pulling the manuscript together. Russell Rhoads and Jaclyn Schuler of the Chicago Board Options Exchange brought me up-to-date on some of the changes in the industry. Brianna Vallesky and Joel Elconin of the Benzinga Premarket Prep show put out a call for questions about options to their listeners. George Avidon of *The TradeXchange,* Mark Longo of *The Options Insider,* Erika Olson, Brian Overby at TradeKing, and Richard Sandor gave me great insight about the day-to-day life of an options trader. The staff at the library of the University of Illinois at Chicago helped me track down some historic trading manuals, and the amazing organizers and attendees of FinCon 2015 shared a lot of ideas and enthusiasm. Marilyn Allen brought me together with Brook Farling of Alpha Books to make it all possible. Thank you, everyone!

Special Thanks to the Technical Reviewer

Idiot's Guides: Options Trading was reviewed by an expert who double-checked the accuracy of what's presented here to help us ensure learning about options trading is as easy as it gets. Special thanks are extended to Gregory Clay.

Gregory is a registered investment adviser, successful trader, and financial writer who shares profitable advice with those who consider themselves novice investors. He loves short-term, low-risk, high-profit trades, in particular option trading. He has a wide range of experience in the investment industry, including an extensive track record of using fundamental and technical investment analysis to increase the probability of profitable trades and minimize risks. He's a regular contributor to several high-level investment services and utilizes a practical application of investment analysis to provide actionable information to active investors. Learn more at theoptionplayer.com.

Introduction to Options Trading

Options are powerful tools in the financial world. They give the holders the right, but not the obligation, to buy or sell an asset in the future at a price determined today. They are used as insurance and as a source of speculative profits. The value is derived from the value of an underlying asset or security, but it is not identical to the value of that asset or security.

Options come with their own set of vocabulary and procedures that are important to know before using them. Chapter 1 covers the very basics, Chapter 2 looks at reading price quotes and placing orders, and Chapter 3 explains how the exchanges and other institutions work. Chapter 4 reviews the mathematics behind options, a key factor needed to value them. Even if the math is more than you had in school, it influences popular trading strategies and is used in discussions of options. Don't worry, you can pick it up.

All About Options

An option is nothing more than a choice. It's a word we use a lot. What *option* would you like for your side dish—the fries or the salad? The movie *options* this weekend are rom-com or sci-fi. The skirt comes in two color *options*—red and black. Our day camp has the *option* of after-care for $10 a day.

In finance, an option gives you the choice between making a trade or not making a trade. Maybe you want to buy a stock but you want to see what news the company announces first. A call option lets you set a price today and gives you the choice of walking away if you change your mind, for whatever reason. This gives them value as tools for making money and tools for insurance.

In This Chapter

- Why we have options
- Basic definitions
- How options operate
- How options are valued

What Are Options?

An *option* is a contract that gives the holder the right, but not the obligation, to buy or sell an asset at an agreed-upon price at any time before an agreed-upon date in the future. This relatively simple contract can be used to help people generate income, buy insurance against money-losing price movements, or speculate on price changes.

An option is a *derivative*, which means its value is derived from the value of an *underlying asset*. In contract law, that asset can be anything. On an options exchange, the underlying asset is usually stock or a commodity, but it also can be the value of a market index or interest rate.

Options have been around in some form or another almost since trade began. They are often a part of contracts. For example, suppose you want to buy a new house, but you want to sell your current house first. You may make an offer on the new house with a *sale contingency*, which gives you the right to walk away from the sale if you don't sell your current house. You have the right, but not the obligation, to buy the new house. In exchange, the seller asks you to pay him or her for that right. If you walk away, you may have to pay the seller a few thousand dollars. That's the price of that option.

> **DEFINITION**
>
> A **derivative** is a financial contract that draws its value from the value of another asset. An **underlying asset** is the asset upon which an option's value is drawn—a common stock, market index, commodity future, or even characteristic of the market such as volatility. An **option** is a derivative that gives you the right, but not the obligation, to buy or sell an asset at or before a predetermined future date at a price agreed upon at the time of purchase. A **sale contingency** is an option included in some real estate sales that gives the potential buyer the right to pay money to walk away from the sale if their current house does not sell in a given period of time.

The modern options market was invented in 1973 with the formation of the Chicago Board Options Exchange (CBOE, pronounced either a letter at a time or as *SEE-bow*). With this, options became standardized contracts anyone could trade. They didn't have to be negotiated every time someone wanted the right to buy or sell something.

Why Options Exist

A stock option is similar to a contingency on the sale of a house, but it involves the stock market rather than real estate.

For example, an *MSFT 2017 Mar 39* call gives you the right to buy Microsoft at $39 per share at any time before the expiration date in mid-March 2017. If Microsoft is trading above $39 per share, you can exercise the option and make a quick profit.

Exercising the option gives you the right to buy the shares at a lower price than the market value and then you can turn around and sell the stock in the market at the higher price. If it is selling below $39, you could buy the stock cheaper in the open market. This means the option would be worthless.

Let's take a closer look at why options exist.

Insurance

One of the main reasons people want stock options is for insurance. They want to guarantee they can buy or sell at a specific price, often to protect something they already own. Stock traders had long wanted a way to manage their risks, but it was only the invention of exchange-traded options that made risk management simple and standardized.

People use options to protect the price of an asset they own from falling too low or one they hope to buy from going too high. They are willing to pay a price, known as a *premium*, to obtain this insurance.

Using options as a way to ensure against price changes is known as *hedging*. Those who use options this way are hedgers.

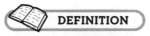 **DEFINITION**

Hedging means to use derivatives to ensure against unfavorable price changes in the underlying asset. A premium is the price of the derivative.

Leverage

Leverage is the use of borrowed money to generate a greater return for your buck. The catch is that increased return comes from increased risk. Because leverage is a central feature of trading in options, you need to know what risk you are taking.

 **DEFINITION**

Leverage is using borrowed money to increase the risk on a trade in the hopes of increasing the return. In the U.K. and countries that use British English, leverage is known as *gearing*, and it works the same way. In engineering, levers and gears allow you to get more power with less force. It's the same in finance.

Options contracts have built-in leverage, which allows the buyers and sellers to make the same profit (or loss) for a lower amount of money than they could by trading in the underlying asset.

Here's how it works: returning to our Microsoft example, if you think the Microsoft stock is going to go up in price, you could buy 100 shares of stock. If the stock is at $43, it would cost $4,300. Or you could buy an option to buy 100 shares with a *strike price* of $45 for a premium of $0.13 each, a total of $13. If the stock increases in price from $43 to $45 before the option expires, your option is out of the money, so you can't exercise it. The stock position would make money, though: $200 (less the commissions).

If the stock goes higher than $45 in price, though, the option becomes much more valuable. At $47, the stockholder has a profit of $400:

$4,700 − $4,300, for a percentage return of $400 ÷ $4,300 = 9.3 percent

The option holder would have a profit of $4,700 − $4,500 = $200 at exercise, but the percentage return would be $200 ÷ 13 = 1,538 percent.

The option holder received a greater percentage return on a smaller amount of initial capital.

But what if Microsoft falls in price to $40? The stockholder has lost $4,300 − $4,000 = $300. The option would expire worthless, so the option holder spent $13 for 100 options that are now worth nothing.

There are two key differences between the stock position and the option position:

- One strategy costs $13 upfront and the other costs $4,300.

- The option can lead to larger losses if the position moves against the *speculator*. The greater potential for return comes with higher risk. Some traders like that; some don't.

DEFINITION

The **strike price** is the price at which an option can be exercised. A **speculator** is a trader who takes risk in anticipation of making a profit. It is the opposite of a hedger, who is trying to reduce risk.

The following tables sum up leverage and option returns.

Initial stock price of $43, exercise price of $45, option premium of $0.13, stock goes to $47, 100 shares.

Strategy	Initial Cost	$ Profit	% Profit
MSFT shares	$4,300	$400	9.30%
MSFT options	$13	$200	1,538%

Initial stock price of $43, exercise price of $45, stock goes to $45, option premium of $0.13, 100 shares.

Strategy	Initial Cost	$ Profit	% Profit
MSFT shares	$4,300	$100	2.32%
MSFT options	$13	$–13	–100%

Initial stock price of $43, exercise price of $45, stock goes to $40, option premium of $0.13, 100 shares.

Strategy	Initial Cost	$ Profit	% Profit
MSFT shares	$4,300	–$300	–6.98%
MSFT options	$13	$–13	–100%

With the options strategy, you have an increased percentage return because you earn the same dollar profit as you would on the stock position for less money. Of course, that assumes your option can be *exercised*. Otherwise, there is no profit.

 **DEFINITION**

An **exercise** is the process of using the option to buy or sell the underlying security.

If the stock price goes down, though, the option limits your loss.

Speculation

In part because of the leverage, many of those who trade in options do so for pure speculation. They are betting on price changes that generate profits and nothing more. These traders like the potential to make large amounts of money relative to the cost of the premium. Of course, this entails risks, but some people are okay with that.

The options exchanges look for products that will appeal to both those looking to hedge and those looking to speculate because a market needs plenty of buyers and sellers with different motivations to operate.

DID YOU KNOW?

Options markets need both hedgers and speculators to function. That not only increases the number of people in the market, but it also helps ensure there will be plenty of people interested in taking different sets of prices and payoffs. When the exchanges consider changing their lineup of options, they consult with both hedgers and speculators.

Basic Options Terminology

Because options are less common than stocks and bonds, the terms used to describe and trade them are not as well known. They aren't hard to learn, though. (In addition to the explanation of the different terms in the text, you can refer to the book's glossary for more information or to refresh your memory.)

Here's one simple bit of terminology before we go on: in market terms, a *bull* market is one going up and a *bear* market is one going down. The origin of these terms is not clear, but many people think it is because bulls charge and bears retreat. Both animals can be nasty if you're on their bad side!

Puts and Calls

An option gives you the right to buy or to sell an asset. The most basic words in the option world are *call* and *put*. The call gives you the right to buy, and the put gives you the right to sell.

Traders buy call options when they expect the market to go up in price because the option allows them to buy the shares at a lower price than they would otherwise. They buy put options when they expect the market to go down.

Puts and calls can be combined in many different ways as part of strategies that take advantage of different market conditions. Each option is based on a specific amount of the underlying asset. Sometimes, people will say their option "controls" 100 shares rather than say it is worth 100 shares. Some options come in mini versions, which control smaller amounts of the underlying asset than regular options. Minis have smaller premiums because of the smaller amounts, which makes them popular with individual traders.

> **MARKET MAXIM**
>
> Here's one way to remember the difference between a call and a put: you *call up* your friend to *put down* your enemy. That is, you buy a call anticipating that the stock goes up in price, and you buy a put anticipating that it goes down.

The person who sells the option is known as the *writer*, and the person who buys it is, of course, the *buyer*.

Bid and Ask

Stocks and options have *bid* prices and *ask* prices. The bid is the price a broker or market maker is willing to pay to buy a security. The broker buys on the bid. The ask is the price the broker or market maker is willing to sell it to someone. The difference between the two is the *bid-ask spread,* and it is a profit to the broker.

The size of the spread is an important market signal. The narrower the spread, the more active the option is and, thus, the easier it is to make the trades. This is especially important for those professional traders using some of the complicated strategies explained later in this book.

Long and Short

In trading terms, to be *long* something is to own it, and to be *short* something is to sell it.

In the world of options, though, *long* and *short* become a bit more complicated because you are also dealing with puts and calls, not a single asset.

For example:

- If you are long a call, you are betting that the price of the underlying asset goes up.

- If you are long a put, you are betting on the price going down.

- If you are short a put, you are also betting that the price of the underlying asset will be above the strike price.

- If you are short a call, you are also betting that the price of the underlying asset will be below the strike price at expiration.

The trader who decides to short an option—in effect, sell it to someone else—is also known as the *writer.*

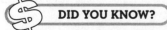 **DID YOU KNOW?**

Underlying is the word used for the asset upon which the derivative is based. For an option on Microsoft, a share of Microsoft stock is the underlying asset and the price of Microsoft is the underlying price. For futures on corn, the underlying asset is the amount and type of corn specified in the contract, and the underlying price is the price of that amount of corn in the market today. In common use, the *underlying* is the price of that asset.

Let's look at some sample transactions.

Trader One thinks Company Uno stock will be trading above $30 at expiration, a month from now.

- The premium for each call option with a $30 strike price is $0.85, so Trader One buys it.

- If Company Uno is trading at $35 at expiration, Trader One can exercise the option and buy shares at $30 each, for a profit of $5 less the $0.85 premium, or $4.15.

- If Company Uno is trading at $30 or less, Trader One is out the $0.85 option.

Trader Two thinks Company Dos will be trading below $40 at expiration, in 2 months.

- The premium for each call option with a $40 strike price is $2.00.

- Trader Two writes (shorts) call options and receives $2 for each option.

- If the price of Company Dos at expiration is $40 or below, Trader Two can keep the $2.

- If the price goes up to say, $44, Trader Two loses $44 − $40 = $4 per share, plus the $2 premium, for a total loss of $2.

Trader Three thinks Company Tres stock will trading below $50 per share at expiration, in 3 months.

- The premium for a put option with a $50 strike price is $0.75.

- If the price of Company Tres at expiration is $47, Trader Three makes $50 − $47 = $3 per share, less the $0.75 premium for a profit of $2.25.

- If the price at expiration is $50 or above, Trader Three is out the premium for a loss of $0.75.

Trader Four thinks Company Cuatro stock will be trading above $60 per share at expiration.

- The premium for a put option with a $60 strike price is $1.02, so Trader Four writes options at $1.02 each.

- At expiration, the stock is at $62 per share, so Trader Four gets to keep the $1.02.

- If the stock were to go to $58, Trader Four would lose $58 − $60 per share, plus the $1.02 premium for a loss of $0.98.

The following table gives you a short summary of what happens to different types of option positions as the underlying asset's price changes.

Basic Put and Call Matrix

Option	Stock Price Goes Up	Stock Price Goes Down
Long call	Profit	Worthless
Short call	Loss	Keep the premium
Long put	Worthless	Profit
Short put	Keep the premium	Loss

You need both buyers and writers in the market. Someone who writes an option is selling it to someone else. The option writer is short, and the buyer is long. And even if everyone had the exact same idea about whether the asset was going to go up or down in price, those who want or need insurance will have to take their positions. Someone who holds an asset might want it to go up in price but need protection against it going down.

The ability to go long and short a few different ways is important to developing options trading cycles.

Strike Price

The *strike price* of an option is the predetermined price where the option can be exercised at any time up until expiration. If the stock pays a dividend or has a split, the price will be adjusted automatically.

A call with a strike price of $30 can be exercised if the underlying price is at $30 or above. At exercise, the trader who wrote the call will receive $30 per share in exchange for a share of the stock. If the trader does not own it, it will have to be purchased at market price. (Some options call for a transfer of the cash value of the underlying asset rather than the underlying asset itself.) The trader who bought the call can buy the underlying for $30, whether it's worth $30.01 or $875 dollars in the market.

A put with a strike price of $20 can be exercised if the underlying price is $20 or less. At exercise, the trader who wrote the put will have to buy the stock at $20 per share, whether it is worth $19.99 or $0.00. The holder of the option receives the difference between the market price and the exercise price.

The following table shows what happens when a call or put expires in the money—that is, when the market price is above the strike price for a call or below the strike price for a put.

	Holder	Writer
Call	Receives cash or security	Delivers cash or security
Put	Delivers cash or security	Receives cash or security

You'll notice that the receiver and deliverer are different for puts and calls, holders and writers. This allows for the structure of many different strategies.

To exercise an option, the holder notifies the clearinghouse, which in then notifies the seller that it is time to settle up. The clearinghouse doesn't know exactly who the buyer and seller of any particular contract are; it assigns the settlement to a random seller.

Expiration Date

The *expiration date* is just that: the day the option is no longer good. Either the holder and writer have to settle up by that date, or the option becomes worthless.

The exercise of the option is handled by the clearinghouse, explained in Chapter 3. You don't have to do anything.

American and European Options

Who knew options had nationalities? Well, they do … of sorts. An *American option* gives the holder the right—but not the obligation—to exercise the option at any point between the purchase date and the expiration date. A *European option* can only be exercised on the expiration date.

> **DID YOU KNOW?**
>
> Before now, the American exchanges only issued American-style options and the European exchanges only issued European-style options. Today, the expiration terms have nothing to do with geography, and exchanges all over the world issue both types. You need to know which type you are trading because it can affect the valuation of the option in question.

Underlying Securities

The first options were written contracts used to cover specific situations, and we still use those customized options all the time. If a hotel charges a cancellation fee, you can think of that as the price you pay for an option on whether or not to pay for the hotel room. If you want the room, it will be there, but you don't have to pay now. If you don't want the room, the hotel receives the option premium.

However, for this book—and for options trading—we're concentrating on exchange-traded options. There are some very specific types of these, tied to different underlying assets.

Commodity Options

The options market developed as an outgrowth of the futures market. The futures markets, in turn, developed to help people hedge and speculate on commodities, especially in the agricultural market.

Commodity options are based on the prices of different agricultural, metal, and energy products. On some exchanges, they are tied to the commodity itself; on others, these are actually *options on futures,* based on the price of a futures contract on that commodity. (A *futures contract* gives someone the obligation to buy or sell at a given price on a given date in the future.)

> **DEFINITION**
>
> **Commodity options** are options listed on such agricultural, industrial, or financial items as corn, cattle, or interest rates. **Options on futures** are options that trade on the underlying value of futures contracts, especially futures on commodities and currencies. This is often the only way to trade options on certain commodities. **Futures contracts** are derivative contracts that give holders the obligation to buy or sell an asset at a specified future date for a specified price.

Equity Options

Equity options—also called *single-stock options*—are options on the common stock of a specific company. They were first issued by the CBOE in 1973, and they are what people usually think of when they think of options trading.

An equity option is an option based on the price of a share of stock. Not all stocks have options attached to them. The exchanges determine whether or not to offer an option, not the companies that issue the stock. If the exchanges don't perceive demand, they won't issue an option.

Most equity options are priced per 100 shares.

Index Options

If you can buy an option on a stock, why not buy one on the entire stock market? That's the idea behind *index options.*

Index options are puts and calls based on the performance of different market indices. There are options on the S&P 500, NASDAQ, and different international markets. You can buy options on some industry-specific indexes, too.

Index options are priced using a multiplier. The contract price times the multiplier, often $100, represents the cash value of each contract.

Interest Rate Options

Interest rate options, sometimes called *yield-based options,* trade on the interest rate on a specific type of bond rather than on the bond price itself.

Interest rate calls become more valuable as interest rates go up, and interest rate puts become more valuable as the rates go down. The settlement is in cash because interest rates aren't securities that can be exchanged.

Keep in mind that bond prices move differently from bond yields. When yields go up, prices go down, and vice versa. Hence, interest rate options move differently from bond prices, too.

Miscellaneous Options

The different options exchanges make money when they develop new types of contracts that meet the needs of hedgers and speculators. As a result, you can find options on different measures of *market sentiment,* different economic outcomes, and even on the weather.

> **DEFINITION**
>
> **Market sentiment** is the overall mood of the market. Is the average trader feeling confident or fearful?

The vocabulary of the overall options market applies to all these options, and the price moves with the underlying.

> **DID YOU KNOW?**
>
> An option is a contract based on the price of another asset. Because of that, options can be drawn up for just about anything for which someone might want to guarantee a price and someone else might want to speculate on that price.

The Least You Need to Know

- An option gives you the right, but not the obligation, to buy or sell an asset on a future date at a price determined today.
- Call options give you the right to buy, and put options give you the right to sell.
- The expiration date is the last date the option can be used, and the strike price is the date at which the asset is bought or sold.
- There are options on many different underlying assets, including stocks, commodities, and interest rates.

CHAPTER 22

How Options Work

Now that you have the basic vocabulary down, it's time to get into the details of how options work. The contracts have lots of different specifications, and the more you understand about them, the more successful you'll be.

The exchanges that handle options have different rules, and they sometimes change the specifications of different contracts. It is very important for you to review the rules for each contract with the exchange itself before you begin. Doing so ensures you won't be surprised if your option doesn't work quite the way you thought it did.

That being said, there is a lot of common ground with different options and different exchanges. Read on for more information.

In This Chapter

- Reading option quotes
- Understanding option premiums
- Managing margin through the mark to market
- Moneyness—it's a thing

Reading the Quotes

The following tables show a series of options price quotes. They list the strike price and the price of the option including the bid-ask spread. The tables also include information on open interest and implied volatility.

Price quotes such as these are known as an *options chain* or *options series*. It is the list of all of the options for a particular expiration date.

> **DEFINITION**
>
> An **options chain** is a list of all the options available on a given security. An **options series** is a list of all the puts and calls on the same underlying asset that have the same exercise price and expiration date.

In the following tables, the *strike price* is the transaction price at which the option may be executed. The contract name, also called the *ticker symbol*, starts with the ticker symbol of the stock, the date of expiration, the type of option, and the strike price.

Expiration: November 21, 2016

Calls							Symbol	Puts						
Strike	Last	Open	High	Low	Change	Volume		Strike	Last	Open	High	Low	Change	Volume
20	0	0	0	0	0	0	IDIO	20	0	0	0	0	0	0
21	7.7	0	0	0	0	0	IDIO	21	0.02	0	0	0	0	0
22	10.8	0	0	0	0	0	IDIO	22	0	0	0	0	0	0
23	0	0	0	0	0	0	IDIO	23	0	0	0	0	0	0
23.5	0	0	0	0	0	0	IDIO	23.5	0	0	0	0	0	0
24	0	0	0	0	0	0	IDIO	24	0	0	0	0	0	0
24.5	0	0	0	0	0	0	IDIO	24.5	0.05	0	0	0	0	0
25	0	0	0	0	0	0	IDIO	25	0.06	0.06	0.06	0.06	−0.09	2
25.5	9.2	0	0	0	0	0	IDIO	25.5	0.01	0.01	0.01	0.01	−0.2	1
26	0	0	0	0	0	0	IDIO	26	0.05	0	0	0	0	0

Expiration: December 20, 2016

Calls							Symbol	Puts						
Strike	Last	Open	High	Low	Change	Volume		Strike	Last	Open	High	Low	Change	Volume
19	0	0	0	0	0	0	IDIO	19	0.31	0	0	0	0	0
20	0	0	0	0	0	0	IDIO	20	0	0	0	0	0	0
21	0	0	0	0	0	0	IDIO	21	0.06	0	0	0	0	0
22	0	0	0	0	0	0	IDIO	22	0	0	0	0	0	0
23	0	0	0	0	0	0	IDIO	23	0	0	0	0	0	0
24	0	0	0	0	0	0	IDIO	24	0	0	0	0	0	0
24.5	0	0	0	0	0	0	IDIO	24.5	0	0	0	0	0	0
25	0	0	0	0	0	0	IDIO	25	0.17	0	0	0	0	0
25.5	0	0	0	0	0	0	IDIO	25.5	0	0	0	0	0	0
26	0	0	0	0	0	0	IDIO	26	0	0	0	0	0	0

Expiration: January 20, 2017

Calls							Symbol	Puts						
Strike	Last	Open	High	Low	Change	Volume		Strike	Last	Open	High	Low	Change	Volume
15	19.3	0	0	0	0	0	IDIO	15	0.02	0	0	0	0	0
16	0	0	0	0	0	0	IDIO	16	0	0	0	0	0	0
17	0	0	0	0	0	0	IDIO	17	0.12	0	0	0	0	0
18	25.52	0	0	0	0	0	IDIO	18	0.18	0	0	0	0	0
19	0	0	0	0	0	0	IDIO	19	0.28	0	0	0	0	0
20	12.5	0	0	0	0	0	IDIO	20	0.07	0.07	0.07	0.07	0.01	1
21	0	0	0	0	0	0	IDIO	21	0.19	0	0	0	0	0
22	0	0	0	0	0	0	IDIO	22	0.1	0	0	0	0	0
23	10.9	0	0	0	0	0	IDIO	23	0.13	0	0	0	0	0
24	8.6	8.6	8.6	8.6	3.45	3	IDIO	24	0.23	0.23	0.23	0.23	0.04	10

Expiration: April 20, 2017

Calls							Symbol	Puts						
Strike	Last	Open	High	Low	Change	Volume		Strike	Last	Open	High	Low	Change	Volume
15	0	0	0	0	0	0	IDIO	15	0.07	0	0	0	0	0
16	0	0	0	0	0	0	IDIO	16	0.1	0	0	0	0	0
17	0	0	0	0	0	0	IDIO	17	0	0	0	0	0	0
18	0	0	0	0	0	0	IDIO	18	0.11	0	0	0	0	0
19	0	0	0	0	0	0	IDIO	19	0.21	0	0	0	0	0
20	12	0	0	0	0	0	IDIO	20	0.2	0	0	0	0	0
21	12.93	0	0	0	0	0	IDIO	21	0.7	0	0	0	0	0
22	13.85	0	0	0	0	0	IDIO	22	0.98	0	0	0	0	0
23	11.2	0	0	0	0	0	IDIO	23	0.44	0	0	0	0	0
24	9.24	0	0	0	0	0	IDIO	24	0.61	0	0	0	0	0

A standard option with the ticker symbol JNJ1721H95-E is broken down as follows:

JNJ   An option on Johnson & Johnson

1721H   With an expiration on August 21, 2017 (month H, the eighth month of the year and the eighth letter in the alphabet)

95   With a strike price of $95

E   European-style

The month of expiration is reported as a letter, as shown in the following table.

Month	Call Expiration	Put Expiration
January	A	M
February	B	N
March	C	O
April	D	P
May	E	Q
June	F	R
July	G	S

Month	Call Expiration	Put Expiration
August	H	T
September	I	U
October	J	V
November	K	W
December	L	X

As new types of options are developed, the ticker symbols have become longer. For example, a weekly option with the ticker symbol JNJ170612C00095000 is broken down as follows:

JNJ   An option on Johnson & Johnson

170612   With an expiration on June 12, 2017

C   Is a call option

00095000   And has a strike price of $95

The next columns in the option chain, moving from left to right, show the last trade price, the bid, the ask, the change in price in dollar terms, and then the change in price in percentage terms.

A note on how volume is reported: the volume number shows the number of options traded in units of 100. The option premium shows the price per option, but you have to buy or sell at least 100. Hence, a volume of 2 means options on 200 shares.

Basics of Orders

The options chain shows you all the available contracts and their price quotes. You can choose:

- The contract you want.
- The type of transaction.
- How you want the order to be executed.

Once you find a put or a call with a strike price and expiration that meet your needs, you place the order. The open interest column reports on how many of these contracts are outstanding, and the *implied volatility* column shows just that—the volatility of the price of the underlying asset based on the current price of the option.

Option Transactions

All of the intricate strategies discussed later in this book use the following four basic transactions to open and close positions:

- A *buy-to-open* transaction gets you a contract to establish a new long position in a put or a call.

- A *sell-to-close* order would close out or end an existing long contract.

- A *sell-to-open* order is used to write a put or a call and to establish a new short position.

- A *buy-to-close* transaction is used to end an existing short position.

Basic Order Types

An options transaction can be executed several different ways, using specifications the trader sets when the order is placed. Almost all brokerage firms handling options allow all customers to set these basic parameters since they meet the needs of an average investor.

Many of these order types are based on prices:

Market orders Market orders are orders to buy and sell at the best price on the exchange at the time the order is placed. These are the most common type of orders.

Limit orders Limit orders are orders to buy or sell only at a specific price or better (higher for a sell order, lower for a buy order). The broker will only execute the order within this restriction. If you place a limit order on a call option at $6 when the option is trading at $8, and the price calls to $6.01, your order will not be executed. Limit orders help enforce discipline, but they might lead to missed opportunities.

Stop orders Stop orders are orders to buy or sell once an option hits a specific price. These are usually entered to limit losses from a position by ordering an automatic close if a particular price is hit. Not only are stop orders used differently than limit orders, but they also continue to be executed if the stop is hit. If you place a stop order of $6 to close out a call position currently priced at $6.50, it will be executed as soon as the price hits $6, even if the order ends up being filled at a worse price.

Stop-limit orders Stop-limit orders are combinations of stop and limit orders. The order is only executed when the stop price is hit. However, the order is only executed at the limit price or better.

Traders also set time limits on their orders:

- *Day orders* will be filled the day they are received and are cancelled if they cannot be filled.

- *Good 'til date* (GTD) *orders* are in place until the date specified, if they cannot be filled earlier.

- *Good 'til cancelled* (GTC) *orders* remain in place until they are filled or until the trader requests it be cancelled.

In addition, a trader can request All *or* None for the order, meaning all or none of the options in the order are bought or sold at the specifications given. Without that qualification, the trader might receive a *partial fill*, meaning only part of the order is filled.

> **MARKET MAXIM**
>
> Prices in financial markets move quickly. The price you see now might be gone in the blink of an eye. Having a range of order types helps you keep the movements in your favor.

Advanced Order Types

Most people who trade options want more control over their orders. That's why some brokerage firms offer additional types of orders that may prove useful:

Contingent orders   Contingent orders are those executed only if the underlying security reaches the specified price. As with stop orders, they will be filled even if the price moves away from the contingent price.

Trailing stop orders   Trailing stop orders start out like stop orders. They are orders to buy or sell once an option hits a specific price. Unlike stop orders, they can be set to move with the market to prevent being exercised when it is no longer advantageous to do so. Trailing stop orders are set as a percentage above or below the option's current market price. If the price moves in a favorable direction, the stop is automatically reset.

One cancels other (OCO) orders   OCO orders are two orders placed together that can be used to automatically close positions when a specified profit or loss target is hit. If one order's stop price is hit, then the other order will be cancelled automatically.

One triggers other (OTO) orders   OTO orders are a combination of two orders placed at the same time. When one is executed, so is the other. For example, if a stop order causes one option position to be closed, another can be opened automatically with the OTO order.

Floor Execution

Almost all market markets work electronically these days, but there are a few exceptions. On the Chicago Board Options Exchange, the VIX (options on market volatility) and SPX (options on the S&P 500 Index) still trade in open outcry pits, with actual human beings on the trading floor in Chicago placing orders to buy and sell.

In addition to the VIX and SPX, some exchanges allow very large trades in single-stock options to be executed through the market maker in person rather than electronically. This might allow for less price disruption in both the option and the price of the underlying asset than a series of large orders sent electronically. It is highly unlikely an individual trader would ever need this service. An institution that wants to use open outcry execution can request it through its broker.

Marking to Market and Margin

Options have built-in leverage. That's good, except the exchange needs to make sure everyone can pay up if necessary when the order to exercise comes around.

You can't place an options trade unless you have money in your account. This is known as *margin*, and it is collateral for your obligations, should you have to meet them. The exact percentage varies with the contract in question, and it is a complicated relationship between the proceeds from writing the option, the value of the option, and the likelihood of the option being exercised.

> **TRADING TIP**
>
> Because margin is complicated, the CBOE maintains a handy margin calculator at cboe.com/tradtool/mcalc/ that will tell you how much cash and securities you must keep in your account for a given options trade.

Every evening after the market closes, the options clearinghouse—the organization that manages money for the exchange—will check the value of each account relative to the value of its option position. This is a process called *marking to market*, and it will determine if there is enough margin to support your position. Depending on whether there is enough margin, one of the following will happen:

- If yes, you are free to continue holding your position into the next trading day.

- If no, you will receive a *margin call*, which is a demand from your broker for money to deposited in your account. If you can't come up with the funds, then your position will be sold.

Moneyness

Yes, *moneyness* is a word—at least in the world of options trading. It is used to describe whether or not an option is *in the money*—or profitable to exercise—relative to the price of the underlying asset. Moneyness has a few different aspects to it.

An option is said to be *in the money* if it is profitable to exercise. It is *out of the money* if it is not profitable. The relationship of the underlying price to the strike price depends on the type of option involved.

In other words, a long call is in the money if the strike price is less than the underlying price. You could make money by exercising the option, taking the underlying asset, and then selling it at a higher price in the market. If the underlying is less than the strike price, then the option is out of the money. Of course, the trader who wrote the option has the opposite situation. The short trader's option will be out of the money when the price of the underlying asset is greater than the strike price and in the money when the price of the underlying asset is less than the exercise.

The situation is reversed for the put position. Let's say a put option has a strike price of $35. If the underlying is trading at more than $35, it would not be profitable to exercise, so the long put position would be out of the money. The long put would be in the money if the underlying were to trade at less than $35. For the short put position, an underlying price of more than $35 would mean the option would not be exercised, so the writer could keep the premium. If the underlying price were to go below $35, though, the option would be exercised and the short position would be out of the money.

The following table offers a neat summary of it all.

The Moneyness of an Option

Position	In the Money	Out of the Money
Long call	U > E	U < E
Short call	U < E	U > E
Long put	U < E	U > E
Short put	U > E	U < E

U = underlying price
E = exercise price

If the strike price and the underlying price are the same, then the option is *at the money*. This is the same whether the option is a put or a call, or whether you are long or short.

Moneyness is not affected by the style of option. Sure, an American option can be exercised at any time, but that doesn't affect how often it is in, out, or at the money.

Open Interest

Open interest is the total number of outstanding options contracts. For the market as a whole, it is used as a measured of sentiment. It is not the same as the number of options traded because many options trades are made to close out existing positions.

Each trader has his or her own open interest, of course. Brokerage firms may set their limits on how many outstanding contracts an account may have based on the amount of margin in the account and the experience of the trader.

Expiration and Exercise

Options aren't in place forever. They expire at regular intervals, creating the need for a set of decisions that go beyond simply whether to buy or to sell. The concepts are related, especially because European-style options cannot be exercised until expiration.

Expiration

First, the *expiration,* sometimes known as the maturity: this is the date on which the option expires. Most options expire on the third Friday of a given month, either in the A.M. or the P.M. However, some high-volume options have expiration dates every Friday. The last time to trade the option is at the close of the market immediately before the option expires. Some options close earlier (the closing time would be specified for the option, so you'd know it before you bought or sold):

- A.M. options stop trading at the close of business on the Thursday before expiration
- P.M. options stop trading at noon Eastern time on the expiration day

Some options are issued on a Monday and close the same Friday. These so-called weeklys take advantage of very short-term moves in the market and they have proven popular.

The *option period,* also called the time to expiration, is the time period that starts with the creation of an option and ends with its expiration.

If you want to maintain the position at expiration rather than exercise the option, you *roll*—that is, you close your open position and simultaneously establish a new position at a different strike price or expiration.

Markets tend to be especially volatile on the third Friday in March, June, September, and December. These are the so-called Quadruple Witching Days, when equity options, index options, stock index futures, and single-stock futures contracts expire simultaneously.

> **(\$) DID YOU KNOW?**
>
> The reason most expirations take place on the third Friday of each month is because that day rarely interferes with any holidays, including Monday holidays when people might take off work the Friday before. This practice ensured there would be enough people at the exchanges and brokerages to handle the paperwork involved with expirations. The convention has stuck even though closing transactions are now handled electronically.

Exercise

To *exercise* is to cash in an option. If you have a call option giving you the right to buy shares of Johnson & Johnson at $100 per share, and the stock is trading at $105, all you have to do is notify your broker that you want to exercise. The exercise happens automatically. Some brokers allow you to turn around and sell the stock immediately, while others require you to wait until the transaction settles.

At expiration, some brokers will automatically exercise any in-the-money (profitable) options you have, and others will not. In almost all cases, automatic exercise is preferable to sending instructions at expiration because everyone forgets important deadlines sometimes.

When it comes time to exercise a given option, the exchange doesn't go back through the records to find out who sold it. Instead, it *assigns* the option, more or less at random, to the brokerage firm involved. This means that broker is responsible for exercising the particular option. The brokerage firm will then assign the exercise to one of its customers, usually at random, but brokers might use different methods to make assignment.

By the way, the vast majority of options expire unexercised. You might never receive an assignment.

Delivery and Settlement

Equity options, and some others, call for *physical delivery,* which means settling an exercised option with the underlying asset. When a call option on common stock is exercised, the writer has to transfer the shares to the option buyer's account. If the writer does not own the stock already, he or she must buy the shares in the open market. Only the actual shares will settle the deal.

With *cash settlement,* the person whose option is profitable receives a cash payment from the person on the other side. This is a common feature of index options. The cash settlement value of an index call option at expiration is the difference between the value of the index and the strike price of the call, multiplied by the multiplier on the option. Here's how that works: suppose an equity index option on the Idiot's 200 Market Index has a multiplier of $100. At expiration, if the index is trading at 561 and the option has a strike price of 541, the cash settlement would be $561 - 541 = 20$; $20 \times \$100 = \$2,000$. That's the amount that will be transferred from the option writer's account to the option owner's account.

Some commodity options and futures require cash delivery from most traders but allow physical delivery for customers in the industry involved. The exchanges actually maintain warehouses and grain silos to make physical delivery possible for someone who does not otherwise have access to grain, or gold, or whatever underlying asset was traded.

Extrinsic and Intrinsic Value

Options have two primary sources of value. The *intrinsic value* is the amount of the option's price that's related to the price of the underlying asset. An option has intrinsic value only if it is in the money because it is the amount that you'd receive if you exercised the option. It may well be zero.

Time value, also known as *extrinsic value,* is the difference between the option's price and the amount that it is in the money. Here's the logic: the amount that an option is in the money is the amount you would receive if you exercised it today. It's the intrinsic value, the hard cash value of the option.

Now, if you're paying more than the intrinsic value of the option, the option is worth more today than what you'd receive if you exercised it. That means if you wait, you might end up with a larger profit or have more time on the insurance value of the option. The time value explains why people sometimes hold onto options even if they are profitable to exercise today.

Options have both extrinsic value and intrinsic value. The more you understand the components of an option's price, the better you can value the option relative to your needs. Valuation is covered in more detail in Chapter 5, but for now, all you need to know is that both time value and intrinsic value come into play.

> **DEFINITION**
>
> **Intrinsic value** is the portion of an option's price attributed to the price of the underlying asset. **Extrinsic value,** also known as *time value,* is the amount of an option's price that's related to the likelihood if it becoming more valuable in the time to expiration. **Parity** is the point at which an option is in the money and has no time value, which usually occurs immediately before expiration.

One additional concept here is *parity*. Parity is the point where an option is in the money but has no time value. Options generally don't reach parity until just before expiration. Weekly options, on the other hand, have almost no time value.

Relationships Among Options

An underlying asset doesn't have just one option. It has a whole range of puts and calls, at different expirations and strike prices. Options traders can find a lot of different ways to play an underlying asset, at a lot of different prices and a lot of different payout possibilities. That, in turn, leads to a range of strategies.

These relationships are described by the options cycle, options series, and options chain. Each has its own structure and its own implications for the market.

Options Cycle

The *options cycle*, also called the *expiration cycle*, is the traditional schedule of expiration dates for a single option. Most options are written for periods that are multiples of three months, but not all options expire on the same months. The options cycle is the pattern of the months on which options contracts expire.

The following table shows the January cycle (JAJO), which has expirations set for January, April, July, and October.

January Cycle

Front Month	Available Expiration Months			
January	Jan	Feb	Apr	Jul
February	Feb	Mar	Apr	Jul
March	Mar	Apr	Jul	Oct
April	Apr	May	Jul	Oct
May	May	Jun	Jul	Oct
June	Jun	Jul	Oct	Jan
July	Jul	Aug	Oct	Jan
August	Aug	Sep	Oct	Jan
September	Sep	Oct	Jan	Apr

continues

January Cycle (continued)

Front Month	Available Expiration Months			
October	Oct	Nov	Jan	Apr
November	Nov	Dec	Jan	Apr
December	Dec	Jan	Apr	Jul

The following table shows the February cycle (FMAN), which has expirations set for February, May, August, and November.

February Cycle

Front Month	Available Expiration Months			
January	Jan	Feb	May	Aug
February	Feb	Mar	May	Aug
March	Mar	Apr	May	Aug
April	Apr	May	Aug	Nov
May	May	Jun	Aug	Nov
June	Jun	Jul	Aug	Nov
July	Jul	Aug	Nov	Feb
August	Aug	Sep	Nov	Feb
September	Sep	Ocy	Nov	Feb
October	Oct	Nov	Feb	May
November	Nov	Dec	Feb	May
December	Dec	Jan	Feb	May

The following table shows the March cycle (MJSD), which has expirations set for March, June, September, and December.

March Cycle

Front Month	Available Expiration Months			
January	Jan	Feb	Mar	Jun
February	Feb	Mar	Jun	Sep
March	Mar	Apr	Jun	Sep
April	Apr	May	Jun	Sep
May	May	Jun	Sep	Dec
June	Jun	Jul	Sep	Dec
July	Jul	Aug	Sep	Dec
August	Aug	Sep	Dec	Mar
September	Sep	Oct	Dec	Mar
October	Oct	Nov	Dec	Mar
November	Nov	Dec	Mar	Jun
December	Dec	Jan	Mar	Jun

After March, of course, you go back to options on the January cycle.

Traders can take advantage of the options cycle to buy options for longer time periods in order to increase the likelihood of making a profit from a given expected event.

Although the introduction of new exchanges and new products has meant the introduction of new expiration schedules, many options traders rely on software that's been programmed based on the traditional schedule, and so it has stuck.

The Least You Need to Know

- The options series gives you a lot of information about prices and trends.
- Orders to buy and sell are placed through brokerage firms.
- At the end of each trading day, profits and losses are noted in each account, a process called mark to market.
- If an option is in the money at expiration, it will be exercised and exchanges for the underlying security, or for cash.

Exchanges, Brokers, and Other Market Institutions

Of course, you'll need a brokerage account to trade options. However, you also will deal with many other institutions that have a critical role in developing options, ensuring that trades clear, and regulating the industry. This chapter gives you an overview of these institutions and how they work together to keep the options markets functioning smoothly.

Keep in mind that the financial services industry has been going through a lot of upheaval in recent years. Tons of mergers, acquisitions, start-ups, and other changes may make some of the information in this chapter outdated almost as soon as I type it, let alone by the time you read it. That's part of the creativity of the industry.

In This Chapter

- The many different options exchanges
- The role of the clearinghouses
- Other organizations handling options
- Brokers who deal with options traders

Pricing and Trading Structures for Options

The main point of competition for many of the exchanges is how they handle orders after the brokers submit them. For the most part, this matters more to an institutional investor than to an individual. Still, it's good to know how orders are handled after the broker submits them, both to understand how the market works and how it might change.

Many years ago, traders used paper notebooks to keep track of orders. Orders are handled electronically now, but the record is still referred to as *the book.*

The Role of Market Makers

Market makers are members of an exchange who agree to place a bid on every order that is entered. Each market maker works with a different set of options. They don't have to place a bid at a price the customer wants, but they do have to be involved in the market. Some market makers are self-employed, most are part of firms that specialize in this aspect of the business, and some are associated with brokerage firms.

> **DEFINITION**
>
> A trader who is in the business of ensuring that there are buyers and sellers for a particular option is known as a **market maker.** If no orders come from the public, the market maker will take the trade. Most market makers then hedge their positions.

Here's what they do: if someone wants to buy a Jan (short for January in standard options lingo) call on XYZ Company, a market maker has to make an offer to sell. The market maker doesn't have to sell at any price, but the offer has to be made.

This is an important function. Market makers ensure there is some liquidity in the market. They ensure someone will take an order and there's a price out there that can be used to determine the value of a given option. Prices carry information, and that helps make the options markets efficient, which means people are willing to turn to it to manage risk. Without the market making function, there would be nothing for speculators to trade.

Most market makers are hedgers rather than speculators because they are taking on risk from their market-making activities. They will make trades elsewhere to protect their business, which is another way they create liquidity.

> **DID YOU KNOW?**
>
> Option pricing is done in cents, which makes the market maker's minimum profit per option just 1 penny. It's a low-margin, high-volume business.

The Order of Trade

Orders come in to the exchanges constantly. There are enough conflicts among them that the exchanges need to set a system to determine which orders are executed first and who pays the exchange.

Here are the different methods exchanges use to handle orders:

Customer priority   If two orders come in at the same price, the customer orders are executed before orders placed by market makers. Market makers pay transaction fees; customers don't.

Maker-taker   Under this model, the market maker—the one who "makes" the orders—pays no transaction fee while the customer—who "takes" the orders—does.

Price-time priority   Orders are given time stamps when they are submitted to the exchange. The order entered earliest at a given price is executed first, and the person placing the order pays the transaction fee.

Pro rata allocation   Orders with the same priority are filled on a proportional basis if they can't be filled completely.

Size allocation   Orders with the same priority are filled largest to smallest.

The transaction fees usually run about $0.20 or $0.30 per lot of 100 options. It's a small fee, but it can add up on large orders or for frequent traders.

Price Improvement

Price improvement means the customer pays less to buy an option or receives more to sell it than the order that was placed. It's a good thing, and some options exchanges promote the ability to receive price improvement as a way to differentiate themselves.

If the market moves as an order is entered, price improvement might occur naturally. Customers placing large orders often want price improvement. In that case, the broker will request it, and the trade will go through an auction process. Market makers can choose to take all or part of the order at a better price.

Price improvement isn't likely on retail orders or even on most institutional orders.

Where to Trade Options

Most options trade on organized exchanges. Unlike stocks and bonds, options are created by the exchanges where they trade and not by the underlying companies. This means the features, benefits, and rules governing different types of options might be specific to the exchange that issued the option. The exchanges were once physical locations in impressive downtown locations, but now they are often nothing more than server farms.

Once a national exchange issues an option, it might be traded on many other exchanges. In exchange lingo, these are *fungible, multiple-listed options*. Some exchanges may have more trading volume, offer better pricing, or allow different order types than others. These differences might matter to your trading strategy or the particular option you want to trade.

> **DID YOU KNOW?**
>
> Once upon a time, the options exchanges were a riot of color and noise, as traders in bright cotton jackets stood in pits on the trading floor to conduct business by hand. This style of trading is known as *open outcry*, and it has mostly disappeared in favor of electronic trading. Some exchanges make open outcry available, and some products seem to trade best this way. However, the number of open outcry floors is dwindling. Some of the strategies and advice you might find in older books on trading no longer work in an electronic world. The new world is less visually interesting but far more efficient.

The first stock options were developed by the Chicago Board Options Exchange (CBOE), and that is still the largest of the exchanges. It's also the default standard for many different explanations of options trading practices. But it is hardly the only one out there.

Options Exchanges in the United States

Exchanges exist all across the United States. Here are the top ones:

BATS Options Market (batsoptions.com)   The *BATS* (Best Alternative Trading System) market was set up to offer better execution for common stock. The company's options exchange, also known as BZX, handles orders on a price-time priority basis. The company has recently announced a new options exchange, EDGX, which accepts orders on a customer priority/pro rata allocation basis. The difference is important to institutions placing large orders via electronic systems, and this is an example of how competition among the exchanges is leading to services that meet the specific needs of some traders.

BOX Options Exchange (boxexchange.com)   This exchange was set up to allow brokers to connect directly with its network. It offers a price-improvement period during the order execution that is designed to mimic the benefits of open outcry trading.

C2 Options Exchange (c2exchange.com)   C2 is an all-electronic exchange started by the CBOE. It uses a price-time order structure.

Chicago Board Options Exchange (cboe.com)   The CBOE is the first and largest of the options exchanges. However, it is no longer the only game in town. The exchange has two key advantages, however:

- It develops most of the option products traded here and on other exchanges.

- It still offers open outcry trading for many of its products, which many in the industry argue allows for better execution of large trades.

Although the CBOE has competition, it continues to set the tone for the rest of the industry.

CME Group (cmegroup.com)   Once known as the Chicago Mercantile Exchange, the CME Group is a holding company for many niche futures exchanges. These exchanges also trade *options on futures,* which are options based on the price of other derivatives contracts. CME Group is comprised of four markets:

- The Chicago Mercantile Exchange, also known as the CME or the Merc, handles options on equity indexes, foreign exchange, and some agricultural commodities.

- The CBOT, or the Chicago Board of Trade, specializes in agricultural options and options on interest rates.

- The New York Mercantile Exchange, or NYMEX, offers options on gas, oil, and other energy commodities as well as some metals.

- COMEX, once known as the New York Commodity Exchange, has options on many different metals contracts.

The Intercontinental Exchange (theice.com)   Also known as ICE, the Intercontinental is owned by the New York Stock Exchange (NYSE) and specializes in energy, metals, and environmental derivatives. It is mostly a futures and physical exchange, but it offers some options, and it handles over-the-counter transactions. ICE also offers contracts on unusual assets and has shown much willingness to experiment.

International Securities Exchange (ise.com)   The International Securities Exchange, or ISE, introduced the first all-electronic options exchange in the United States in 2000. It uses a customer-priority, pro rata (or proportional) market structure. The company also operates a separate options exchange, ISE Gemini, which uses pure maker-taker pricing. Most of the offerings are traditional equity options, but the ISE folks have been willing to experiment with options on such things as cybersecurity.

> ### DID YOU KNOW?
>
> The Chicago Climate Exchange was founded in 2003 to allow for active trading in carbon credits generated by cap-and-trade regulation so market forces could create environmental change. Regulators would allow companies a maximum amount of greenhouse gas emissions. Companies that used less could sell their credits, and companies that used more could buy them, creating a free market approach to a vexing environmental problem. The exchange was set up as a voluntary program in anticipation of forced regulation. But the regulation never happened, and trading dropped to nothing by 2010. The exchange was then acquired by the ICE, where it handles trading in voluntary environmental offsets and waits for regulation to make it a big business.

MIAX Options Exchange (miaxoptions.com)   This is a fully automated exchange that uses a hybrid of transaction charges, maker-taker fees, and rebates in its fee structure. The parent company has plans to open an equity exchange that would specialize in Latin American stocks, which could become a point of differentiation for the options business, too.

NASDAQ OMX (nasdaq.com/options)   NASDAQ, an electronic equity exchange that started life as the National Association of Securities Dealers Automated Quotation System, operates an options exchange in addition to its better-known equity market. NASDAQ specializes in options on foreign currencies and financial assets. The company operates three electronic options exchanges:

- NASDAQ BX has customer priority for retail orders.

- NASDAQ NOM uses a price-time priority structure.

- NASDAQ PHLX uses both electronic and open outcry floor trading for institutional customers.

NYSE Options (nyse.com/products/options)   The venerable NYSE issues options on equities and on different exchange-traded funds. It also has two options exchanges:

- NYSE Amex Options uses a customer priority/pro rata structure.

- NYSE Arca Options uses a price-time priority model. Both have electronic and open outcry models available.

In most cases, your broker will decide on the exchange for the trade based on the order flow on any given day. Some brokers allow customers to direct trades to a specific exchange, although there might be a fee involved.

Over-the-Counter Options

Over-the-counter (*OTC*) *options* do not trade on an organized exchange. Instead, they are issued by brokers and rarely have a secondary market. These are sometimes known as *exotics* because they cover unusual assets or situations, often customized to meet a specific customer's needs.

> **DEFINITION**
>
> **Over-the-counter (OTC) options** are options that do not trade on an organized exchange. They're often customized by a broker to meet a particular customer's needs.

As an options trader, you might never come across an OTC option, but it's nice to know that they exist.

Finding a Broker

Options trades are executed by brokerage firms, and almost all of them handle options trades. However, that doesn't mean just any firm will be able to meet your particular needs. The occasional options trader might not need to shop around, but someone who is day trading options or who plans to make a significant number of trades should check into different features that distinguish options brokers from the rest. The benefits in information and execution could be significant for you.

Some brokers use different brand names for their options trading services than their primary business. For example, TD Ameritrade's options brokerage is known as *thinkorswim*. The difference is usually related to the types of trading platforms (discussed later in this chapter) available to different types of customers.

> **DID YOU KNOW?**
>
> Most brokers allow you to open a free demo account to let you test their services with play money.

How important the different features are depends on your own needs. The following sections highlight different features to help you comparison shop.

Commissions and Trade Execution

Brokerage firms charge commissions to make trades. That's fair, because they have to make money. Traders often fixate on the pretrade commissions different brokers charge, but it is only part of what you pay. You also pay any exchange fees, and then there's the price at which you buy or sell. Would you rather buy at a lower price or pay a lower commission? As a customer, you should look for the lowest overall price, especially if you will be trading options on a regular basis. Commission is just one part of the price.

Many brokers have different fee schedules based on how much money you keep in your account or how many trades you place. Keep that in mind as you check out different firms.

The discussion of the exchanges earlier in this chapter included information about different pricing and priority structures. They often include tradeoffs between, say, paying an exchange fee and receiving priority in execution or getting a better price and having the order executed right away. Brokers must disclose information about trade execution prices and speeds once a quarter, so you can get that information to make comparisons.

> **TRADING TIP**
>
> Some brokerage firms don't charge commissions. That doesn't mean their services are free. They will be passed on to you in other ways, usually in the form of worse execution from their own market makers. When evaluating firms, look at the total cost of trading, and not at any one line item.

Position Limits

Brokerage firms have to manage their own risks, and one way they do this is by setting limits on what customers are able to do in their accounts.

The broker might set a *position limit*, for example, which is the maximum number of open contracts an investor can hold in one account. This might be expressed in terms of number of contracts on one side of the market or in terms of total long or total short delta. If you plan on being an active trader, you'll want to check on this.

> **DEFINITION**
>
> **Position limit** is the maximum number of contracts any one account holder can have in the same underlying asset. It may be set by either the exchange or the brokerage firm.

Choosing a Software Platform

Active traders often make decisions based on the information on their computer screens. Hence, the software offered by the brokerage firm is really important.

Later in the book, I cover information about different types of research and services people use (see Chapter 16). For now, though, compare brokerages based on the following:

- Additional fees for the use of software
- Sources of real-time price quotes
- News feeds
- Charting services
- Backtesting
- Performance tracking

Most active traders find that the platform is more important than the other aspects of the broker's services, so be sure to look for a system that works for you.

Futures Commission Merchants

Most options trade through regular brokers, but some types of derivatives don't. If your trading strategy will include futures contracts, options on futures contracts, retail off-exchange foreign exchange, or swaps, you'll need to trade through a *futures commission merchant* (FCM), a broker registered with the futures exchanges. Many FCMs are the same brokers who also handle stocks and options, but not all stockbrokers are FCMs.

MARKET MAXIM

A future is similar to an option in that it allows you to buy or sell something at a date in the future at a price agreed upon today. The big difference is that a futures contract must be exercised if it reaches expiration, so most futures contracts are closed out with an offsetting transaction before expiration hits. An option on a future is a way to get exposure to the price change of the underlying asset without actually having to buy or sell.

Signing the Options Agreement

In order to trade options—in your existing brokerage account or a new one—you need two pieces of information on file to ensure you understand the risks of option trading and can cover them:

- The *margin agreement* covers the borrowing of funds inherent in options trading.

- The *options agreement* covers all the information about the risks of options trading, as well as details about any limits that may be placed on your account and information about exercise assignment.

Not all options strategies are risky, but a few have the potential for huge losses, and the brokers aren't taking chances.

> **DEFINITION**
>
> The **margin agreement** is the contract a customer signs with a brokerage firm that states he or she understands the risks and costs involved with margin. The **options agreement** is the contract a customer signs with a brokerage firm in which the customer acknowledges receiving a guide to options from the broker and understands the risks and fees involves with trading options.

Other Institutions in the Options Game

The options industry has its own set of regulators and related organizations that oversee the industry. They have their own rules and quirks, and you might not know much about them if you are new to options trading.

Some of these organizations were invented to handle aspects of options trading that are different from stock and bond trading.

Options Clearing Corporation

The Options Clearing Corporation (OCC) ensures that options trades clear. This means they guarantee that options orders go through and options exercise takes place as contracted. A key part of the OCC's job is setting and enforcing margin requirements. It also operates the centralized system used by clearing brokers to help the system work efficiently.

The clearing brokers, or clearing members, are the people who handle the transactions involved. They guarantee that a market maker will deliver on his or her trades. Clearing brokers also provide different cash management and account services.

The OCC itself doesn't make transactions, but it oversees the work that takes place.

Options Industry Council

Whether you are new to options trading or want to keep current on all the new products, the Options Industry Council (OIC) is your best friend. This industry-sponsored organization offers educational programs about options at every level: speculation, hedging, beginner, advanced, retail, and institutional. Its purpose is to help people be successful with options trading so they will keep it up.

At the OIC website, optionseducation.org, you'll find lots of webinars, courses, publications, and other information to help you learn about options and refine your strategies.

The Regulators

The options industry is highly regulated. To complicate matters, different types of options are handled by different types of regulators. That will probably change some day, but not in time for my deadline on this manuscript.

The first line of regulation is made up of the exchanges themselves. They determine which firms are allowed to trade with them and what practices they must follow.

Beyond that, many different government and industry regulators are involved:

U.S. Commodity Futures Trading Commission   The first equity options exchange, the CBOE, was founded by the CBOT, which specializes in agricultural futures contracts. This organization, also known as the CFTC, oversees the commodity exchanges. Given that options on futures, swaps, and other derivatives contracts trade on the commodity exchanges, the CFTC plays a role in the options market.

Financial Industry Regulatory Authority   The Financial Industry Regulatory Authority, or FINRA, handles the licensing of brokerage firms and their personnel. This is not a government agency, but rather an organization made of people in the financial industry. It works closely with the Securities and Exchange Commission (SEC).

National Futures Association   This private organization, also known as NFA, works closely with the CFTC to regulate the futures exchanges, and that includes exchanges that handle options on futures. It provides licensing examinations for futures commission merchants and their personnel.

U.S. Securities and Exchange Commission   More commonly known as the SEC, this government agency oversees the operations of stock and bond exchanges as well as exchanges that trade options on stocks and bonds.

The Least You Need to Know

- Options trades are executed through market makers who use different fee and priority structures.
- Many exchanges in the United States issue and trade options.
- Brokers expect customers to sign option agreements before allowing them to trade options.
- Options trading is overseen by both equity and commodity regulators.

The Greeks

Not only do options draw their value from an underlying security, they also have features that give them extra value. The relationship between the price of the option and the price of the underlying, the time to expiration, and the market rate of interest is complex.

How complex? We're talking college-level-math complex. I'm not kidding. Many options strategists, market makers, and traders are PhD-level mathematicians, actuaries, and physicists who prefer the excitement of trading to the drama of teaching undergraduates or calculating car insurance rates. These people can develop and use valuation models for complex option positions and just about any market situation.

You don't need to have taken calculus to be a good options trader, but it helps to have a mathematical brain. There are many traders without formal schooling who do well, but they are nevertheless comfortable with math and with information shown on graphs. The better you can grasp the relationships among all of the different factors that go into an option's price, the better off you will be.

In This Chapter

- Basic concepts of options pricing
- The calculus of options price changes
- Understanding the role of volatility
- Using the Greeks for insights on valuation

This chapter is an introduction to the math of options. For some people, this will be all they need. For others, there are more advanced classes, offered by the exchanges and by private vendors. Some people want to see the equations while others just want to watch the prices in action.

The key mathematical variables used in options trading are known collectively as *the Greeks.* Here's an introduction to get your started.

Delta

In math, *delta* is a rate of change. The term is from calculus—it's used for the first derivative—but you don't need calculus to understand it. Here are some examples:

- The difference between 1 and 2 is 1. In percentage terms, it is 100 percent.

- The difference between 2 and 3 is also 1, but in percentage terms, it's 50 percent.

- The difference between 3 and 4 is also 1, but the percentage change is now just 33 percent.

The amount by which the numbers change from 1 to 2, 2 to 3, and 3 to 4 is the same, but the rate at which they change is different. That's the delta.

In these examples, delta was the percentage relationship between one number and the next. To an options trader, delta is the relationship between the price of the underlying asset and the premium of the option, scaled by dollars. If the premium goes up $1 for every dollar the underlying increases, then the delta is $1. If the premium goes up $0.50 for each dollar increase in the underlying, then the delta is $0.50.

Delta in Pictures

The following graph shows the delta for a call and for a put. The delta is the curve of the line—also known as the slope or the first derivative—and you can see how the size of the delta changes as the price changes.

Delta is very much related to the moneyness of the option, which is how close the option is to being in the money. The closer the option is to being in the in money, or if it is already in the money, the closer the delta will be to 1.00.

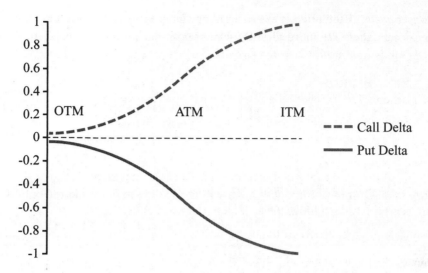

OTM *stands for "out of the money,"* ATM *for "at the money," and* ITM *for "in the money."*

Delta in Use

Delta is sometimes known as the *hedge ratio* because it can be used to determine how many options are needed to hedge a share of stock. This makes it useful for many different types of trading strategies.

Here's how it works. Suppose the delta of a put is 0.75.

- This means one call's change in price would match the change in price of 0.75 shares of stock.

- If you have 100 options and 75 shares of stock, and the stock price goes up by $1 per share, you now have a profit on the stock of $75.

- The put options will decline in price by $0.75 each, for a loss of $75, so the movements cancel each other out. This is what you would expect from a hedge.

- Likewise, if the stock falls $1 per share, the put options increase by $0.75 each, and once again, the movements cancel each other out.

The opposite would happen with a call option. If the delta is 0.75 and the stock increases by $1, the option would increase by $0.75. Although "hedge" is in the name, the hedge ratio can be used to design speculative positions.

The delta changes as the price of the underlying changes. It's not a "one and done" number. Hedgers in particular may need to readjust their positions in order to maintain the hedge.

> **$ DID YOU KNOW?**
>
> If the price of an option changed at a consistent rate when the price of the underlying asset changed, then it would be graphed along a straight line, with delta being the slope. However, delta is a curve, which is why calculus comes into play.

Delta is one of the most important measures for those using options to hedge. There's only one catch: delta doesn't follow a straight line. It will change as the stock and the option change in price.

Gamma

Gamma tells you how fast delta changes. If gamma is high and the price of the underlying asset moves against you, then your option value will fall fast. It's an important number to know to manage your risk.

In mathematical terms, gamma is the second derivative, or the rate of the rate of change. (Note *the rate of* is repeated on purpose, as gamma tells you the speed at which the rate of change changes.) It is getting into hard-core calculus.

But what does "rate of the rate of change" mean? Well, go back to the explanation for delta. When the numbers change from 1 to 2, 2 to 3, and 3 to 4, they change by 1. The rate of change—the delta—differs; it is 100 percent, 50 percent, and 33 percent as you move along the line. In other words, delta is the rate of change of the numbers.

Now, the difference between the rate of change from 100 percent to 50 percent is 50 percent, and the rate of change from 50 percent to 33 percent is 34 percent. That rate of change of the rate of change (whew!) is the gamma. (And if you struggled with calculus back in the day, this is a great example of how it's a really cool, really powerful tool used in many different fields.)

The graph shows gamma, which would be the slope of the relationship between the delta and the stock price. It's the rate of change in the rate of change—the speed at which the delta changes—in the price of the option. It varies depending on how much the price of the underlying asset changes.

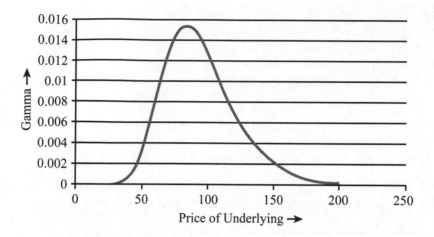

How gamma changes with the price of the underlying asset for a particular asset. When the underlying asset is way out of the money or deep in the money, the rate at which delta changes is very small.

If the gamma is 0, the price won't change much if delta changes. This happens if the option is deep in the money (so any price change in the underlying asset will affect the price of the option one-to-one) or if the option is so far out of the money the value of the underlying is almost irrelevant. At the other extreme, a gamma of 1 indicates the delta will change really fast when the underlying asset changes price, so the price of the option will change quickly, too.

The gamma will be greatest when the option is at the money, which you may remember is the point at which the price of the underlying asset is the same as the strike price of the option. As the option moves in the money (where it is profitable to exercise) and out of the money (where it is not profitable to exercise), the gamma will be smaller. The greater the gamma, the faster an option price will change when the underlying price changes.

Delta tells you how much an option moves, and gamma tells you how fast it is moving. Consequently, gamma is used in risk management more than it is in actual trading. Someone looking to manage risk needs to know how quickly a given situation could move in the wrong direction. Anyone who wants to prevent an option account from going to 0 should pay attention to the gamma of their open options positions. Traders should close out their options positions if the gamma becomes too large for comfort.

MARKET MAXIM

If you find yourself at the bottom of a hole, the first thing to do is stop digging. Risk management is important because losses can multiply.

Gamma is important for another reason. It is a reminder that the option price relationships are not linear. Actual price movements form a curve, and that means price changes can be more dramatic than you might expect.

Theta

Theta is a measure of time decay, or how much an option's price falls over time. It's another calculation made using calculus, and it shows the rate of change of the option over time. It is used to figure out how long to keep a trade in place, especially in combination with delta.

Delta tells you how much an option's price changes with the price of the underlying asset. Theta tells you how much it changes with time. Another way to think of it is:

- Delta shows you the move in the intrinsic value of an option.

- Theta shows you the move in the time value.

Both affect valuation in different ways.

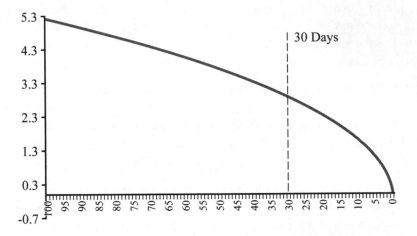

How option prices fall as time passes. In mathematical terms, the theta of the option declines to 0.

This graph shows the theta for a call and for a put. The theta is the curve of the line—also known as the slope or the first derivative—and you can see how the size of the theta changes as the time to expiration changes. Theta is a negative number because the time value declines over time as the option gets closer to expiration. A share of stock, which never expires, has a theta of 0. An option at the moment of expiration has an infinitely negative theta because it will go to 0 as soon as it expires.

Theta is expressed in dollar terms. A theta of −0.05 means if everything else stayed the same, the option would decline in value by $0.05 in the next day.

Other First Derivatives

Delta and theta are the most important of the Greeks to traders, and they are both first derivatives in calculus. They have company, though, with lesser (but still useful) Greeks that define how much the option price changes relative to other variables.

Vega

Vega is not a Greek letter, but it's lumped in with the Greeks. The letter used in calculus is nu. A lowercase nu looks like the letter v, so traders decided to call it *vega*, which is the Greek name for the brightest star in the constellation Lyra.

Vega represents how much an option's price changes due to a change in volatility. It is also a derivative, just like delta. Some underlying assets gyrate a lot in price, while others are steadier. The less predictable the asset's price, the more valuable the insurance provisions of an option will be. Also, the less predictable the price for an asset, the more likely a speculator will find the option ends up in the money.

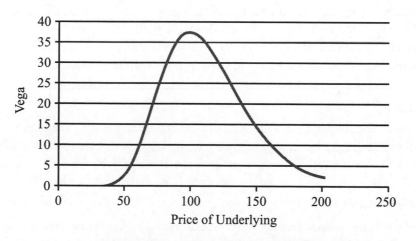

How vega changes with the price of the underlying asset.

This graph shows the vega for a call and for a put. The vega is the curve of the line, and it changes as the price of the underlying asset becomes more volatile. Because vega is discussed in the form of price, it is easy to use. If the amount of volatility increases, the option's premium will increase by a dollar amount equal to the vega multiplied by the percentage increase. In other words, if the vega is .20 and the option's volatility increases by 3 percent, the option's price would increase by .20 × 3 = $0.60.

Changes in volatility have a larger effect on the value of an option than do changes in time, but both matter. The difference is that time changes constantly; every moment, the time value of an option declines. Volatility doesn't change as fast, but when it does change, the effect on the option's price can be significant. That's in part because changes in volatility are usually caused by unusual events; the change in time is predictable.

> **DID YOU KNOW?**
>
> In the stock market, volatility is the primary source of risk. It is hardly the only source of risk, though. In the options market, it is the change in the value of the underlying asset, which might or might not be related to volatility.

Rho

Rho is another first derivative, but it is based on changes in interest rates rather than changes in underlying prices. The interest rate that matters here is the rate that is used to finance the option position. These are the rates brokerage firms and clearing firms charge traders. These rates are keyed off of the interest rates in the economy, but they aren't the same at every firm.

The assumption behind rho is the option is being used to hedge an underlying position. This means the trader will either give up a return on cash in order to buy the stock, or she will borrow from the broker in order to *short sell* it. (To sell short, the trader will borrow shares of the stock from the broker and then sell the shares in the open market. The bet is the price will fall. Later, she will buy the shares back in the future at a lower price in order to repay the loan.) When she sells the stock short, she can invest the cash received and earn interest on it until the position is closed.

This graph shows the rho for a call and for a put. The rho is the curve of the line, and it changes as interest rates change. An increase in interest rates makes call options more valuable because of the interest earned on the cash from the short position. It makes put options less valuable because of the interest expense involved in holding the underlying asset longer rather than investing the money elsewhere.

The value of rho is the dollar effect on option premiums on a 1 percentage point change in interest rates. In other words, a rho of .25 means if interest rates change from 2 to 3 percent, the option price will change by $0.25.

Rho will be greater the longer the time to expiration and the higher the price of the underlying security.

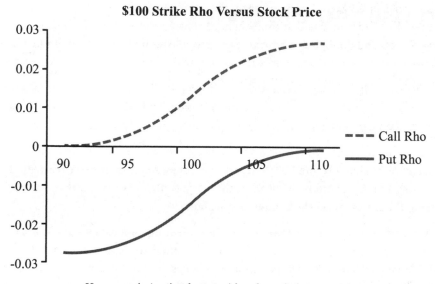

How an option's price changes with a change in interest rates.

Every option has exposure to interest rates, but options written on interest rates themselves and on different economic factors have even more exposure. For these, interest rates affect both the value of the underlying asset as well as the price on their options.

The following table gives you a summary of the Greek letters used in options trading.

Greek Letter	What It Tells You
Delta	How the option price changes with the price of the underlying asset
Gamma	How the delta changes with the price of the underlying asset
Theta	How the option price changes over time
Vega	How the option price changes with volatility
Rho	How the option price changes with interest rates

DID YOU KNOW?

The Greek alphabet begins with the letters alpha and beta. Those letters are skipped over in options trading, as the Greeks go straight to gamma and delta because alpha and beta already have use in trading. Beta is a measurement of volatility relative to the stock market. The market has a beta of 1. A stock as volatile as the market has a beta of 1; if it is twice as volatile, it has a beta of 2. Alpha refers to the portion of an investment's return that is not explained by risk. If a stock with a beta of 1 returned 10 percent more than the market, that additional 10 percent would be considered alpha.

How to Use the Greeks

The math is well and good, but it has to be used, yes? And how often have you used algebra since high school?

Well, you've used algebra more often than you probably like to admit and more often than you probably realize. Do you ever stand at the grocery store and figure out how many boxes of sale-priced cereal you can buy and still have enough money left over for milk? Then you have used algebra.

As with algebra, traders use the Greeks every day. They sometimes don't realize it because they aren't running the calculations themselves; there are computers that do that. Instead, they are interpreting the information the computer spits out.

And so it is with the Greeks. The primary factors affecting an option's valuation are the price of the underlying asset and the time to expiration—in other words, the delta and the theta. Both of these change constantly. Volatility and interest rates change all the time, too, but these have a lesser effect on the price.

Options valuation models, covered in detail in Chapter 5, will generate the value of the Greeks at any one point in time. Traders then use those results to forecast how an option's price might change with different changes in price, interest rates, volatility, or time. If, for example, something happens that will make underlying prices more volatile, which options will benefit the most? How should positions be managed accordingly?

Delta and theta are always the starting points, but the other Greeks are in the back of every trader's mind.

The Least You Need to Know

- Delta is a measure of how much an option's price changes with a change in the price of the underlying asset.
- Theta is a measure of how much an option's price changes as time passes.
- Options prices are also affected by the volatility of the underlying asset and interest rates.
- Different computer models will generate these figures, but they are also second nature in an option trader's brain.

Options Valuation and Trading Strategies

Before options can be used, you must know what they are worth. Option valuation is so complicated, many traders rely on computer models to determine their positions and strategies.

Not all options strategies are difficult, though. Many are simple to assemble once you have an understanding of how they work. Chapter 5 covers the math behind options valuation. Chapter 6 discusses volatility in the options market and why it matters to anyone in the financial markets. Chapter 7 is an introduction to the basics of trading options, Chapter 8 is an overview of basic strategies using calls, and Chapter 9 is an overview of puts. Puts and calls are combined in the strategies reviewed in Chapter 10.

This information helps you use options to accomplish your goals and to better understand what is happening in the financial markets.

CHAPTER 5

The Basics of Options Valuation

People trade options for many different reasons. Regardless of why someone trades an option, the trader needs to know what a particular contract should be worth and why. Options are a type of derivative, and derivatives were named that because their value is derived from the value of the underlying security.

The value of the underlying is important, but it is not the only factor involved. The same is true with the time to expiration. Options and other derivatives have features that the underlying asset does not. Those features add value.

Options add value to a portfolio by offering choices about whether and how to conduct transactions in the underlying asset. How much value do these things add? That's what will be covered in this chapter.

In This Chapter

- Put-call parity: the foundation of valuation
- Basic forms of return
- Adding risk through leverage

Put-Call Parity

Put-call parity is the most basic relationship between the value of the underlying asset, the value of a put, and the value of call. It gives you a way to think about how much an option should be worth without getting into the weeds of calculus and statistics. It is simple, and it serves as a great check on how well the market is valuing options on any given day. It is the relationship between the price of a put and the price of a call.

Put-call parity holds means the relationship between the price of a call, the price of a put, and the price of the underlying will remain fixed for European options with the same strike price and same expiration date. In easy-to-remember equation form, this is:

Underlying asset price = strike price + call premium – put premium

For European options with the same strike price and expiration date, the strike price plus the call premium minus the option premium should equal the stock price.

Stock price = strike price + call premium – put premium

This means that you can create the same payoff of the stock by buying a call and a put, then exercising whichever is in the money.

It also means if one component of the equation changes, then the others should, too. For example, if a stock pays a dividend, then the stock price will go down. This will make the call premium decline, too. Also, it will make the put premium go up.

The put-call parity equation has a big effect on *arbitrage*, which is the process of making a riskless profit because an asset is at the wrong price. If a trader notices the put premium is higher than it should be, given put-call parity, he can sell puts and buy calls to make a profit with no risk. It does not happen often—in fact, it's rare—but it does happen.

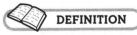 **DEFINITION**

> **Arbitrage** literally means "riskless profit"; it is the process of taking advantage of a mispricing in the market by buying the underpriced asset and simultaneously selling the overpriced asset.

The put-call parity relationship is used to design trading strategies. Also it tells you what the price of an option should be without running through all the math of Black-Scholes or running a Monte Carlo simulation. Those complex models are covered next.

Basics of Valuation

Options markets didn't take off until people understood how they could be valued. Options valuation is a complicated process because there are several variables involved, namely these:

- Price of the underlying asset
- Volatility of the underlying asset
- Strike price
- Time remaining until expiration
- Option type (American or European)
- Current interest rates

Obviously, this is not a back-of-the-envelope calculation. The math involved in options valuation is complicated, and many options trading firms hire actuaries and mathematicians to develop valuation models.

You probably won't be doing that, but you will be using models that others have created, or you will be trading against people who use them. That's why it's important to know what goes into the valuation systems that are used most often.

At the most basic level, there are two factors that affect an option's price:

- *Intrinsic value*, or the value based on the underlying asset
- *Time value*, also known as *extrinsic value*, which is the value based on the fact that the option's moneyness will change until the time to expiration.

These aren't the only two factors, of course. That's why options valuation gets a lot more technical.

Intrinsic and extrinsic values are the most important factors in options valuation, and so they are the most important for a new trader to learn. Most of the changes in an option's price are related to changes in the price of the underlying asset and to the passage of time. However, other factors do come into play, especially with complex trading strategies.

Understanding Pricing with the Binomial Option Model

The *binomial model* isn't really a usable model for options pricing, but I'm putting it in here anyway. That's because it's a good way to think about how options prices should work. This will help stimulate the mathematical part of your brain without throwing too many equations or terms at you all at once. Also, the binomial model is the basis for *Monte Carlo simulation* models that are used by some traders.

Let's assume that you buy a call option that will be worth either $10 or nothing at expiration. This is a really simplistic assumption, but that's okay. We can build on it. When the option in this scenario expires, it will be worth either $10 or nothing. If those two events are equally likely, then the option is, on average, worth $5:

$$(\$10 \times .50) + (0 \times .50) = \$5$$

Of course, these two states won't be equally likely. So then what?

The value of the option is determined by the value of the underlying asset during the time that you hold the option. What are the possible prices that the stock could reach in that time, and what is the probability of each? Suppose the stock price could lead to an option value at expiration of $15, $10, and $0, all of which are equally likely. If that's the case, then the option is worth $8.33:

$$(\$15 \times .333) + (\$10 \times .333) + (\$0 \times .333)$$

The idea behind the binomial model is that you continue finding all the outcomes and probabilities until you finally reached the right price. It's unreasonable to try to do this by hand, but many computer algorithms used to value options follow the binomial process to reach a value in seemingly no time at all.

> **WARNING**
>
> Binary valuation is different from *binary options*. Binary options are a yes/no proposition about the value of the underlying asset. A binary option could be placed on whether the underlying stock will be worth $15 per share on the expiration date. If yes, the option will pay off an amount predetermined at the time of purchase; if no, it will be worthless. Some binary options are listed on organized exchanges, with the same clearinghouse regulations as traditional options. Others trade over-the-counter through offshore brokerage accounts operating online. These markets are sometimes fraudulent or manipulated. The Securities and Exchange Commission recommends trading in binary options only listed on bona fide exchanges and only through registered brokers.

Pricing in Detail with the Black-Scholes Model

The *Black-Scholes model* is the fundamental theory for the valuation of options. Like all models, it explains how everything works in a perfect world. The world is hardly perfect, but the model gives traders a good starting point for how an option's price should behave when everything goes right. Then, traders can determine what will happen when reality interferes.

Options pricing is difficult to do by hand. One reason the exchange-traded options were not introduced until 1973 is the market could not function without enough computing power to handle the valuation. Experienced traders often internalize the math, meaning that they've seen enough options trade to know how they should be trading without running through the calculations.

The calculations are complex, too. In 1973, economists Fischer Black and Myron Scholes published a paper called "The Pricing of Options and Corporate Liabilities" and economist Robert Merton published "Theory of Rational Option Pricing." Scholes and Merton received the 1997 Nobel Prize for Economics for their work; Black had died and so was not eligible.

DID YOU KNOW?

Myron Scholes and Robert Merton joined the board of a hedge fund called Long-Term Capital Management in 1994. In 1998, that fund failed, nearly bringing down the world financial markets. Having academic smarts doesn't necessarily translate to investment success.

The Black-Scholes model explains how European call options on nondividend-paying stocks better than anything before or since. In a way, it's a binomial option model with the factors that influence the underlying price thrown into the mix.

Here, in its gory glory, is the Black-Scholes model.

C_0 = the price of the call option today, which is equal to $C_0 = S_0N(d_1) - Xe^{-rT}N(d_2)$, where

$$d_1 = \frac{ln\left(\frac{S_0}{X}\right) + \left(r + \frac{\sigma^2}{2}\right)T}{\sigma\sqrt{T}} \text{ and } d_2 = d_1 - \sigma\sqrt{T}.$$

No, you don't need to be able to calculate this in order to trade options! But you might find it helpful to understand the factors that go into the model to get a better understanding of how they affect both the price of an option and the rate at which the price changes (you know, the Greeks, as we discussed in Chapter 4).

The variables are as follows:

S_0 = the price of underlying stock today.

$N(d)$ = the probability that a random number in a normal distribution will be less than d.

$ln\left(\dfrac{S_0}{X}\right)$ approximates the percentage amount by which the option is currently in or out of the money.

r = the *risk-free rate of interest,* usually assumed to be the U.S. Treasury bill rate. (Yes, it has some risk, but if the U.S. government fails, we have bigger problems than the price of a call option.)

T = the number of years until the expiration of the option. If it expires in 3 months, then T would be .25.

σ = the *standard deviation* of the annualized return on the stock. The combined term $\sigma\sqrt{T}$ is a measure of how much the option is in or out of the money.

> **DEFINITION**
>
> **Standard deviation** is a term from statistics that measures how much any one item in a series of numbers might be different from the average of all of the numbers in the series.

Finally, *ln* and *e* are related to natural logarithms. They are used to work the calculation and are not related to the options themselves.

With that in mind, the first equation needed to solve the Black-Scholes model is more or less the call price multiplied by a change in the price of the underlying. It is a measure of intrinsic value.

$$d_1 = \frac{ln\left(\dfrac{S_0}{X}\right) + \left(r + \dfrac{\sigma^2}{2}\right)T}{\sigma\sqrt{T}}$$

The second equation is used to determine the contribution of time value.

$$d_2 = d_1 - \sigma\sqrt{T}$$

Intrinsic value and time value are the most important components of option value, but they are not the only components.

Combining all of this, the Black-Scholes equation says that the current price of a call option is determined by interest rates, time to expiration, and how much the current stock price varies from what it is expected to be given the historic rate of return. The Black-Scholes equation incorporates delta, which is the change in the option price based on a change in the price in the underlying security. It also incorporates theta, vega, and rho.

The Black-Scholes model was revolutionary at the time, but it has some flaws:

- It only applies to European options on stocks that do not pay a dividend. That excludes most of the equity options trading today.

- Then there's the theoretical issue about what a risk-free rate really means. Most models assume that U.S. government bond rates are the next-best thing to risk free, but next-best thing leaves a lot of leeway in markets that trade almost instantaneously and in fractions of a cent.

- It assumes that the interest rate and the standard deviation of the stock returns remain consistent. That doesn't happen.

WARNING

A model is a good way to explain how things would work in a perfect world. It is used to figure out what can go right and what can go wrong, which allows the trader to adjust accordingly. Black-Scholes is a starting point for valuation models developed by others rather than a plug-and-chug formula that you can use for trading. It is not a practical tool for trading.

Value of the Underlying

An option allows you to make a transaction on the underlying asset at a given price. The closer the underlying price is to making the option in the money, the more valuable the option.

The value of the underlying is the most important part of option valuation, but not the only factor.

Here's a way to think about the value of the underlying asset using the Black-Scholes model. Suppose you buy a call on an underlying asset with an underlying price of $50. If the price of the underlying asset goes to $51, the call should increase in value, all else being equal.

Now, how much will that call price increase? That depends on the delta because delta is the rate of change. Delta isn't a static number, though. How fast delta changes depends on the gamma—the rate of the rate of change.

What we do know is that the price of the call will go up in this example. Because a put has the opposite payoff, an increase in the underlying asset's price will make the put less valuable, all else being equal.

In other words, Black-Scholes accommodates intrinsic value as well as other factors.

It accommodates intrinsic value another way. Think about what happens when the exercise price of a call option is high relative to the price of the underlying asset. If the price of the underlying is $20 and a call has a strike price of $50, it probably won't be exercised. A call with a strike price of $25 is more likely to be exercised, so it will be more valuable. For puts, the situation is reversed. A put with a high exercise price relative to the price of the underlying asset is more likely to be exercised than a put with a really low strike price, so—all else being equal—it will have a lower price.

Time Value

The longer the time to expiration, the more likely it is that the option will end up being worth something. After all, the more time you have, the more that can happen. Every day is a new day with a new opportunity for a company to have a news announcement that will drive the option's value up or down.

Time value is second to the price of the underlying in determining an option's valuation. This is the option's extrinsic value. The longer the time, the greater the extrinsic value and the more valuable the option.

Interest Rates

The role of interest rates in option valuation might not seem logical at first, but think of it this way: if you weren't buying or writing options, you would be doing something else with the money. That something would probably involve investing or borrowing, so the return or the cost would be determined by market interest rates.

Generally, an increase in interest rates is good for call prices and bad for put prices. That's because a call writer is receiving income and will expect a higher premium in times when interest rates are high, in order to make options writing more attractive than putting money in the bank.

Keep in mind that this is an average tendency, not an absolute. Interest rates affect time value, intrinsic value, and economic risk, so a change in rates might end up affecting options in different ways. On average, an increase in interest rates is good for calls and bad for puts. However, there are plenty of situations in history where the opposite has happened. Interest rates are affected by the overall level of economic activity, the amount of inflation in the economy, and the risk of a particular investment. Black-Scholes is a model that helps traders think about valuation, not a road map to profits.

The effect of interest rates is small, but it is not zero.

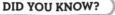
DID YOU KNOW?

An interest rate is simply the price of money expressed in percentage form. Three factors go into an interest rate: the *real rate of interest* (the supply and demand for money in the economy), inflation, and the risk of the investment in question.

Volatility

Volatility is a measure of how much an underlying asset moves around in price. If you had statistics, it's simply another word for *standard deviation.*

If you haven't had statistics, this little illustration will help. Stock A has a return of 3 percent in year 1, 3 percent in year 2, and 3 percent in year 3. The average return for those 3 years is 3 percent, and the return never varies from that 3 percent number.

Stock B has a return of 6 percent in year 1, –2 percent in year 2, and 5 percent in year 3. The average for return for those years is also 3 percent, but the return bounces around a lot and, in fact, is never exactly 3 percent.

Because the price of Stock B is less predictable than the price of Stock A, Stock B is more volatile. Even though the expected return is the same, Stock B's return is going to vary a lot more in any given year than will Stock A's return.

The more volatile a stock price is, the more a hedger will want insurance on it and the more opportunities a speculator will have to make money. The greater the volatility, the more likely an option is to be exercised. That means that the greater the volatility, the more valuable the option. And, to get back to the earlier discussion of the binomial model, the greater the volatility, the more price points to consider when evaluating the probability of the option being in the money.

The option doesn't have to be in the money for long to be profitable to exercise either. Plenty of traders have made big money on a position that was in the money for 10 minutes. In general, both puts and calls are more valuable if the underlying asset is volatile than if the asset is a steady performer.

The big criticism of standard deviation, which is the most common measure of volatility used in valuing common stock, is that it is calculated with historic information. That's all well and good, but expiration is a point in the future. The future may be very different from the past. Options traders care about volatility between the purchase day and the expiration, and all sorts of things could happen—or not—that are very different from the historic level of volatility.

Now, if you calculate the option's theoretical price using price of the underlying, the strike price, the time to expiration, and interest rates, you'll get a number lower than the price of the option. The difference in value is based on the *implied volatility,* which is the volatility that the market is using to justify the current price of the option. Your job is to compare this to the information you have to see if the option is cheap or expensive.

American or European?

European options can only be exercised on the expiration date, while American options can be exercised at any time. That makes the American options more valuable because there might be situations in which it is better to exercise them early instead of holding them until expiration.

The Black-Scholes model was developed by looking at European options because the analysis is simpler. This model can be used as a basis to analyze American options, with the difference being that the American option will be worth more. After all, the more things you can do with an option, the more valuable it will be.

The Effect of Dividends

A *dividend* is a payment that a company makes to shareholders out of its profits. Not all companies pay dividends, but most of the largest do. When a dividend is paid, the value of the stock declines by the same amount as the dividend. That decline, of even a few cents, makes a call option less likely to be in the money and a put option more likely to be in the money. The result is that a dividend makes a call option less valuable, all else being equal, and a put option more valuable.

The effect of the dividend payment is not included in the Black-Scholes model, but it has a very real effect on the price of an option.

Putting Together the Black-Scholes Model

To help you keep all this straight, the following table gives a simple overview of the factors in the Black-Scholes model and their effects on the direction of call and put option prices. It also includes stock dividends, which are not in Black-Scholes but have an effect on options prices, too.

The Black-Scholes Model, Summarized

Market Factor	Call Prices	Put Prices
Underlying price	Increases	Decreases
Exercise price	Decreases	Increases
Volatility	Increases	Increases
Time to expiration	Increases	Increases

Market Factor	Call Prices	Put Prices
Interest rate	Increases	Decreases
American option	Increases	Increases
Dividend	Decreases	Increases

Keep in mind that these relationships assume that all else is equal, so there will often be situations where you notice deviations from Black-Scholes. Black-Scholes is a model that shows what would happen in a perfect world, and real-life trading isn't perfect.

Also, these factors don't play out one by one. They often operate in conjunction with each other. A major news event might cause a stock price to fall and increase the expected volatility. The decrease in the price of the underlying will cause the price of the call option to fall, but the increase in volatility will cause the price of the option to rise. Does one of these factors become more important than another? Will they cancel each other out? I don't know!

That's the problem. The Black-Scholes model was a major revolution in option valuation because it broke out all of the different factors, but it can't provide an exact price useful for a trader. Use it as a framework to think about prices, not to find out where to buy and where to sell.

Heston Volatility Model

In 1993, Steven Heston, a professor at the Yale School of Organization and Management, published a paper titled "A Closed-Form Solution for Options with Stochastic Volatility with Applications to Bond and Currency Options." It was a revision of Black-Scholes with one change—it assumes that the rate of volatility is itself changeable. The Black-Scholes model, meanwhile, assumes that the rate of volatility is fixed for every asset.

This refinement, known as the *Heston Volatility model,* has been incorporated into many options trading models. Like Black-Scholes, it can't be used by itself for options trading, but it has influenced the work of other trading systems.

The Heston Volatility model is one of several models that have been developed to address problems in the Black-Scholes model, by the way. If you're inclined to learn more, make a trip to your library and check out databases of academic journals. It's interesting, although not necessarily practical unless you are programming your own trading models.

The Least You Need to Know

- Options valuation requires advanced math, heavy computing power, or both.
- The Black-Scholes model is the basis for most option valuation programs, but it has some flaws that make it impractical for use on its own.
- Other mathematical models have been developed to address problems with Black-Scholes, but the math is even more complex.
- The simplest option pricing relationship is put-call parity, and the only math it requires is arithmetic.

The VIX and Other Market Indicators

Financial markets are driven by information. Traders gather information about the market by looking at different market statistics to give them some insight. Even those who are not options traders often use the options market as a way to evaluate the overall financial markets. Options traders give people a window into what speculators see and what risks concern hedgers on any given day.

In the options market, strategies of countless market participants come together to create an aggregate view of the market. The signals given off by the options exchanges help options traders and other investors evaluate the mood of the market, its volatility, and other expectations about the future.

Remember vega, from Chapter 4 on the Greeks? Vega is the measure of implied volatility in an option. The greater the vega, the more valuable the option.

You might be familiar with such indexes as the Dow Jones Industrial Average and the Standard & Poor's 500 Index. These are indicators of how the stock market is performing for a given time period. These indices give market observers a lot of information about the underlying market. For example, in the derivatives market, there are options on the index and

In This Chapter

- How volatile is the market
- Volatility and volume indicators
- Measuring the market's mood
- How the market is moving

on the stocks in it. Using that information, traders can calculate an implied volatility for the entire market. This calculation offers observers even more information.

Just as options derive their value from the value of an underlying asset, they derive their volatility from them, too. When translated to the level of the market as a whole, an understanding of volatility can help traders of all types see how the market's behavior affects their positions.

Working with Volatility, Implied and Otherwise

To refresh your memory, volatility is a measure of how much prices vary over time. For example, you can have an average return of 10 percent with returns of 10 percent, 9 percent, and 11 percent over 3 years; or you can have an average return of 10 percent with returns of 30 percent, −10 percent, and 10 percent. The second series has a lot more variability than the first, so we would say that it is more volatile.

Remember that when valuing an option, the component that is not related to underlying value or time value is known as implied volatility, or vega. It's a key reason for trading in options, whether the objective is to hedge or to speculate.

Underlying assets become more volatile as traders become more uncertain of what the value should be. This could happen because of a lack of information or because the underlying asset operates in an environment where the range of outcomes is really wide. For example, the size of the wheat crop is affected by the weather. The price of wheat is affected by the size of the crop. If the weather becomes more volatile, then so will the price of wheat.

People like steady and predictable performance, even though it is very rare. One reason people use options is to insure against volatility in the price of the underlying asset. The greater the volatility in the underlying, the more important the insurance function is.

In the financial markets, a bull market is one that is going up, so *bulls* are those who believe the market's next move is up. A bear market is one that is going down, and *bears* believe the market's next direction is downward. The options market offers many clues as to whether the overall direction is bullish or bearish.

> **MARKET MAXIM**
>
> Anyone who can predict the future with certainty is retired and living on a beach in Maui. Everyone else is taking a risk.

Sentiment

The market isn't human, although sometimes it seems like that to traders. The market has no emotion. The computers that direct a lot of the trades aren't human, either, although they were programmed by human beings. They, too, have no emotion, but they read a lot of indicators about what's happening in the markets.

Humans are emotional creatures who are a mess of nerves, feelings and ideas. And as human beings trade in the financial markets, at least some of these emotions play out in price and volume activity. The introduction of electronic trading hasn't eliminated this, either. If anything, electronic trading magnifies the trends created by humans rather than tamping them down.

Sentiment indicators give you information about the broader market. Sentiment indicators fall into three categories:

- **Leading**   Leading indicators show where the market will be moving.

- **Lagging**   Lagging indicators show what happened and may confirm trends or indicate changes.

- **Contrary**   Contrary indicators mean the opposite of what it seems. A positive signal from a contrary indicator means that the market may be expected to go down.

However, none of these indicators should be confused with clairvoyance. Sentiment indicators can be misread, and they can change. Strange and unexpected events can take place to change the mood of the market faster than the blink of an eye.

> **DEFINITION**
>
> **Sentiment indicators** are metrics used to help options traders and other market observers discern whether prices will be going up or going down.

Put-Call Ratio

Want to know how people feel about a particular stock? Then check out the *put-call ratio*. The ratio is just that: the number of put options written divided by the number of call options written. The higher the put-call ratio, the more bearish the sentiment.

> **DEFINITION**
>
> The **put-call ratio** is the number of put options divided by the number of call options written on a particular underlying asset. The more puts that are being purchased, the more people are betting that the market is going to fall.

After all, if people are negative on a stock, they will want to buy put options in order to see if they can make a profit on the decline. If they think the stock is going up, they will buy call options. Of course, some of the buyers and sellers are acting without information, while other buyers and sellers are market makers and hedgers. There will always be both puts and calls outstanding on any underlying asset. A big change in the ratio, though, could signal a change in sentiment signaling an upcoming price move.

Traders tend to look at changes in the ratio rather than its absolute level. They also look for information explaining why the ratio is changing. A change that is driven by institutional investors who are hedging is viewed as more important than a change driven by retail customer volume. This difference is because retail speculators tend to be overly emotional in their trading.

Put-call ratios can be calculated different ways, depending on what's being measured. The put-call ratio for one particular individual underlying asset is a way to measure sentiment for that asset, which may have nothing to do with sentiment for the broader market. A look at the put-call ratio for the entire market, or for a section of it, provides information about how bullish or bearish sentiment is for a broader market. Some traders look at the put-call ratio for index options to get a quick read on the overall market. You may see this metric used many ways to gauge sentiment.

These measures offer different perspectives on what might be happening in the market, and traders use a combination of them to gauge the current market direction.

Each day, the stock exchanges publish put-call ratios for the exchange as a whole, as well as put-call ratios for different types of options.

The following tables show really broad ranges of sentiment associated with different put-call ratios. Some traders use different ranges, depending on what they are trading and what market conditions are at any given time.

Put-Call Ratios for Index Options

If the Ratio Is ...	It Is Considered ...
1.50 or higher	Bearish
0.75 to 1.50	Neutral
0.75 or lower	Bullish

Put-Call Ratios for Single-Stock Equity Options

If the Ratio Is ...	It Is Considered ...
0.75 or higher	Bearish
0.40 to 0.75	Neutral
0.40 or lower	Bullish

There's a wrinkle, though—there is always a wrinkle. Some people take a contrarian approach to the market, which means they assume the conventional wisdom is wrong. Hence, they will reverse the measures, buying when put-call ratios are really high and selling when they are low.

In addition to the general put-call ratio, some exchanges and research services have developed modified numbers designed to show clear bullish or bearish signals.

Put and Call Volume Indicators

The ratio of puts to calls provides one measure of sentiment. Changes in the level of trading volume in puts and calls offer another measure. As trading volume increases, traders begin to feel stronger about the likelihood of a change in market direction.

Some people buy puts as insurance, but others buy them because they are speculating on a price decline. Either way, the more put buyers out there, the more people are expecting the market for the underlying asset to go down.

Put indicators tend to be taken more seriously than call indicators because most financial markets have an upward bias. People would not invest in the underlying asset if they expected it to go down!

Open interest itself is not a sentiment measure because every long position is matched by a short position. It is the change in open interest that matters. (Have you forgotten these terms? They are covered in Chapter 2.)

Volume and open interest numbers are published daily by the exchanges.

DID YOU KNOW?

Different indexes and indicators are parts of big businesses. Publishers such as Dow Jones, and exchanges such as the Chicago Board Options Exchange give the basic information away for free as a way to promote their other services. Analysts who want more detailed information about how the prices change must pay for it. Detailed information is often included in a brokerage account's services.

Premium Levels

For all the math that goes into determining a fair valuation for an option, the basic determinant of price for an option is that same for anything else: supply and demand. If people want to buy (or sell) more of a given option, then the price will go up (or down) accordingly.

Hence, options traders look for trends in prices to see if there are changes in demand that might indicate future direction. Prices are tracked with price charts, and they are often analyzed using technical analysis (see Chapter 14 for more information). Technical analysis of prices is a way to see how market psychology affects the price of different underlying assets, as well as the options on them.

The options exchanges publish indices of put premiums and call premiums so people can see how they have changed over time. An increase in the put premium index tends to be a bearish signal, and an increase in the call premium index tends to be bullish.

Confidence Index

Many years ago, *Barron's*, the weekly business newspaper, started publishing what it calls its *confidence index*. The confidence index is found by dividing the yield on high-quality bonds by the yield on intermediate-quality bonds. The idea is that the greater the return people want for intermediate-quality bonds, the more concerned they are about the economy. The greater the ratio, the more confidence held by investors.

The options-market version for the confidence index is based on the spread between the call premium index and the put premium index. This works because, if put-call parity holds, the primary difference between the two should be carrying costs (that is, interest and commissions). Carrying costs are highly sensitive to interest rates.

Here's how you calculate that: take the difference between the put premium index and the call premium index and multiply by two. The result is an annualized spread between the two indices. The higher that spread is, the better the signal for the underlying asset in question—at least until the point of overconfidence. That's that wrinkle in using sentiment indicators I discussed earlier in the chapter.

Implied Volatility

Implied volatility, also known as vega, is one of the key factors in option valuation. The more volatile an underlying asset is, the more likely an option on it is to end up in the money. Also, the more volatile the underlying asset, the more value it has to both hedgers and speculators.

And what causes volatility to increase? In almost all cases, uncertainty.

In fact, the Volatility Index (see the next section) and related volatility index options are followed for this very reason. They are looking at the implied volatility of the market as a whole.

Traders in single-stock options don't need a specialized index because they can track the implied volatility in their options class to see what the expectations are for that company.

MARKET MAXIM

The four most dangerous words in the English language are: this time is different. Markets move in cycles, and human beings tend to respond in predictable ways. Yes, sometimes there are significant new economic factors. However, in most cases, the market is the same old, same old. If people lost money the last time this cycle came around, they probably will lose money this time, too. Learn from history.

The VIX

VIX is short for Volatility Index, a measure introduced by the Chicago Board Options Exchange in 1993 as a way to communicate with the world about implied volatility. The index is calculated on the volatility of options on the Standard & Poor's 500 stock index. The VIX is often thought of as the fear index, and it is followed by many market commenters and strategists for clues about the direction financial markets might be moving.

A high VIX indicates that investors perceive a lot of volatility, while a low VIX shows a lot of market confidence—maybe even too much confidence.

DID YOU KNOW?

The VIX and other market indicators are used for both straightforward readings and contrarian reads. A rising VIX means that uncertainty in the market is increasing. However, at some point, the uncertainty becomes so high that traders assume people are overly fearful and the markets will actually improve. Thus, a rising VIX is negative, but a very high VIX is actually positive. Thus, a high VIX is thought of as contrarian. One reason for this is that a lot of traders are not very sophisticated. Often, speculators are not as informed about the market as they could be. This means that they often jump in just as a trend noticed by professionals is ending.

Calculating the VIX

The VIX is calculated based on the CBOE's SPX contract, which is an option on the value of the S&P 500 Index. The S&P 500 Index, in turn, is a measure of the stock market based on the market values of 500 of the largest companies in the United States.

The SPX options are traded to speculate on, or hedge, the global financial markets. Although the S&P 500 is an index of American companies, it is heavily weighted toward multinational companies. The size of the U.S. economy relative to the rest of the world makes the S&P 500 the best world proxy we have now. It's not perfect, but no sentiment indicator is.

The math that goes into the VIX calculation is complicated, but it pulls out the expected 30-day volatility of the S&P 500 Index from the other factors such as underlying value and time to expiration. These are the same factors that go into the valuation of the index options. It uses both standard and weekly options to back out the volatility expected in the next 30 days.

In other words, the VIX is an index based on the volatility of options that are based on the value of the S&P 500. Yes, I know, that's a complicated definition. It takes a few different steps to isolate the volatility of the market as a whole. The calculation method itself isn't terribly important to a beginner trader. What is important is how it is used to measure market sentiment.

Using the VIX

VIX options can be used to speculate on the future direction of the market and to hedge changes in market direction. For example, equity investors might want to reduce the amount of market risk in their portfolios. They can do this by writing puts on the VIX. This would let them sell the market volatility to someone else. By offsetting the effect of volatility on the overall portfolio, they reduce risk, and that's valuable.

The basic idea of the VIX as a sentiment indicator is this: If people expect the market to be volatile, then they will be more likely to want insurance and thus to buy VIX options. This will push up the price of the VIX, even if the underlying market remains flat. Hence, the VIX is used to isolate expectations about future market volatility.

The VIX now trades almost around the clock so that speculators and hedgers alike can consider events in Asia and Europe as well as in North America. This improves its significance as an overall market indicator despite being based on the S&P 500. The CBOE has both options and futures contracts on the VIX, including options with weekly expiration.

Because the VIX has been around since 1993, it has a long history of data for researchers to analyze. The track record of the VIX for predicting problems in the stock market is mixed. Volatility is an important component of valuation, for the market as a whole and for individual underlying assets. However, a change in the VIX might not show a change in market volatility, and a change in market volatility might not indicate a change in market valuation. The VIX is one signal among many, but one that has proven popular as a way to trade on volatility.

Extending the VIX Concept

The VIX has proven so popular that the CBOE has issued options on other forms of volatility, including energy, emerging markets, and a handful of very large stocks such as Apple and Goldman Sachs. Other exchanges have introduced versions for other markets, such as Hong Kong.

Some brokerage firms and research services have different volatility measures that are based on the VIX or VIX-like measures, with adjustments to improve the performance of their chosen measure as a leading indicator. (The index market is really competitive, believe it or not.) The idea behind these measures is huge, but there is room for improvement on the execution.

MARKET MAXIM

John Maynard Keynes once noted, the market can remain irrational longer than you can remain solvent. Sometimes, the market makes no sense at all. Someone will make money when the market moves from irrationality to rationality. However, a lot of people will lose money. This is especially true when the broker asks you for money to cover your losing position.

Using Indicators

Market indicators are goofy. They exist because circular trading activities generate indicators that other traders use to plan their trading activities. The exchanges then develop derivatives products based on these indicators that, when traded, generate more indicators used by traders to plan more trading activities.

Options traders use market indicators to figure out where the market is going, how strong that movement is likely to be, and what strategies they want to use to hedge or speculate on those changes. Some of this information is good, and some is noise. It may take some time to figure out which indicators work for you. However, if you know a bit about how they are used, then you can better monitor and evaluate them for your trading.

Don't let the terms bullish, neutral, and bearish confuse you: there are profit opportunities in every type of market. (Of course, there are ways to lose money in every type of market, too, which is why you need to prepare before placing an order.)

Bullish Strategies

If the indicators point to a strong market, then speculators will want to take on more risk in order to profit from it. The simplest, and most bullish strategy, is to buy a call, or to place an order with the broker for a call option.

Bullish strategies look to maximize the upside return. Pushing off risk is less of a concern, but traders should be aware that nothing goes up in price forever.

Neutral Strategies

For all the excitements of bull and bear markets, they aren't as common as you might think. The financial markets have long periods of being sideways, which is trader lingo for a neutral market. Prices move up a little bit and down a little bit, in no discernable direction, for periods ranging from minutes to months.

During these periods of sluggish activity, options traders tend to focus on income strategies. These neutral strategies include writing puts and calls in order to collect the premium as well as straddles and spreads (covered in Chapters 8, 9, and 10).

Bearish Strategies

Bearish strategies fall more along the line of hedging than speculation. Bearish strategies are designed to protect asset values. Nevertheless, options markets give traders quite a few ways to make money on market weakness, including the most bearish strategy, buying calls.

Some people think it's distasteful to make money with a play on prices going down. However, if traders didn't speculate on the downside, overall economic losses from declines could be far greater than they would be otherwise. Options markets have an insurance component; people buy options as much to hedge a position as to speculate on it. Furthermore, speculation on both sides of the market ensures that markets perform their important price discovery functions, helping everyone find the price where both buyers and sellers are satisfied.

The Least You Need to Know

- Successful trading starts with evaluating the mood of the market.
- The options markets have many indicators that traders can use to gauge market sentiment.
- The VIX and other volatility indexes are ways to trade directly on market sentiment.
- Bulls expect market prices to increase, and bears look for them to fall. Both can make money.

Beginning Options Trading

Let me start with a warning. I once talked to the management of a derivatives brokerage that specialized in day traders—smaller investors interested in fast trading. The firm's problem was customer retention because a huge percentage of new customers lost money and quit. (The phenomenon is so common that some trading scams have involved simply taking customer money and not executing any of the trades placed. These scams are only uncovered when the rare successful trader tries to cash out.)

It is easy to lose money in the financial markets, and there are people with a vested interest in helping you do just that. Meanwhile, very simple strategies often make enough money that even big hedge funds and money management firms—with all their fancy MBAs and sophisticated investors—are using them. This book has a lot of information on complex strategies, but that does not mean they are right for you.

Take a careful approach. Think through what you want to accomplish. Options are powerful tools that can help you make money and reduce risk. They can also do some serious damage to your portfolio.

How to Open an Account

You can't trade options without an options account. Most brokerage firms that handle stock trades also handle options trades. Some brokerages specialize in options trading, which are great for experienced traders. However, their services might be overkill for a newbie.

A basic brokerage account is known as a cash account. You deposit cash and buy securities with it. If you sell the securities or receive dividend and interest payments, the money goes into the account. Some options transactions can be handled in a cash account.

The Options Agreement

Before you can trade options in your cash account, though, you'll need to sign an options agreement. This is a standard contract that shows that you understand the risks involved with options trading. Before you trade any options, your broker must give you a standard document prepared by the Options Clearing Corporation titled "Characteristics and Risks of Standardized Options," also known as the Options Disclosure Document or ODD. It's readily available online, so the broker probably will send you to a web page or have you download the file.

As part of this process, the broker will ask for information about your level of trading experience, and the types of options trades you want to make. The broker isn't being nosy. The broker is required by law to collect information about its customers in order to manage its own risks.

Margin Accounts

In addition to the basic account documentation, you might need to be approved for a margin account, which allows you to borrow money from the broker and is a requirement to trade options. The requirements will come in two forms.

The first is the amount of cash and securities that must be in your account before you can be approved to trade on margin. Most brokers set a few different margin levels: one for trading stocks, another for trading *covered options,* and another for trading *naked options.*

> **DEFINITION**
>
> A **covered option** is a short position in an option and the asset needed if the option is exercised. This includes writing a call on shares of stock you already own, or writing a put with enough cash in your account to buy the underlying if the option is exercised. A **naked option** is a short option position in which you do not own the underlying (for a call) or the means to buy it (for a put), so you have greater financial exposure if the option is assigned.

The second is that you must meet a maintenance margin requirement while you are trading. This is the percentage of equity (in the form of cash or securities) relative to your open position that must be kept in the account. This equity is required to protect the broker from default. Minimum maintenance margin requirements are set by the Federal Reserve Board, and your broker might set higher requirements. If your account does not meet the requirements, you will receive a margin call, which is a notice to either deposit more cash and securities, or to sell out your position.

Accounting in Your Account

Obviously, the value of a standard brokerage cash account is equal to the value of the cash and securities in it.

However, the value of an options account is expressed in terms of the credit and debit position. When you buy an option, the cost of the premium is debited from your account. When you sell (write) an option, the cost of the premium is credited to your account. Because some options strategies involve buying and writing simultaneously, the usual term is the "net credit position," which is the net value of all premiums paid and all premiums received.

The value of the premiums changes with the market, and those changes will be reflected in your account.

Also, the options account will show a number called *open interest*, which is the number of options contracts held in the account.

What Do You Want to Do?

This is the big question, isn't it? In both life and trading, figuring out what you want to do is of utmost importance. Do not place a trade without knowing why you are placing it. "To make money" is not the right answer.

Chapter 17 covers trading plans, and it's really important. Planning a trade from entrance to exit is a key discipline in successful trading.

A trading plan does not have to be fancy or complicated. Think: are you trying to hedge a position? Generate income? Reduce the costs of buying and selling stocks?

This chapter covers a few basic strategies—so read on. The strategies discussed in this chapter might be all you ever need to know to find a workable strategy. Whatever you do, be sure you figure out the strategy before you place the trade.

> **MARKET MAXIM**
>
> When it comes to financial markets, simpler is usually better. Making a complicated trade doesn't make you a more sophisticated trader. In fact, making a complicated trade might make you more likely to lose your entire account. The goal of hedging is to protect your position. The goal of speculating is to get a return relative to the amount of risk taken. Impressing people at a cocktail party is not a goal of responsible trading.

Simple Speculative Strategies

If you're interested in options as a way to increase your investment returns by taking risks, then consider some simple speculative strategies. These are not fancy by any stretch of the imagination, but they work well.

Covered Calls

A covered call is a short-call position against an underlying asset that you already own. You collect the premium from selling the option. If the option is then exercised, you fill the order with shares you already own.

This is a simple strategy. And it's effective. It is a way to generate a return without taking on high levels of risk, and it is a good introduction to options for equity investors.

Covered calls can be used to generate a dividend or to close out an equity position with lower transactions costs than a straight sale.

Synthetic Dividend

We're going to get into some financial theory with this one, specifically the work of Nobel Prize winners Franco Modigliani and Merton Miller. Here goes! A company should be generating cash from its business operations, or it is not going to stay in business long. That cash can be reinvested in the business, or it can be paid out as a dividend. In theory, it doesn't matter. (It's one of Modigliani and Miller's propositions, if you are inspired to do more research on this.) In practice, companies don't pay a dividend for a lot of reasons, the main one being that management believes that there are good opportunities to use the cash to fund growth opportunities. Under this reasoning, a dividend payment would reduce the value of the business.

That's all well and good, but maybe you would like some income from your investment. Modigliani and Miller said that all you have to do is make your own dividend by selling some of your shares.

If you have a position in a stock you like but does not pay a dividend—and if you would like a dividend—you can write covered calls on part of your position. The premium generated will bring in some cash. On occasion, the call might be assigned and you lose some of your underlying shares. That is to be expected. The occasional loss of stock will be the equivalent of selling some of your stock to create your own dividend—Modigliani and Miller said so, and who are we to argue with Nobel Prize winners?

Selling the Position

Do you have a stock you want to sell? If you sell it through a broker, you will have to pay a commission. If the stock went up in price, you may owe capital gains taxes, too.

Wouldn't it be nifty if you could actually generate some income when you sell the stock? Well, you can! How? By writing covered calls! To do this, you write calls with an at-the-money strike price to generate some premium income. (This is a strike price that equals the current market price of the underlying asset.) There is a high likelihood that the option will be assigned and the underlying asset called away. In other words, you get out of a position that you wanted to get out of, and you make money in the process.

Playing a Hunch with Weeklys and Binary Options

Weeklys are options that expire at the end of the week. They have a 5-day time horizon. Because of the short time horizon, the price decays quickly.

Essentially, with a weekly, you are betting the option is in the money or that it is worthless, with very little middle ground.

Here's an example. Pretend it's Monday. Your research indicates that a company's earnings are likely to be lower than expected when they are reported tomorrow. If that's the case, the stock is likely to fall in price, so you buy a put. Then you wait. If the news is as bad as you expect, you can either exercise your option or sell it for a higher price. If the company reports good news— or if the news is bad but the stock price stays steady (it happens)—your option will begin its fast decline toward 0 when it expires on Friday.

Binary options are another way to play a hunch. They pay out a fixed amount or nothing, depending on where the price of the underlying asset is relative to the strike price. A long binary put pays off if the underlying security closes at or below the strike price. Most binary options are offered by exchanges outside of the United States, where regulation is less favorable for the trader. Some U.S. exchanges have begun offering binaries because they are popular.

Binaries and weeklys are very much the province of speculators. If you want to speculate, they are the way to go—as long as you understand that you can lose money.

Writing Deep Out-of-the-Money Puts

A popular and risky income strategy is to write deep *out-of-the-money* puts. For example, if a company's stock is currently trading at $75, you could write puts with a strike price of $50. Some traders need these puts for their own reasons, and you can keep the premium. Hurray! Because it's not likely that the stock is going to go up to $50, is it?

While this strategy might work, it's really risky. Many new options traders are happy following this strategy. Of course, their happiness fades when they get stuck with shares of stock in a company they know nothing about and do not want to own. The losses on that underlying asset can outweigh the gains they made from premium income.

There are ways to use this strategy to improve your odds. First, look for companies you might want to own but that have very expensive stock prices. These businesses might not always be wildly successful stock market darlings, but they are likely to be in business for the foreseeable future. In particular, look for companies that are expensive but that pay a steady dividend. This strategy allows you to earn some return even if the underlying price languishes. The dividend acts as a cushion to help reduce the potential loss. Then, write deep out-of-the-money puts on these stocks.

You'll get the income from the puts. If the price falls and the put is assigned, you are likely (but not guaranteed) to end up with a stock that has relatively less risk than many others, which cushions your losses on the downside. Sure, you'll occasionally end up losing money on a terrible underlying asset, but that is a risk you take in the quest for return.

A bull-spread transaction—in which you write a put with one strike and then buy a put with a lower strike price—can cushion the potential for losses by giving you a way to sell the asset to someone else if prices fall. However, it will cut your profit a bit because you'll have to pay for the downside protection.

Reducing Transaction Costs with the Wheel Trade

Stock traders often use limit orders to control their buy and sell prices. A *buy-limit order* tells the broker to buy shares only at or below a predetermined price. A *sell-limit order* tells the broker to sell only when a certain price has been reached. Limit orders are useful forms of discipline and risk management. *Wheel trades* allows you to use limit orders and make money at the same time using options.

> **DEFINITION**
>
> A **buy-limit order** is an order to buy a financial asset that includes instructions to the broker to execute the order only if the asset is at or below a predetermined price.
> A **sell-limit order** is a sell order placed with the broker for a financial asset with instructions to execute it only if a predetermined price is met or exceeded.

The wheel trade is good for people who buy and sell common stocks. It works like this: write puts with a strike price that is at your target purchase price. You'll collect the premium, and if the option is assigned, you'll be able to buy the stock at your purchase price.

Once you have the stock, write calls at your target sell price. Again, you'll collect the premium, and you'll be able to close out your equity position if the option goes in-the-money.

Sometimes, you might end up buying the stock cheap through your put when the company's value slides all the way to 0. Also, you might end up selling a good company's shares too soon. These are the same risks you'd have with a limit trade. The difference is that with the wheel trade, you earn some income as you wait for the underlying price to move to your target range.

MARKET MAXIM

The way to make money in the markets is simple: buy low and sell high. Well, it's simple to state but hard to do in practice. The thoughtful use of options can make it easier for you to buy low and to sell high, which can improve your returns.

Hedging

A key part of the value of options is that they can be used as a form of insurance. They can help people manage their risks. As with any insurance, you pay for coverage, and you are out the price of the policy if you don't use it. The more comprehensive the coverage, the higher it costs.

The simplest hedge is a protective put. This is a put on a security you already own, with a strike set to the maximum loss you are willing to accept. If the price of the underlying goes below the strike price, you can exercise the option and limit the loss.

More complex hedging can be accomplished with the use of options on financial futures and indicators. If you want to hedge the risk of the market, you could sell puts on a major market index. Or, you could hedge volatility with calls on the VIX. If the market fell in value or became more volatile, the gains from these options would offset losses elsewhere in your portfolio.

Finally, if you are trading options on underlying assets that you do not own, you might want to find ways to hedge those risks. Earlier in this chapter, I talk about writing deep out-of-the-money puts and hedging them with the purchase of puts with a lower strike price. This simple spread greatly reduces a trader's risk.

The more you understand about the risk of your position, the better you'll be able to respond to changing markets or find hedges.

Closing Out Your Position

Options come with an expiration date. That's why they have time value. That's also why part of your trade plan must include closing the position. As the name implies, you have options with options.

An option position can be closed out with an offsetting trade by letting it expire, or through exercise and assignment. Part of your trade plan should include thinking about what will happen to the trade between the day you initiate it and the day it expires.

As a rough estimate, 60 percent of options are closed out with offsetting trades. Another 30 percent or so expire worthless. The remaining 10 percent are exercised.

Offsetting Trades

Most option positions are closed out before expiration with an offsetting trade. If you buy a 50 July put, you sell a 50 July put, and then—blam!—you have no net open interest.

Options traders often place positions with the expectation that the price of the premium will change in their favor. Many of the complex trades—such as butterflies and condors—are as much about speculating on the prices of options as they are on the underlying asset.

You can make an offsetting trade to lock in a profit, limit a loss, or prevent assignment. For example, if you write a covered call and would prefer to keep the underlying asset, it might be worth offsetting the trade with the purchase of a call—even at a loss—than to have the underlying asset called away.

Expiring Worthless

Most options that are not closed out end up expiring. If you wrote the option, you get to keep the premium. If you purchased it, then you're out the money. You can roll your position out to a new expiration date or walk away.

Many of those who write covered calls or cash-secured puts figure that they will be safe because most options expire worthless. That's a dangerous train of thought. Option writing is not free money. You are writing a real contract and taking real risks. You might very well be better off making an offsetting trade than crossing your fingers and hoping to avoid exercise.

Exercise and Assignment

If you want to exercise an option, you will need to contact your broker. Some firms require you to call rather than order the exercise online. Also, the Options Clearing Corporation has the right to automatically exercise any option that is in-the-money by at least a penny on the day before expiration. This matters because it could create a short position and a margin call. For example, if you wrote a naked call that is automatically exercised, your account will reflect the short position. If you don't have the margin, your account will be closed.

When an option is exercised, the Options Clearing Corporation does not track down the specific trader who wrote the specific contract in question. Instead, it randomly assigns the option to someone who wrote one just like it. If you sell a 30 August call to Bob, and Bob decides to exercise it, the OCC may bypass you and assign the call at random to Jenny, who wrote 30 August calls to someone else. She can't argue that she wasn't the original writer. She has an obligation to exercise upon assignment.

If an option is assigned to you, then the brokerage firm will automatically exercise it. If you wrote a call, then the cash will be transferred to your account and the underlying asset transferred out. If you wrote a put, then the cash will be transferred out of your account and the underlying asset transferred in.

What About Employee Stock Options?

This book is about exchange-listed options, but many individual investors have experience with a different type of option: employee stock options. These are call options written by an employer and given to employees. In most cases, they are given to employees as incentive compensations. The idea is that you will do such a great job that the stock price will go up and you will make a lot of money when you execute the option.

I've known people who have made a lot of money from their employee options, and I've known people who had a crazy number of options expire worthless when their employer went bankrupt.

There are a few things to keep in mind:

- Your option is worth nothing unless and until you exercise it.

- You might owe tax when receiving the option, executing the option, or selling the stock you received when you exercised it.

- You might very well have a taxable event even though you didn't receive any cash. Check with a tax expert to be sure your option won't generate a headache. IRS Publication 525, Taxable and Nontaxable Income, has all the details.

The Least You Need to Know

- You need a margin agreement with your broker to trade options.
- Simple strategies are best for beginners—and for most advanced traders, too.
- Plan your trade and trade your plan.
- Close out your trade when it's time.

Call Strategies

Calls are options that give you the right—but not the obligation—to buy something in the future at a price agreed upon today. You can exercise that right at any point until the option expires. Calls are bets that the price of the underlying asset will be higher than the strike price by the time the expiration rolls around. That's why calls are often considered to be a bullish derivative.

At the most basic level, people buy calls as bets that the underlying will increase in price. They are hoping that the call will allow them to buy the underlying asset at a price below the market.

Traders use calls in many ways, from the simple to the complex. This chapter covers many of their uses. Not all of these calls will be appropriate for you. However, learning more about calls might help you better understand a simple strategy.

In This Chapter

- How call options work
- Potential payoffs
- Using calls to speculate
- Hedging with call options

Basic Uses of Calls

A call is an option that gives you the right to buy a share of stock at a specified price in the future. If you buy a call option, your payoff looks like the following graph:

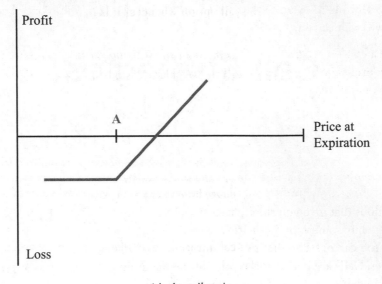

A is the strike price.

The vertical axis is the amount of profit you receive, and the horizontal axis is the price of the underlying asset. The line drawn at zero profit is the *x* axis and is the price of the underlying asset. Showing it helps illustrate when the option is profitable and when it is unprofitable to the holder. Until the option is exercised, the position is at a loss equal to the premium.

For example, let's say you buy a American-style March 2017 call with a strike price of $120 on an stock with an underlying price of $106. You pay $1.08 for the call. Although you can exercise the option at any time, you probably won't do so until the price of the underlying asset is above $120 because you can buy the stock cheaper in the open market. Below $120, you lose the $1.08 cost of the call. Above a stock price of $121.08 (or the strike price plus the call premium), your position is profitable. At stock prices between $120.00 and $121.08, exercising the option will reduce the loss. If you exercise when the market is at $120.50, you'll have a profit on the stock of the $120.50 market price less the $120.00 strike price, or $0.50. That $0.50 offsets some of the $1.08 premium, for a total cost of $0.58.

With a long call position, you are out the amount of the premium. Part of that loss might be offset by an increase in the value of the underlying asset. Your position is considered to be in-the-money if the underlying is above the exercise price. However, it is only profitable to exercise when the underlying asset hits a price above the sum of the strike price plus the call premium.

Still, it is worthwhile to exercise the call option whenever it is in-the-money because exercising the option will reduce your loss.

If you write a call—also known as the sale of a call, or being short a call—you receive the premium. In exchange, you agree to sell the stock at the strike price, should the buyer choose to exercise the option.

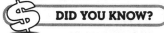 **DID YOU KNOW?**

> The basic option payoff graph will show up over and over again in this book. It's a useful way to work out a strategy and to see exactly what could happen to a position that you establish. Some brokerage firms offer payoff graph generators as part of its service array.

Here's what the payoff from the short call position looks like:

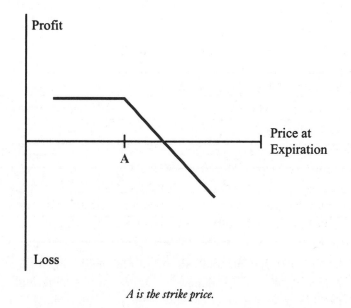

A is the strike price.

As with the call payoff graph, the vertical axis is the amount of profit you receive, and the horizontal axis is the price of the underlying asset. The line drawn at zero profit helps illustrate when the short call becomes is unprofitable to the writer. The writer keeps the premium no matter what happens to the underlying. The writer must transfer the underlying asset if the call holder decides to exercise it. This will most likely happen if the call is in-the-money. However, holders are free to exercise at any level of moneyness they choose.

For example, suppose you write an American-style call option on a common stock that has a current price of $32.50 per share. This option expires in a year and has a strike price of $40. The premium is $0.48. And you, dear writer, get to keep that $0.48 no matter what happens. The trader who buys the option from you won't be in-the-money until the stock price is above $40. (Of course, people exercise options for different reasons, and you could hit it lucky and be assigned to receive $40 per share for a stock with a market price of $35.00. Cha ching! Don't count on that, though.) If the market price is $41 when the option is assigned, you must deliver the stock to the option holder. At a market price of $41 and a strike price of $40, you'll have a loss of $1. Of course, you also have the $0.48 premium, so your total loss is $1.00 − $0.48 = $0.52.

With a short call position, you keep the amount of the premium, no matter what happens to the strike price. The position is considered to be in-the-money at prices below the exercise price.

The following table summarizes the economics of a call option for both the buyer and seller.

Economics of a Call Option on a Single Stock

	Buyer	Writer
At purchase	Pays premium	Receives premium
In-the-money	Receives stock	Transfers stock
Out-of-the-money	Loses premium	Keeps premium
Upside potential	Market price − strike price − premium	Premium received
Downside potential	Premium paid	Market price − strike price + premium
Market view	Bullish	Bearish

The buyer of a call pays a premium and will receive the underlying asset at exercise. The option is profitable to exercise if it is in-the-money—meaning that the underlying price is higher than the exercise price. The most the buyer can lose is the premium paid. The most the buyer can make is the market price of the underlying asset, less the strike price, less the premium paid. Call buyers are generally bullish.

Call writers have a different set of economics. They receive the premium in exchange for writing the option. If the option is exercised, the writer has to transfer the underlying asset to the option holder. If the option is not exercised, the writer's profit is the premium amount. If the option is exercised, the writer's loss is the difference between the market price and the strike price, offset by the premium. (Note that the writer's cost might be different than the market cost of the underlying. Many option sellers write options on stocks they already own.) Option writers have a more bearish view of the market than option buyers.

Why Use Long Calls

Let's start with the simple proposition of buying a call. You are taking a position on the underlying asset increasing in value. Why?

Hedging with Long Calls

It might seem strange to want insurance against the price of the underlying asset going up, but that is exactly what people want when they hedge with long calls. There are situations in which an increase in the price of the underlying asset is a problem:

- Being short the underlying stock

- Needing to pay bills in a different currency

- Running a business in which profits will be hurt by rising energy prices

Speculating with Long Calls

Being long a call is the most bullish of ways to speculate on the price of an underlying asset. It's a bold statement when you expect the asset to go up in value, and you want to make a profit when it happens!

Being Short a Call

The person who writes the call is short, meaning that he hopes the underlying asset stays flat or goes down. Short calls have many uses in trading.

Hedging with Short Calls

The value of a short call as a hedge comes from the income generated on a covered position. If you write a call on an asset you already own, you will make some money if it falls in price or stays flat. That gain is offset by the loss of the asset should the option be exercised. Some stock holders use a call as a way to sell an appreciated stock. They use the premium to offset the capital gains tax obligation.

Short calls don't really offer price protection, but they are a way to make money if the market is flat or down. Short calls might be part of complex hedging strategies because the premium income might offset the cost of purchasing other derivatives used to build the hedge.

Speculating with Short Calls

Short-call speculation strategies are tied to income. The option writer receives the premium and hopes to avoid exercising the option in question. The bet is that the price of the underlying asset will be below the strike price at expiration.

A covered-call strategy involves writing options that are out-of-the-money on assets already owned.

Some covered-call strategies are written in-the-money, with the intention of having the underlying asset called away. This strategy offsets the transaction cost and capital gain on an asset sale.

Naked-call writing has more risk than covered-call writing. Writing naked calls is covered later in this chapter.

The Call and Its Premium

As with any option, the value of a call is affected by a variety of factors. The following table summarizes how the value of long and short call positions change as different market factors increase. The option price will be the same, but its relative value will be different to the holder and the writer.

Market Factor	Long Call	Short Call
Underlying Price	Increases	Decreases
Exercise Price	Decreases	Increases
Volatility	Increases	Decreases
Time to Expiration	Increases	Decreases
Interest Rate	Increases	Decreases
American Option	Increases	Decreases
Dividend	Decreases	Increases

This is related to the Black-Scholes model discussed in Chapter 5. If you compare, you'll see that the value of the short call is similar to the value of the long put. The two have similar payoffs.

If the value of the underlying asset increases, the value of the long call increases, too. The short call becomes less valuable, all else being equal. The relationship to the exercise price is the opposite. For the long call, a high exercise price will be less valuable, but it will be more valuable for the call writer.

The big difference between the valuation of the short call and the long put are the factors that increase the likelihood the option is exercised. The person taking the long side of the option probably wants to exercise it, while the person on the short side would like to keep the premium and not be assigned. The greater the volatility and the more time to expiration, the more valuable the option is to the holder. Likewise, if volatility is low, the option has less value for the holder.

American options, which can be exercised at any time before expiration, are more valuable for the holder because the option could be in-the-money for a short period before expiration. The writer, on the other hand, would prefer a European-style option because, all else being equal, it is less likely to be assigned.

This background can help you think about the risk and return of the position that you are considering.

Call Strategies

Calls are traded on a standalone basis, but they are also used as part of different strategies. Some are simple, some are more complex. Following is the rundown.

Writing Covered Calls

A *covered call* is a call option written on an underlying asset. This is also known as a *buy-write strategy*. It's a way to generate income with relatively little risk. Because you already own the underlying asset, you won't lose much money if you have to sell it to the option buyer. If it's an asset that you are already thinking of removing from your portfolio, the premium from the call option will help cover the transactions costs when it is called away.

The profit payoff for a covered call is the same as that of a short-call position. The difference is that the cash loss is smaller because you own the asset in question.

This strategy is popular in a neutral market. It also has the potential to perform well. The CBOE publishes the S&P 500 BuyWrite Index, which looks at a hypothetical trade involving the purchase of the S&P 500 Index and then writing calls on the index—a covered-call strategy on the entire market. Over the years, the BuyWrite Index has outperformed the S&P 500, but with less risk.

DID YOU KNOW?

Although buying the entire S&P 500 Index seems impossible, it's really not. Index mutual funds, exchange-traded funds, and index futures are different ways that traders can buy these funds for use in different strategies.

Writing Naked Calls

This is the practice of writing a call option on an underlying asset that you do not own. Because you are not covered, you're naked.

The writer keeps the premium as long as the option is out-of-the-money. If the option is assigned (most likely because it is in-the-money), then the writer must buy the underlying asset in order to sell it to the option holder. This is an expensive proposition if the market is moving fast.

There is demand for deep out-of-the-money options that meet the needs of people pursuing complex portfolio hedging strategies. These also have low premiums. The problem is the premium generated will rise the closer the option is to being in-the-money. However, that also increases the risk.

Replacement Therapy

Replacement therapy is a strategy that involves selling a stock and replacing it with long calls to get your capital out of the market. The calls may be in-the-money or out-of-the-money, depending on how anxious the shareholder is to sell. This allows you to get out of a stock position while still retaining some upside potential.

Call Spreads

Call spread strategies involve the purchase of one call and the sale of another. The two differ on only one feature, such as strike price or expiration.

Call spreads also add an element of complication to a position. Instead of having to track an option and an underlying asset, you now must track two options. These aren't beginner strategies.

Bull-Call Spread

A bull-call spread means you purchase a call with one strike price and then write a call with a higher strike price. The premium received will be less than the premium paid because the call with the higher strike price will be further out-of-the-money. This position has limited risk, but that comes with limited profit. (This is not necessarily a bad thing.)

For example, suppose you buy a June call on a stock with a strike price of $140 and a premium of $0.87. You then write a call with a strike price of $145 and a premium of $0.58. Your cost of the position is $0.87 − $0.58 = $0.29, and that's the most you can lose.

The option you wrote will be in-the-money if the stock price goes above $145. The option that you bought will be in-the-money then, too. So you could exercise your option to buy the stock at $140, then sell it to the call holder at $145, for a net profit of $5.00. Of course, you have to take out the $0.29 cost of the position, for a maximum profit of $5.00 − $0.29 = $4.71.

The following graph shows the payoff:

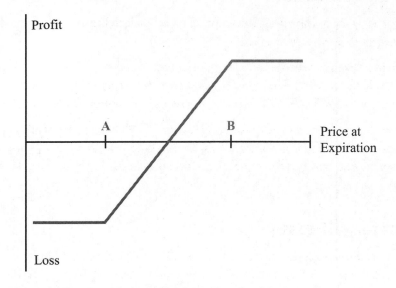

A is the strike price of the long call and B is the strike of the short call.

The profit is limited to the difference in the strike prices less the difference in the premiums (also known as *net debit* or net premium paid). The loss is limited to the difference in the premiums. These are used by traders who are bullish, but not so bullish that they want to take a risk on the downside.

Bear-Call Spread

A bear-call spread involves buying a call with one strike price, and then selling a call with a lower strike price.

Suppose you buy a September call with a strike price of $39 for $0.15. You then write a September call with a strike price of $32 for $1.27. You now have a *net credit* position of $1.27 − $0.15 = $1.12. Now, your overall position is out-of-the-money and profitable to you as long as the underlying price is below $32. At that price, the option is likely to be exercised. You would have to buy the underlying asset in order to cover the assignment, so your loss would be the market price less $32. However, if the underlying price were at $39 or above, you could exercise your long call to limit your loss. Hence, your maximum loss would be $39.00 − $32.00 − $1.12 = $5.88.

The payoff looks like this:

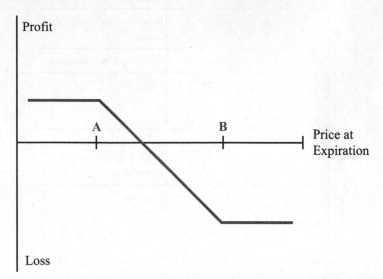

A is the strike price of the short call, and B is the strike of the long call.

The maximum payoff is the difference between the premium received and the premium paid (the net credit position). The maximum loss is the difference between the strike prices minus the difference between the underlying premiums. This is a mildly bearish strategy. It is profitable when the underlying price is below the strike price on the short call on the expiration date, but its losses are limited.

Married Calls

A married-call strategy is similar to a bull spread except that the trade involves shorting the underlying asset while purchasing calls to cover the amount of the asset. The calls act as insurance against the short position moving against the trader. Married calls can be used to repurchase the asset and to close out the short, which is a fine insurance policy.

The following table is a summary of the costs and payoffs of call spread strategies.

Economics of Call Spread Strategies

	Bull Spread	Bear Spread	Married
To establish	Pay premium on one call, receive premium on another call with a higher strike	Pay premium on one call, receive premium on another call with a lower strike	Receive proceeds of stock sale, pay premium on calls

	Bull Spread	**Bear Spread**	**Married**
In-the-money	Deliver underlying	Receive the underlying asset	Receive the underlying asset
Out-of-the-money	Lose net premium	Receive net premium	Lose premium
Upside potential	Difference in strikes minus difference in premiums	Premium	Difference between stock price and strike price minus premium
Downside potential	Difference in premiums	Difference in strikes minus difference in premiums	Premium paid
Market view	Bullish	Bearish	Bullish

Calendar Spread

A *calendar spread,* also called a time spread or a horizontal spread, involves buying a call with one expiration date and selling a call on the same underlying asset with the same strike price but a different expiration. This is a play on the time value and volatility of the options, because the value of the underlying asset nets out.

> **DEFINITION**
>
> A **calendar spread** involves buying a call with one expiration date and then selling a call on the same underlying asset with the same strike price but a different expiration date.

For example, you could buy a call with a strike price of $80 and an April expiration for $0.10. Then, you could write a call with a strike price of $80 and a July expiration for $0.60. You now have a profitable net credit position of $0.60 − $0.10 = $0.50.

However, you still have to make a decision about how to handle the underlying asset. The call you wrote for the July expiration could be exercised and assigned to you at any point up to and including the expiration date. You could minimize the risk by exercising your long call for $80 to keep on hand if the short call is exercised. However, if the price is below $80 when the July call expires, you have taken a loss on the asset position. A calendar spread is a speculative position that is usually closed out before the expiration date of either option.

Butterfly Spreads

Butterfly spreads get their name for the wings that form on the payoff graph, which you can see later in this chapter. Butterfly spreads are designed to play on expectations about volatility. Keep in mind that these are speculative positions, so they can do a lot of damage to your account. Also, the more transactions you make to establish a position, the higher the commissions and fees, which can wipe out profits no matter what happens to the price of the underlying asset. These strategies are for advanced traders only.

Long-Butterfly-Call Spread

A long-butterfly-call spread is the combination of a bear-call spread and a bull-call spread. A trader sets it up by selling two calls that are at or in-the-money and buying one in-the-money call and one out-of-the-money call on the same underlying asset with the same expiration date. The two short calls have the same strike price.

For example, let's say that September calls are $8.50 for a strike price of $47, $5.80 for a strike of $52.50, and $3.15 for a strike of $3.15. First, you set up a bull-call spread, buying the option with the $47 strike and writing the option with the $52.50 strike. Then, you set up a bear-call spread, writing the $52.50 strike and buying the $57.50 strike.

The following table shows what your position looks like.

Long-Butterfly-Call Spread

	Strike	Premium
Bull-Call Spread		
Buy	$47	($8.50)
Write	$52.50	$5.80
Bear-Call Spread		
Write	$52.50	$5.80
Buy	$57.50	($3.15)
Net credit		($0.05)

Now, if the underlying asset trades above $57.50, then all of the options will be exercised. You'll be able to buy shares at both $47 and $57.50, and then sell them to the traders who bought your calls at $52.50. In this situation, your profit will be $52.50 + $52.50 − $47.00 − $57.50 = $0.50, less the $0.05 cost of the premium, for a net profit of $0.45.

If none of the options are exercised, you've lost $0.05.

The following diagram shows the payoff:

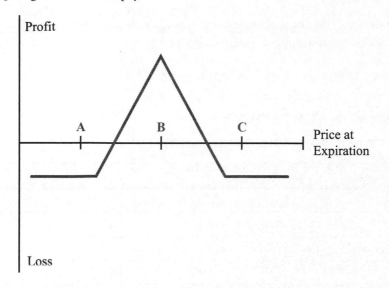

A and C are the strike prices of the long calls, and B is the strike price of the short call.

The profit on a long-butterfly-call spread is equal to the difference in strike prices minus the difference in premiums. The loss is limited to the net premium paid. A long-butterfly-call allows a trader to profit when the underlying asset is not expected to change much in price, but with much less downside risk than either a straddle or a strangle (covered in Chapter 10).

> **MARKET MAXIM**
>
> If you want action, go to Vegas. A lot of good options trading strategies are slow and steady. They might not be glamorous, and they might not lead to lots of jumping and screaming, but that doesn't make them bad strategies.

Short-Butterfly-Call Spread

Just like the long-butterfly-call spread, a short-butterfly-call spread is the combination of a bear-call spread and a bull-call spread. However, the short-butterfly-call spread has different price points for the long and the short. A trader sets it up by buying two calls, either at the money (i.e., with a strike price that is the same as the current market price of the underlying asset) or out-of-the-money. The trader then sells one in-the-money call and one out-of-the-money call on the same underlying asset with the same expiration date. The two long calls have the same strike price.

Here's an example. Let's say that February calls are $12.35 for a strike price of $155, $5.57 for a strike of $165, and $1.82 for a strike of $175. First, you set up a bear-call spread, writing the option with the $155 strike and buying the option with the $165 strike. Then, you set up a bull call spread, buying the $165 strike and writing the $175 strike.

The following table shows what your position looks like.

Short-Butterfly-Call Spread

	Strike	Premium
Bear-Call Spread		
Write	$155	$12.35
Buy	$165	($5.37)
Bull-Call Spread		
Buy	$165	($5.37)
Write	$175	$1.82
Net credit		$3.43

If the underlying asset trade is above $155, you can keep the $3.43 credit.

If the asset trades above $175, all the options will be exercised, and the strike prices net out. The assignment of the call option written at $155 can be filled with the call option purchased at $165, for a loss of $10. The call option written at $175 can be filled with the second call purchased at $165, for a gain of $10. The underlying value nets out and you can keep the $3.43.

Between $155 and $175, this position will lose money. The amount you lose depends on the price of the underlying asset. If the price of the underlying asset is at $160, the option written at $155 is in-the-money. Your position is down $5, offset by the $3.43 credit, for a net debit of $1.57. The maximum loss occurs at $165 exactly, with the option position down $10 but offset by the $3.43 for a net loss of $6.57. As the underlying increases beyond $165, the gain on the bull spread offsets the loss on the bear spread.

The following diagram shows what the payoff looks like:

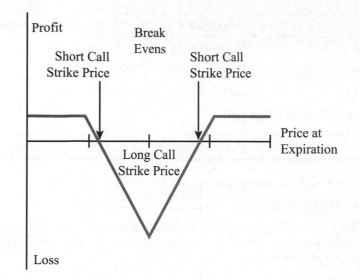

The figure crosses the x axis at the strike prices of the short calls. It loses the most at the strike price of the long calls.

The potential profit on this transaction is limited to the net premium paid. The potential loss is equal to the difference in strike prices minus the difference in premiums. A short butterfly allows a trader to profit from volatility, but with much less downside risk than either a straddle or a strangle (covered in Chapter 10).

Keep in mind that premium prices change frequently, so it might be difficult to set up a profitable butterfly. Also, you will probably want to close it out before maturity.

Economics of Butterfly-Call Strategies

	Long Spread	Short Spread
To establish	Net premiums	Net premiums
In-the-money	Difference between underlying, strike, and net premium	Net premium
Out-of-the-money	Lose net premium	Lose difference between the price of the underlying asset, strike, and net premium

continues

Economics of Butterfly-Call Strategies (continued)

	Long Spread	Short Spread
Upside potential	Difference between underlying, strike, and net premium	Net premium
Downside potential	Net premium	Lose difference between the price of the underlying asset, strike, and net premium
Market view	Neutral	Volatile

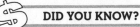

DID YOU KNOW?

There are a lot of fanciful names for options strategies. Some are named after their payoffs, but others might simply be named by traders doing something interesting on a slow day. That's okay.

Condors

Condors are like butterflies except that they have a spread on the strike prices. This gives them a wider wingspan than the butterfly (hence the name).

Long-Condor-Call Spread

A long-condor-call spread is similar to a long-butterfly-call spread, but with a wider range of prices where the position is at peak profitability. A trader sets it up by selling two out-of-the-money calls with different strike prices. She then buys one in-the-money call and one out-of-the-money call on the same underlying asset with the same expiration date, making sure that those strike prices are above and below the prices of the short calls.

The profit on a long-condor-call spread is equal to the difference in strike prices minus the difference in premiums. The loss is limited to the net premium paid. A long-condor-call allows a trader to profit when the underlying asset is not expected to change much in price. However, long-condor-calls have much less downside risk than either a straddle or a strangle and more flexibility than a butterfly.

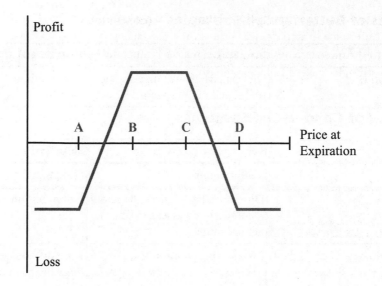

A and D are the strike prices on the long calls, and B and C are the strikes on the short calls.

Short-Condor-Call Spread

Just like a long-condor-call spread, a short-condor-call spread is the combination of a bear-call spread and a bull-call spread. A short-condor-call spread is made by buying two in-the-money calls, and selling one in-the-money call and one out-of-the-money call on the same underlying asset with the same expiration date. The long calls should have a strike price between the two short calls.

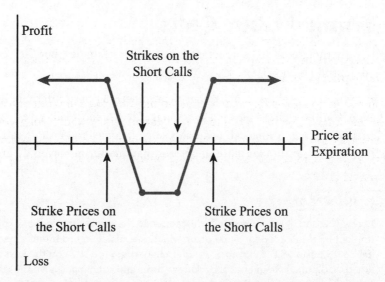

The strike prices on the short calls are above the x axis, and the strike prices on the long calls are below it.

The potential profit on this transaction is limited the net premium paid. The potential loss is equal to the difference in strike prices minus the difference in premiums. A short condor allows a trader to profit from extremes in volatility, but with much less downside risk than either a straddle or a strangle (covered in Chapter 10).

Economics of Condor-Call Strategies

	Long Spread	Short Spread
To establish	Net premiums	Net premiums
In-the-money	Difference between the price of the underlying asset, strike, and net premium	Net premium
Out-of-the-money	Lose net premium	Lose difference between the price of the underlying asset, strike, and net premium
Upside potential	Difference between underlying, strike, and net premium	Net premium
Downside potential	Net premium	Lose difference between the price of the underlying asset, strike, and net premium
Market view	Neutral	Volatile

How to Think About Calls

Calls are generally thought of in conjunction with bullish strategies, but they can be used as part of bearish and neutral positions, too.

The key is to think about calls as tools, rather than something particularly bullish or bearish. A long call gives you the right to buy at a particular price. A short call gives you the obligation to sell at a particular price. A long call generates some income, and a short call costs money. Understanding those basics are far more important than mastering payoff diagrams.

DID YOU KNOW?

Every now and again, something will happen in the market that defies explanation. It might be a so-called *fat finger* error, which is a mistaken order entry made by a keyboard mistake. For example, a trader might press too hard on the keys and buy 1,000,000 puts instead of 100. Brokerage firms and exchanges have the right to cancel trades that appear to be the results of order entry errors. Let's hope it's not you!

The Least You Need to Know

- A long call position pays off when the underlying increases in price. A short call pays off when the asset stays flat or declines in value.
- Long calls are generally used as bullish strategies.
- Writing calls is a popular strategy for generating income, especially by those who own the underlying asset.
- Long and short calls can be combined to play different aspects of price volatility.

Put Strategies

Want to get rid of something? In trader terms, you put it to someone else. If that item has gone down in value, the ability to put it to someone else is a great thing. A put option gives the holder the right to sell an asset to someone else at a pre-determined price. If the asset falls in value, the put holder makes money.

Because puts come in-the-money as the underlying price falls, they are often considered to be bearish. Some people even think it's bad to profit on a decline in price. But puts don't have to bearish, and a price decline isn't always bad news. Put strategies offer different ways to speculate and hedge on the prices of stocks and other assets.

In This Chapter

- How puts work
- Using puts for hedging and speculating
- Complicated strategies for occasional use only
- Other put strategy information you need to know

Basic Uses of Puts

A put, of course, is an option that gives you the right to sell a predetermined amount of an underlying asset at a specified price at or before a specified future expiration date. The following graph below illustrates the payoff of a long-put position:

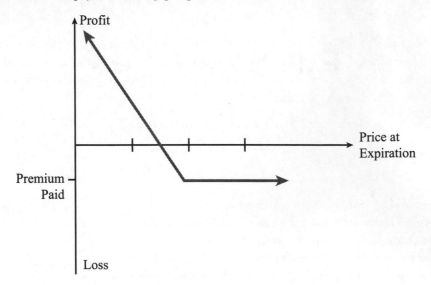

The vertical axis is the amount of profit you receive, and the horizontal axis is the price of the underlying asset. The axis crosses at 0 profit to show when the option is profitable and when it is unprofitable to the holder. When a put option is purchased, the position is a loss equal to the amount of the premium.

For example, you buy a March put on an asset with an underlying price of $118. The strike price on your put is $100, and you pay a premium of $4.55. If the asset falls to $90, you would be able to buy the stock at $90 and sell it to the put writer for $100, for a profit of $10. Of course, you'd have to subtract the $4.55 premium paid, so your profit would be $10.00 − $4.55 = $5.45.

If the underlying asset is at $100 or above at expiration, you would not ordinarily want to exercise the option, so you'd be out the $4.55 cost.

DID YOU KNOW?

If you read Chapter 8, you might think this graph and the others in this chapter look familiar. And in fact, the payoff of a long put is similar to the payoff of a short call. Because of this, the payoffs of other put strategies look similar to those of call strategies. The relationship between puts and calls is important for designing combination strategies, which will be covered in Chapter 10.

With a long put position, you lose the premium amount, no matter what happens to the strike price. Your position is considered to be in-the-money as soon as the underlying price exceeds the exercise price, but it is only profitable to exercise when the underlying hits a price below the sum of the strike price minus the put premium.

Still, it is worthwhile to exercise the put option at any time that it is in-the-money, because exercise will reduce the amount of the loss you have.

If you write a put—also known as the sale of a put, or being short a call—you receive the premium. In exchange, you agree to buy the underlying at a specified price in the future, should the buyer choose to exercise it. In general, the price that makes assignment profitable is a price that is higher than the market value.

The payoff from the short put position can be illustrated like this:

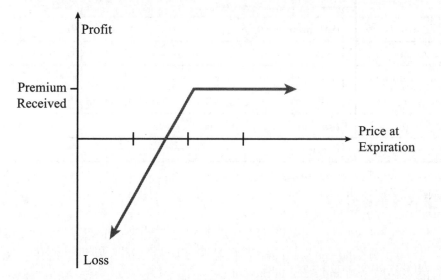

A short put is profitable as long as the price of the underlying asset is below the strike price.

As with the long put payoff graph, the vertical axis is the amount of profit you receive, and the horizontal axis is the price of the underlying asset. The axis is drawn at 0 profit helps illustrate when the short put becomes unprofitable to the writer. The writer keeps the premium no matter what happens to the underlying. The writer must buy the underlying asset if the put goes into the money. (Sure, the holder has the right to exercise at any time and at any market price, but it is only profitable to do so if the put is in-the-money. It makes things easier to assume that traders are rational. However, who knows what goes through people's heads some days.)

And just as the long put profits from the same market conditions as a short call, the short put behaves similarly to a long call.

With a short-put position, you keep the amount of the premium, no matter what happens to the strike price. The position is considered to be in-the-money at prices above the exercise price.

The losses on a naked short put can be huge—you might have to buy an asset that goes all the way to 0. One way to hedge is with the purchase of a put with a lower strike price (also known as a bull-put spread). Don't assume that it can't happen to you! The financial markets are very strange.

The following table offers a summary of the profits and losses involved with different put positions.

Economics of a Put Option on a Single Stock

	Buyer	Writer
At purchase	Pays premium	Receives premium
In-the-money	Sells stock	Receives stock
Out-of-the-money	Loses premium	Keeps premium
Upside potential	Strike price minus market price minus premium	Premium value
Downside potential	Premium value minus market price	Strike price plus premium
Market view	Bearish	Bullish

Long Put Strategies

The starting point for a review of uses of puts is simple: what happens if you buy a put? You want to be long a put if you want to bet on the price of the underlying asset going down. The reasons for taking this proposition may differ.

Hedging

A put holder might be hedging against the decline of a price in the underlying security. A put is a great form of insurance on prices, which is useful for anyone who does not want to lose wealth from a price decline.

Speculating

A speculating put holder is betting that the underlying asset will decline in price. This is a bit risky because most markets have an upward bias in prices. If we assume that the economy is growing, then prices should increase by the rate of inflation. That's the tendency that a put holder is fighting when he or she is speculating on the market.

> **DID YOU KNOW?**
>
> Some people think it's bad to speculate on price declines because it's a way of making money from someone's misfortune. However, a price decline doesn't always mean suffering. A decline in grain prices, for example, is bad for the farmer but good for the consumer. Markets need to have two sides to function. That means for any good or service, a price change that benefits one side won't benefit the other.

Short Put Strategies

A short put is the mirror of a long call. It is bet that the price of the underlying will close above the strike price at the expiration date. And like any put or call, it has many uses.

Hedging with Short Puts

Short puts are a way to hedge against the price of an asset rising in the sense that an increase in the asset price is offset by the premium received for writing the put.

Now, you might be thinking that an increase in the price of an asset is a good thing, but that is not always the case. Think of a business that has expenses in yen. If the yen increases relative to the dollar, then the business's costs will go up. One of the many ways to hedge against this would be to write puts, collecting income to offset the effect of a stronger yen.

Speculating

When writing a put, the seller is looking to generate income. She will be able to do so as long as the price of the underlying does not fall below the strike price at expiration. There is considerable risk, though, so few put sellers are willing to write puts without using other types of options for protection.

But, you might be thinking, wouldn't a call writer have the same risk? After all, a stock can, in theory, go up to infinity, and it can only go down to 0. That's absolutely true, but most call-writing income strategies are based on covered calls. If you write calls on assets you already own, then you have some protection if your call is exercised. It doesn't work that way with puts. If you write puts on an asset you already own that go down in price, you still must buy more of the asset at the strike price when the underlying goes down.

The Put and the Premium

Put options are affected by the price of the underlying, the price and date of exercise, the amount of volatility, and interest rates. The following table summarizes the effects of the price factors.

Market Factor	Long Put	Short Put
Underlying price	Decreases	Increases
Exercise price	Increases	Decreases
Volatility	Increases	Decreases
Time to expiration	Increases	Decreases
Interest rate	Decreases	Increases
American option	Increases	Decreases
Dividend	Increases	Decreases

Put Strategies

Some buyers and sellers of puts are interested in puts alone, but most use them as part of more complex strategies. This section is a rundown of many of the different ways that puts can be used, alone and with other contracts.

Protective Puts

A *protective put*, sometimes called a covered put, is a long-put position combined with a long position in the underlying asset. This is one of the most common uses of puts because it's obvious and it works.

For example, suppose you own an underlying asset with a market value of $100. You do not want to lose more than 15 percent of its value, so you buy a put with a strike price of $85. If the price of the asset falls by more than 15 percent, you can exercise the option and sell your underlying for $85. If the underlying is above $85, then you lose the cost of the premium. That's how insurance works, after all.

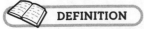 **DEFINITION**

A **protective put** is a put option purchased by the owner of the underlying asset as insurance against a price decline.

Naked Puts

The thing about writing puts is that there's no way to hedge it with assets you already own, other than with cash. Most put writers are using other options to manage their positions, but some choose to write options naked—that is, with no coverage. This is risky, but if you want to do it, here's the usual technique: writing deep out-of-the-money puts. These are puts that are very unlikely to go in-the-money during the holding period, such as puts on a 20 percent decline in a stock market index over the next month. Can it happen? Sure. There are a few huge one-day declines in the history of the financial markets. Is it likely? Well, it's hard to say.

For example, consider OEX put options. These are Chicago Board Options Exchange options on the S&P 100 Index. On a day when the index is at $875, you see that the premium for December put options with a strike price of $320 are trading at $2 each. How likely is it that the index will fall by more than half between now and expiration? Not very. Could it happen? Sure! And if that happens, you will be out a lot of money.

Some algorithmic programs use puts on unlikely price declines as part of complex portfolio insurance strategies. The downside, of course, is that a calamity in the financial markets will make these go in-the-money with very little warning—and very big losses for the writer. Tread carefully.

> **DID YOU KNOW?**
>
> A common hedging strategy is portfolio insurance, which an investor uses to protect against an overall market decline. The simplest form of portfolio insurance is the purchase of market index puts. That's why there's a market for them.

Put Spreads

Put spreads involve the purchase of one put and the sale of another. They not only help manage the risk of writing a naked put, but they also offer a range of ways to hedge and speculate. All you have to do is put them together! (I know, bad pun.)

The two options in a put spread differ on one feature, such as strike price or expiration. Because of this, they have different premiums and different expected price movements.

Bull-Put Spread

Although the put is a bearish option, put strategies are not necessarily bearish. A great example is the bull-put spread, also known as a credit spread. In this, you sell a put with one strike price and buy a put with a lower strike price. You have the premium and some protection.

For example, say you write a put with a strike price of $37 for a premium of $0.08. Then, you buy a put with a strike price of $30 and a strike price of $0.01. Your net credit position from the premiums is $0.07. If the underlying closes above $37, you keep the premium. If the price slides below that, you might be assigned the option and buy the stock at $37. If the underlying goes below $30, then you can put it to the trader who wrote your option for a maximum loss of $37.00 − $30.00 = $7.00, offset by the $0.07 premium credit for a net loss of $6.93.

Here's what that looks like on a graph:

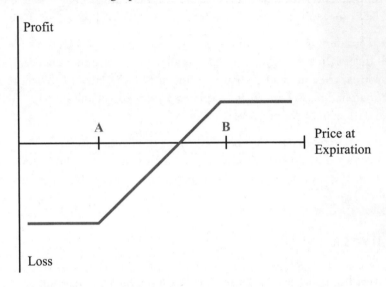

A represents the strike on the long put, and B represents the strike on the short put.

The maximum payoff is the difference between the premium received and the premium paid. The maximum loss is the difference between the strike prices minus the difference between the underlying premiums. This is a mildly bullish strategy because it is profitable when asset prices close above the strike price at expiration, but its losses on the downside are limited.

Bear-Put Spread

A bear-put spread involves buying a put with one strike price and then writing a put with a lower strike price. The premium paid on the put purchased will be higher than the premium received on the put written. This is because the put purchased will be closer to the money in value.

The maximum profit on a bear-put spread is the difference in the strike prices minus the net debit position from the net premium paid, provided the underlying security is below the lower of the two strike prices. The maximum loss is the difference in premiums paid—much less than with a naked put.

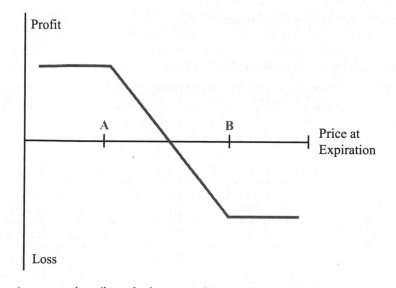

A represents the strike on the short put, and B represents the strike on the long put.

Married Puts

A *married put strategy* is the purchase of stock and put options to cover the same number of shares. It's a form of protective put strategy, and it is a form of a put spread. It's like two strategies in one!

The put position limits the risk of the stock because if it falls in value, then it can be sold at the exercise price of the puts.

Let's say you buy 100 shares of stock at $22.61 and one put options contract with a strike price of $22 to cover 100 shares at $1.85 per share. If the stock increases in value by more than $1.85 between the initiation and the expiration, then you profit from the upside. If it sells for less than $22, you can exercise the option.

Of course, you can set any strike relative for the option, which is where the spread part of the strategy comes in. Normally, the put would have a strike at or below the current price of the stock, but how much lower would depend on how you're feeling about the market. The further out-of-the-money, the lower the cost of the put—but the less protection you have.

The following table offers more information on put-spread strategies.

Economics of Put-Spread Strategies

	Bull Spread	Bear Spread	Married
To establish	Pay premium on one put; receive premium on another put with a lower strike	Pay premium on one put; receive premium on another put with a higher strike	Buy stock; pay premium on puts
In-the-money	Deliver the underlying asset	Receive the underlying asset	Deliver the underlying asset
Out-of-the-money	Lose net premium	Receive net premium	Lose premium
Upside potential	Difference in strikes minus difference in premiums	Premium	Difference between stock price and strike price minus premium
Downside potential	Difference in premiums	Difference in strikes minus difference in premiums	Premium paid
Market view	Bullish	Bearish	Bearish

Calendar Spread

A calendar spread, also called a time spread or a horizontal spread, involves buying a put with one expiration date and selling a put with a different expiration. This is a play on the time value and volatility of the options.

For example, you can buy an April 40 put for $0.39 and then sell a July 40 put for $0.66. The net premium here is $0.66 − $0.39 = $0.27. If the underlying is below $40 at or before the April expiration, you can exercise the put that you bought. Of course, if the underlying is below $40 at or before the July expiration, you might have to buy it at a loss.

Butterflies

If you squint, the payoff graphs for these spreads look a little like butterflies. Maybe? Sort of?

No matter what they look like to you, butterfly spreads are plays on volatility more than on prices going up or down. The trader is trying to determine if the market is likely to be extremely volatile or have no volatility at all when structuring butterflies.

Long-Butterfly-Put Spread

A long-butterfly-put spread is the combination of a bear-put spread and a bull-put spread. A trader sets it up by selling two at-the-money puts and buying one in-the-money put and one out-of-the-money put on the same underlying asset with the same expiration date. The two short puts have the same strike price, with one long put having a greater exercise price, and one long put having a lesser one.

Let's say you set up one spread with the purchase of a 32 June put at $1.56 and the sale of a 34 June put for $1.98. Then, you set up a second spread with the purchase of a 36 June put at $3.05 and the sale of another 34 June put at $1.98. Your net premium here is −$1.56 + $1.98 − $3.05 + $1.98 = −$0.65. This net premium is the cost of your position, and the most money that you can lose.

The following graph shows the prices where the long butterfly put spread pays off and where it doesn't.

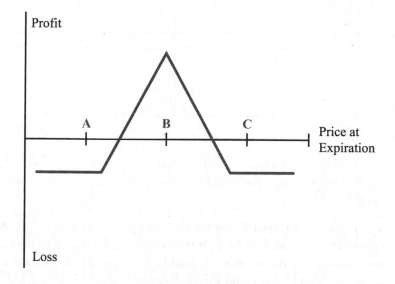

A and C are the strike prices on the short puts, and B is the strike price on the long puts.

The loss on a long-butterfly-put spread is equal to the net premium paid to set it up. The potential profit is the difference between the long and short strike prices ($2 in the earlier example), less the net premium paid. A long butterfly allows a trader to profit on a modest decline in the underlying asset, but with much less downside risk than either a straddle or a strangle (covered in Chapter 10).

Short-Butterfly-Put Spread

As with the long-butterfly-put spread, a short-butterfly-put spread is the combination of a bear-put spread and a bull-put spread. However, the short-butterfly-put spread has different price points for the long and the short. A trader sets it up by buying two at-the-money puts, and selling one in-the-money put and one out-of-the-money put on the same underlying asset with the same expiration date. The two long puts have the same strike price. One of the short puts has a greater exercise price, and the other short put has a lower exercise price.

For example, let's say you buy two 75 August puts at $2.86 each, for a total cost of $5.72. Then, you sell one 65 August put for $0.73 and another put, an 85 August put, for $11.02. You collect a total of $11.75 and paid $5.72 for a net premium of $6.03. That premium is yours to keep, and is your maximum profit.

The short butterfly put spread's payoff is limited, as shown on the following graph.

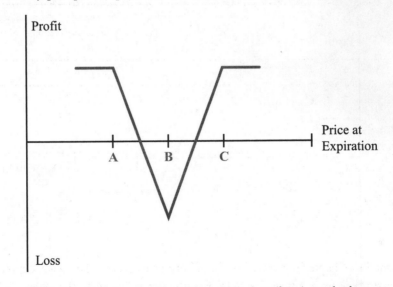

A and C are the strike prices on the long puts, and B is the strike price on the short puts.

The potential gain on this transaction is limited the net premium paid. The potential loss is equal to the difference in strike prices minus the difference in premiums, or −$10 + $6.03 = −$3.93 in the preceding example. A short butterfly allows a trader to profit from volatility, but with much less downside risk than either a straddle or a strangle (covered in Chapter 10).

If you're interested in butterfly strategies, consider the range of payoffs summarized in the following table.

Economics of Butterfly-Put Strategies

	Long Spread	Short Spread
To establish	Net premiums	Net premiums
In-the-money	Difference between the price of the underlying asset, strike, and net premium	Net premium
Out-of-the-money	Lose net premium	Lose difference between the price of the underlying asset, strike, and net premium
Upside potential	Difference between the price of the underlying asset, strike, and net premium	Net premium
Downside potential	Net premium	Lose difference between the price of the underlying asset, strike, and net premium
Market view	Neutral	Volatile

MARKET MAXIM

When the circus comes to town, it's time to go out and sell some peanuts. No matter how efficient the market may be, there are some people in it who are irrational. And that is an opportunity for you to make money.

Condors

As you learned in Chapter 8, condors are like butterflies except they have a spread on the strike prices. This gives them a wider wingspan than the butterfly, hence the name.

They also offer more flexibility because they pay off on a wider range of prices. Like a butterfly, a condor is a bet on volatility. Unlike a butterfly, the volatility position need not be one of extreme volatility or extreme stability.

Long-Condor-Put Spread

A long-condor-put spread is similar to a long-butterfly-put spread, but with a wider range of prices where the position is at peak profitability. A trader sets it up by buying two out-of-the-money puts with different strike prices. She then sells one in-the-money put and one out-of-the-money put on the same underlying asset with the same expiration date, making sure that those strike prices are above and below the prices of the long puts.

The long condor put spread's payoff is broader than with the butterfly, but it is still limited, as shown on the following graph.

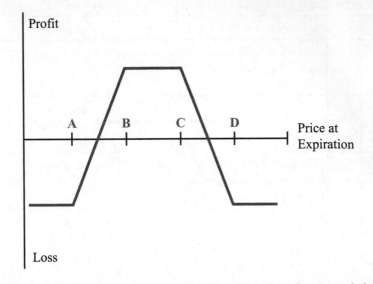

A and D are the strike prices on the short puts, and B and C is the strike price on the long puts.

The profit on a long-condor-put spread is equal to the net premium received. The loss is limited to the difference in strike prices minus the net premium paid. A long condor allows a trader to profit when the underlying asset is not expected to change much in price. A long condor also has much less downside risk than either a straddle or a strangle and more flexibility than a butterfly.

Short-Condor-Put Spread

Just like the long-condor-put spread, a short-condor-put spread is the combination of a bear put spread and a bull put spread. It is established by selling two in-the-money puts, and buying one in-the-money put and one out-of-the-money put on the same underlying asset with the same expiration date. The short puts have an exercise price between that of the two long puts.

The following graph shows the payoff of the short condor put spread.

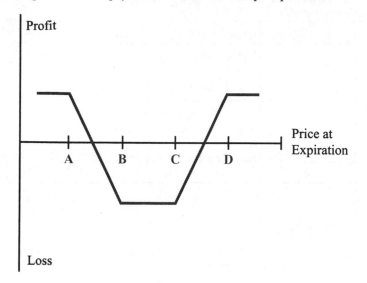

A and D are the strike prices on the long puts, and B and C are the strike prices on the short puts.

The potential profit on this transaction is the difference between the strike prices and the net premium paid. The potential loss is equal to the difference in premiums. A short condor allows a trader to profit from extremes in volatility, but with much less downside risk than either a straddle or a strangle (two volatility plays covered in Chapter 10).

If you're interested in butterfly strategies, consider the range of payoffs summarized in the following table.

Economics of Condor-Put Strategies

	Long Condor	Short Condor
To establish	Net premiums	Net premiums
In-the-money	Net premiums	Difference between the price of the underlying asset, strike, and net premium
Out-of-the-money	Lose difference between the price of the underlying asset, strike, and net premium	Net premium

continues

Economics of Condor-Put Strategies (continued)

	Long Condor	Short Condor
Upside potential	Net premium	Difference between the price of the underlying asset, strike, and net premium
Downside potential	Lose difference between the price of the underlying asset, strike, and net premium	Net premium
Market view	Neutral	Volatile

MARKET MAXIM

Hope is not a strategy. Even if you're hedging, trading is an active game. Pay attention to what you see and act on it instead of hoping that things go your way.

How to Think About Puts

Puts are bearish options, but often used as part of bullish strategies. Some of that is because of the risks inherent with naked puts and the inability to do a true covered put in the same manner as a covered call. (The analogue is a protective put. For that, you will be charged a premium instead of receiving it.)

The key is to think about puts as a way to buy a payoff, rather than something particularly bullish or bearish. Then, you can work puts to fit your needs.

The Least You Need to Know

- A long put position pays off when the underlying asset decreases in price. A short call pays off when the asset stays flat or increases in value.
- Long puts are generally used as bearish strategies.
- A protective put is a common hedge against a long position in the underlying asset.
- Long and short puts can be combined to play different aspects of price volatility.

CHAPTER 10

Combination Strategies

Puts and calls work together. In essence, owning the underlying asset is the same as being long a call and short a put. You make money when the underlying asset goes up in price and you lose it if it goes down.

Furthermore, a long call has a similar payoff to a short put, and a short call has a similar payoff to a long put. There might be times when prices on the different options are out of alignment, or where you're looking at different movements in prices over time. That's just the first of many reasons to think of puts and calls in combination.

That's the starting point for trading strategies that rely on a combination of puts and calls. This chapter will cover the terms and strategies involving option combinations.

Keep in mind that many of these strategies are used by professional traders. Low-risk, low-profit strategies might bring in pennies for an individual. A proprietary trader with access to leverage and low transactions costs might find that a strategy that's not a good use of your time is a great trade for him. Other combination strategies might be used by trading firms to hedge their own risks, or to offset other positions. You might hear about these combinations and want to learn what they are. However, they might not be good for your trading.

In This Chapter

- How puts, calls, and the financial market work together
- Using puts and calls together to manage risk and return
- Risks of using combination strategies
- Strategies you can use when trades don't work out

Combination Spreads

A basic spread involves owning a combination of puts and calls, or owning them in different forms, in order to profit from price changes.

Back Spread

A *back spread* occurs whenever a trader has more long options than short options on a given underlying asset. This is something that a trading firm might get into but not one that an individual will face. A trading firm would want to determine the risk of loss and then manage it appropriately.

For example, suppose that a brokerage firm risk manager looks at the open interest and finds that there are 100 long calls and 80 short calls on the same underlying asset. If the price of the underlying asset moves up, then she can exercise the long calls. The short calls will be exercised, too, but the profit will be greater than the cost of fulfilling the option assignment.

If the underlying asset falls in value, then the short options expire worthless and the firm can keep the premium. However, it will have spent more on the long calls (probably), so it will have a net debit position.

The opposite happens if the back spread involves puts. If the underlying asset falls below the strike price, then the long puts are in-the-money but the short puts will be assigned. If the underlying asset closes above the strike, then the short puts will expire worthless. This means the firm can keep the premium—but it will have lost premium on the long puts.

Diagonal Spread

To set up a diagonal spread, a trader buys one option and sells another of the same type with different strike prices and different expiration dates. This combination profits from a change in the direction of the underlying over time.

For example, you sell a 37.50 March call for $0.55 and then buy a 42.50 May call for $0.29. You now have a net credit position of $0.55 − $0.29 = $0.26. If the March option is assigned, then you lose the cost of the stock, but that would increase the value of the May call. (By how much? Who knows?) If the March call expires, you then sell a May 42.50 call to close out the position, increasing your net premium. This has somewhat less risk than a naked-short-call position, but it requires paying attention to the price of the underlying asset.

MARKET MAXIM

Every exit is an entry somewhere. Financial markets only work if there are buyers and sellers. When you write an option, someone has to be on the other side. And when you close out a position, you have funds to put into another position. The constant trading keeps the markets functional and efficient. It's okay to close a position and move on.

Christmas Tree Spread

A *Christmas tree spread* is another option strategy with a cute diagram. A long-call Christmas tree spread involves one call at the lowest strike, selling three calls at the third strike, and then buying two calls at the fourth strike.

This strategy has limited risk, but it also has limited profit potential. It may be one of these strategies that exists because it makes for an interesting payoff graph, not because it's particularly useful.

Box Spread

A *box spread* is so called because the payoff diagram forms a box. It involves a long call and short put at one strike price, along with a short call and a long put at another strike price. This matches the payoff of a long stock position at one price with that of a short stock position at another price. Your payoff, therefore, is within the box.

Here's what it would look like. Start with the first part: a long call and short put. You buy a 55 October call for $2.85 and sell a 55 October put for $6.95, for a net credit of $6.95 − $2.85 = $4.10. Then, you sell a 57.50 October call for $2.05 and buy a 57.50 October put for $8.60, for a net credit of $2.05 − $8.60 = −$6.55. Your total cost of this position is $4.10 − $6.55 = −$2.45.

Now, what do you receive in exchange for that $2.55 cost? If the price of the underlying asset is below $55 at expiration, then the long call expires worthless. The short put will be exercised, so you'll have to purchase the asset for $55. The short call will also expire worthless, and the long put will be in-the-money, so you can sell the stock that you bought at $55 for $57.50, for a $2.50 profit. Subtract the $2.45 cost, and your profit is $0.10.

That's all well and good, but what happens if the underlying exceeds $57.50 at expiration? Your long call will be in-the-money and your short put will expire worthless. Your short call might be assigned, so you'll end up with the difference between the stock's purchase price and its sale price, or $57.50 − $55.00 = $2.50. Subtract the $2.45 cost, and you have a profit of $0.10.

This only works if you can establish the box at a lower cost than the maximum profit. You might not find many situations that fit.

Straddles and Strangles

Straddles and strangles seem dangerous, don't they? In reality, they are more like the butterflies and condors of Chapters 8 and 9. The difference? They are established with puts and calls, rather than only puts or only calls.

Straddles

A *straddle* is similar to a butterfly. It is a way to play volatility. You can think of it as two options that "straddle" a common strike price, looking for prices that deviate from that central point.

Long Straddle

A *long straddle* involves the purchase of a call and a put with the same strike price. If the options expire at the strike price, then the loss is the maximum of the combined premium on the two options.

This trade moves in-the-money if the asset goes up or down in price, but the amount made over the premium paid might be pennies unless there is a significant movement in the underlying price. If the asset goes up or down, the profit is equal to the underlying price minus the premiums paid.

Here's an example: 100 May calls cost $2.85, and 100 May puts cost $5.70 on a particular asset. You buy both for $8.55. If the underlying is at $110 on expiration, then the call can be exercised and the put expires worthless, for a profit of $10.00 − $8.55 = $1.45. If the underlying is at $90 at expiration, the call is worthless and the put can be exercised for a profit of $10.00 − $8.55 = $1.45.

The payoff diagram looks like this:

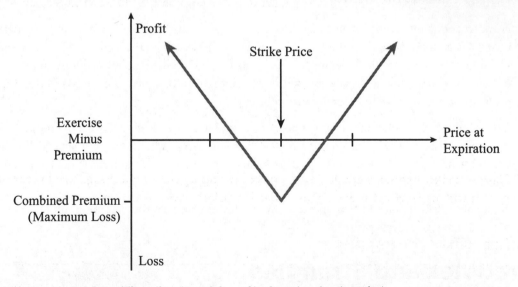

The strike price and the combined premium (maximum loss).

A long straddle is used when a trader perceives volatility in the market but is uncertain which direction it will take.

Short Straddle

A *short straddle* involves the sale of a call and a put with the same strike price. If the options expire at the strike price, then both options are in-the-money, and the profit is at a maximum: the combined premium on the two options.

This position loses money if the asset goes up or down in price. If the asset price is anything other than the strike price, the loss is equal to the strike price minus the premiums paid. The problem here is that you will need to maintain margin in your account to cover the short positions. Doing so can get really expensive really fast. As a result, short straddles are the province of deep-pocketed professional traders.

The payoff looks like this:

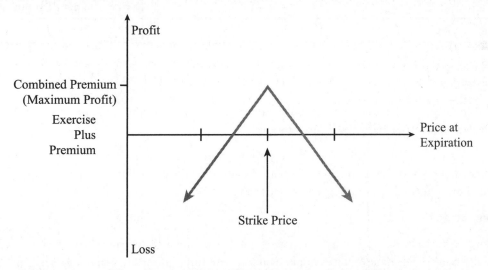

The strike price and the combined premium (maximum profit).

Short straddles are used by traders who expect very little volatility in the market. Because a market with no volatility is not common, this is a risky trade.

Economics of Straddles

	Long Straddle	Short Straddle
To establish	Net premium	Net premium
In-the-money	Difference between the price of the underlying asset, strike, and net premium	Net premium

continues

Economics of Straddles   (continued)

	Long Straddle	Short Straddle
Out-of-the-money	Lose net premium	Lose difference between the price of the underlying asset, strike, and net premium
Upside potential	Difference between the price of the underlying asset, strike, and net premium	Net premium
Downside potential	Net premium	Lose difference between the price of the underlying asset, strike, and net premium
Market view	Volatile	Flat

Strangles

Options strategies have so many fanciful names! A *strangle* is a trade using options with the different strike price on the same expiration.

Strangles are similar to straddles, but they allow more wiggle room on the amount of volatility tolerated. The payoff is identical to that of a condor (see Chapters 7 and 8), but they are set up using both puts and calls rather than one or the other.

Long Strangle

A long strangle is established by purchasing both a call and a put with different strike prices, usually out-of-the-money. For example, you buy a 45 July call for $1.52 and a 33 July put for $2.75 on an underlying asset trading at $39. The net credit position of the combined premium is the $4.27 that you paid to establish the position.

The maximum loss is that $4.27 combined premium, should both positions expire out-of-the-money. The maximum profit is the difference between the underlying price and the premiums paid.

The following graph shows the range of maximum profit for the long strangle.

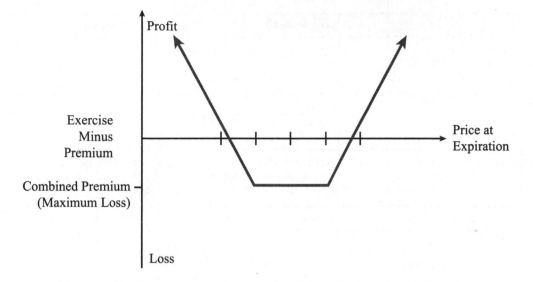

The range of maximum profit for the long strangle and the combined premium (maximum loss).

This allows a trader to take advantage of volatility at a lower cost than with a straddle. The strangle can be arranged with either out-of-the-money or in-the-money options. Using in-the-money options minimizes the break-even point, but also has a larger potential loss if the position expires worthless.

> **DEFINITION**
>
> **Strangles** and **straddles** are options strategies designed to take advantage of volatility. They pay off if the price of the underlying goes up or down, but not if it stays in a small range. The difference is that the strangle has two different strike prices while the straddle has only one. A **long strangle** is the purchase of a call with one strike price and put with a higher one. A **short strangle** is the sale of a call with one strike price and a put with a lower one. A **long straddle** is the purchase of a call and a put with the same strike price. A **short straddle** is the sale of a call and a put with the same strike price.

Short Strangle

A *short strangle* is established by writing both a call and a put with different strike prices and the same expiration. The maximum profit is the combined premium, should both positions expire out-of-the-money, and the maximum loss is the difference between the underlying price and the premiums paid.

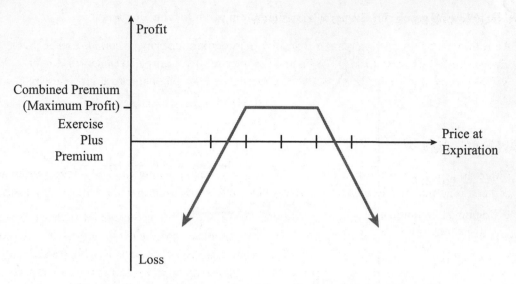

The range of loss for the short strangle and the combined premium (maximum profit).

This position allows a trader to generate income in a sideways market. As long as the underlying asset stays in the range between the strike prices, the trader will see a profit. A short strangle has much less risk than a short straddle, but it still has risk, and it has very large margin requirements.

Economics of Strangles

	Long Strangle	Short Strangle
To establish	Net premiums	Net premiums
In-the-money	Difference between the price of the underlying asset, strike, and net premium	Net premium
Out-of-the-money	Lose net premium	Lose difference between the price of the underlying asset, strike, and net premium
Upside potential	Difference between the price of the underlying asset, strike, and net premium	Net premium
Downside potential	Net premium	Lose difference between the price of the underlying asset, strike, and net premium
Market view	Volatile	Flat

Iron Butterflies and Iron Condors

An iron butterfly or an iron condor is similar to a regular butterfly or condor except that it involves selling the midstrike straddle and buying the surrounding strangle. It's simply another way to arrange the strike prices, using both puts and calls. The names are just irresistible, aren't they?

Collars and Fences

Collars and *fences* are synonyms for the same strategy: having a long call and a short put, or a short call and long put, at different strike prices above and below the price of an underlying asset.

For example, suppose you wanted to hedge against the price of a stock market index falling. To do this, you would buy puts on the index with an exercise price below current levels. To offset the cost of the puts, you would write calls on a price above current levels. If the market falls, your long put position protects you. If the market goes up, though, your appreciation potential is limited.

You do not need to have a position in the underlying asset to set up a collar or a fence, although the combination is often set up in order to hedge an underlying position.

A *conversion* is related to the collar. It is an arbitrage strategy that involves purchasing stock, a long put, and a short call. The put and call should have the same strike price and expiration. The result is a nearly riskless profit on the downside. The main risk is having the short call exercised, which would mean you lose the underlying asset.

> **MARKET MAXIM**
>
> If you're going to panic, panic early. When a trade isn't working out, it's usually better to cut your losses and move on than it is to wait it out.

Rolls, Jelly and Plain

A *roll* is a trade that involves closing out one open option position and opening a new position at a different strike price, different expiration, or both. It the new strike price is higher, this is a roll up; if lower, it's a roll down; and if it's for a later time period, it's a roll out.

A jelly roll is a special form of roll that involves a long call and a short put with the same strike price and same expiration coupled with a short call and long put with the same strike price with a later expiration. This is a form or a collar or fence that extends out over time.

> **DEFINITION**
>
> A **roll** is a trade that involves closing out an open option position while at the same time establishing a new one at a different strike price.

Strips and Straps

Sometimes, a trader wants to reduce risk but not eliminate it entirely. *Strips* and *straps* fit the bill in these situations, and are often used by professionals in managing the risk of a large options portfolio.

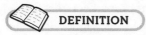

> **DEFINITION**
>
> A **strap** is a risk-management transaction used by institutional options traders. It involves two long calls and one long put. A **strip** is similar to a strap. It involves two puts and one call.

A strap involves two calls and one put, usually long. (You can short two calls and a put as a bear strap, but that's a risky proposition.) All options have the same strike price and expiration, and they work on the same underlying asset.

A strip is similar, but it involves two puts and one call. Like a strap, it can be long or short. It can be bullish, if long, or bearish, if short.

Repair Strategies

Your trading positions are not always going to go according to plan. There are options strategies you can use to increase the probability of profit or reduce the size of losses.

Closing out the position is one alternative—and that should be done if research shows your original idea no longer holds—but repair strategies increase the tools in your toolbox. The idea is to look for a similar payoff, but buy some time and space by changing expirations or strike prices. Furthermore, the ability to generate income from writing options can help increase return for very little additional risk.

Option Repair

An *option repair* starts with assessing the problem. Why is the trade not working out?

If the problem is that you are dead wrong in your analysis, but you are wishing and hoping that is not the case, you should get out now. If you check your research and still feel confident about the basic approach you are taking, a repair gives you some alternatives that might increase your likelihood of being in-the-money, albeit at the cost of some profit potential.

If the problem is that your option position is starting to look unlikely to pay off for you, the first step is to look for ways to trade in those options that are looking unlikely to work out for some that are more promising. Buying a little more room on the exercise or a little more time to expiration is unlikely to cost a lot, especially after the old position is closed.

A second strategy is to replace a single option position with a spread. A bull spread can replace a long call, and a bear spread can replace a put. This gives you a wider range of possibilities for profit.

Stock Repair

If you hold shares of stock that are not performing as you expect them do based on your research, a repair strategy might help. Consider buying one call and writing two calls for each share of stock held. The calls should be for the same expiration, but the short strike should be higher than the long strike, with both above the current stock price. Now, you have a combination of a call—to profit when the increase finally happens—with a covered call position to generate some income while you wait.

> **MARKET MAXIM**
>
> There are a million ways to make money in the market, but none of them are easy to find. There's no one way to make money in the market, and there is no one way to lose money. Be very leery of anyone who promises a sure-fire strategy, and recognize that you'll need to experiment.

The Least You Need to Know

- Puts and calls are usually used in combination.
- Different strategies can achieve the same risk management or profit goals.
- Combination strategies are especially popular as hedges.
- Repair strategies help correct problems with other trades using options.

PART 3

Advanced and Synthetic Strategies

Because the value of an option is derived from something else, there are ways to use options to mimic the performance of many different financial assets—and vice versa. Much of the power of options comes from their ability to replicate other assets; how the price of different strategies relates to the price of the underlying is another way to use the options market for information.

Chapter 11 covers other types of traded derivatives, and Chapter 12 looks at synthetic versions of assets created with options and futures. Chapter 13 shows how these different combinations are used to set up arbitrage trades, and Chapter 14 shows how to look at the trading history of an underlying asset or a derivative to find trends that might indicate future prices. Chapter 15 discusses fundamental analysis, which drives a lot of options trading. The stronger the evidence is backing that belief, the less risky the position. Chapter 16 helps you sort through the different sales pitches out there so you can find what works for you to trade with more success.

This information helps you learn more about the importance of options in both financial theory and actual practice. With it, you will be in a better position to develop strategies for hedging and speculation, no matter the underlying.

Futures, Forwards, and Related Derivatives

Just as with options, futures contracts are derivatives. They derive their value from the price of something else. They are standardized contracts traded on organized exchanges, used by both hedgers and speculators. They are valued based on the price of the underlying asset, the exercise price, the expiration date, interest rates, and the volatility of the underlying asset—the same as options.

However, one key difference is the holder of a futures contract carries the obligation to buy or sell. An option holder does not have this same obligation. Futures are sometimes used in conjunction with options as part of a trading strategy.

Futures contracts are one of the most common types of derivatives. Along with options, they are standardized and trade on organized exchanges. In fact, the options market is an outgrowth of the futures market.

This chapter will cover some of the other derivatives in the financial markets and discuss how they work with options to help people create new strategies. All of them are making bets on how prices differ from the *spot price*—that is, the price of a given item in the market today.

In This Chapter

* Learning about futures and forwards
* The mark to market process
* Swaps, CDOs, and other nonstandard contracts
* Using options with other derivatives

Defining Futures

A *futures contract* is an obligation to buy or sell a predetermined amount of a given item at a future date, and at a price determined today. The big difference between a future and an option is that with a futures contract, you must buy or sell if you hold the contract until expiration. (Most futures contracts are closed out with an offsetting position prior to expiration, so buying cattle futures doesn't mean a bunch of cows will show up in your backyard.) In some cases, the settlement of the future is in cash, meaning the buyer and seller exchange the cash value of the item involved. In other cases, though, the settlement is in the physical asset.

Futures contracts are standardized by the exchanges. The contracts are traded in preset amounts, and they have set expiration dates. Traders use a clearinghouse account in order to *mark to market*.

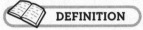 **DEFINITION**

> **Mark to market** is the process of updating the value of trading accounts at the end of the day to reflect the official closing price for the day.

When trading closes for the day, the futures *clearinghouse* (the organization that manages the money for the exchange) will value all traders' accounts to reflect the official price at the end of the trading session, also known as the *settlement price*. (This is usually the price of the last sale.) The process is known as marking to market, and it is a key way to ensure traders have the money to settle up when expiration occurs. After all, if they have to come up with a little money every night, they can't be in denial about the value of their position.

Almost all futures contracts are closed out before expiration with an offsetting trade. Someone who is long a future sells an identical contract to close out the position, for 0 net exposure to the asset price.

Types of Futures Contracts

The futures markets were established to create markets for agricultural commodities, and that's still a large component of the market. Grain, cattle, and pork bellies (yes, that's a thing, it's the futures market for bacon) trade electronically these days, rather than on the floor of the Chicago exchanges. Over the years, the futures markets expanded to include financial futures. The market now has futures on currencies, interest rates, and market indexes. They often trade in mini-sized contracts, which are smaller value positions for individual investors.

Options on Futures

The futures market has expanded to include *options on futures,* a way to trade options on agricultural commodities and currencies. These trade like other options. The difference is the value is drawn from the value of another derivative, rather than the value of the asset itself. Settlement is in cash, not the underlying asset.

Forward Contracts

A *forward contract* is similar to a futures contract. Both involve a commitment to exchange an item at a date in the future at a price determined today. The difference is a forward contract is not standardized.

People often use forwards in their lives. A simple example is making a hotel reservation. You agree today you will receive the use of the room in the future, at a price agreed upon today. You then use your credit card to guarantee that settlement.

Some types of forward contracts trade amongst institutional investors in the over-the-counter market. For example, banks might trade different currency forward contracts. As an independent options trader, it is unlikely you will be working in forward contracts.

 DID YOU KNOW?

If there's a stream of payments and time period, there's a valuation. As long as traders can value a contract, they are willing to trade it.

Environmental Credits

One of the more interesting derivatives markets is in environmental credits. It started in 1990 under an amendment to the Clean Air Act. The goal was to reduce the amount of sulfur dioxide electric utilities could emit in order to reduce the incidence of acid rain, an effect of pollution that damaged trees. Each utility was given a number of allowances for pollution. A utility could use those or sell them to another utility. If a utility emitted more sulfur dioxide than it was allowed, it could either spend money on technology to reduce the emissions or buy more credits from other utilities. Thus, a utility didn't have to make changes; it had alternatives to consider.

And alternatives add value.

This system, called cap and trade, was a huge success—so much so people figured it would be used for other types of pollution. For whatever reason, that didn't happen.

That being said, there is a voluntary market in environmental credits, the Chicago Climate Exchange, operated by ICE. It can be expanded at any time regulators in the U.S. or elsewhere establish a new cap and trade program—and that creates a potential opportunity for traders.

> **DID YOU KNOW?**
>
> The founder of the Chicago Climate Exchange, Richard Sandor, had been an executive at the Chicago Board of Trade. He is passionate about the power of the financial markets to create change. He says that the agricultural futures markets have gone a long way to improving the distribution of food in the world to alleviate hunger, and that cap and trade programs could do the same thing for the environment.

Swaps

A *swap* is a contract that allows someone to trade one type of contract for another. For example, suppose you have a floating rate bond, and you'd rather receive fixed interest payments. Someone else has a fixed-rate bond but would rather receive floating rate payments. You swap your payments, and everyone is happy.

> **DID YOU KNOW?**
>
> A swap is not a matter of aesthetics. There are sound economic reasons for trading payments. For example, if you have liabilities with floating interest rates, you might want to receive income in the same way in order to match the risk. If you have expenses in one currency, you might want income in the same currency to better manage exchange rates.

Swaps are almost always negotiated contracts, often with the bank as the counterparty and with a variety of unique features. However, there are some standard practices that allow banks to trade swaps with each other.

Currency Swaps

Currency swaps allow two parties to trade commitments to pay in one currency for another. This is a way to manage exchange-rate risk and to get around problems of currency controls, which is an issue in some emerging markets.

Interest Rate Swaps

Interest rate swaps are usually exchanges of fixed-rate payments for floating-rate payments. They are based on a predetermined amount of principal, called the notational principal amount. Only interest payments are exchanged, not the underlying. This can help portfolio managers hedge interest rate risks.

Commodity Swaps

Commodity swaps are contracts based on the price of an underlying commodity. They are similar to futures contracts in that they allow parties to lock in the price of a sale. These are useful for commodities that are not covered by exchange-traded futures contracts.

Swaptions

A *swaption* is an option on a swap. Clever, huh? A payer swaption gives the holder the right, but not the obligation, to enter into an interest rate swap at a predetermined fixed rate at a predetermined time. A receiver swaption gives the purchaser the right, but not the obligation, to receive fixed payments at a predetermined time.

Collateralized Debt Obligations

A *collateralized debt obligation* isn't a true derivative, but it is often included in lists of derivatives. It's a bond issued against a pool of loans. A bank or mortgage company collects a group of loans and then sells bonds on it. The loans might be mortgages, car loans, credit card debts—anything that generates cash flow.

Instead of the lender keeping the principal and interest payments it receives, it passes shares of those onto the bond holders. In a sense, the bond buyers are receiving payments derived from the value of the underlying loans. Collateralized debt obligations are also the reason for the development of another type of derivative, the credit default swap, as buyers were looking for a form of insurance.

Credit Default Swaps

Credit default swaps, also known as CDSs, are contracts in which a bond holder insures the position against default by the issuer. If the bond goes into default, the seller of the swap must pay the buyer the funds. In exchange, the seller keeps the premium. These contracts then trade over the counter. As long as the loan does not default, everyone is happy.

If the loan defaults, though, problems can arise.

DID YOU KNOW?

Credit default swaps on mortgage-backed securities were a major contributor to the financial crisis of 2008. Many of those who sold credit default swaps did so under the assumption there was no risk to residential mortgages. As defaults increased, they were on the hook to pay more than they could afford to insure the CDS buyers. Many of these sellers were brokerage firms, banks, and insurance companies made insolvent by their CDS position.

Repurchase Agreements

A *repurchase agreement,* also called a repo, is an agreement between a buyer and a seller in which the seller agrees to buy back the asset at an agreed-upon price at a future time. In most repos, the asset in question is a U.S. government security, so there is virtually no risk on the value of the underlying asset. In essence, a repo is a loan structured as a forward contract. The treasury bond is the collateral. The seller is receiving money and agrees to repay it in the future at a price high enough to compensate the buyer—the lender—for the use of the funds.

Repos are common transactions between banks and large corporations that need to borrow money for short-term purposes, such as meeting payroll, often for as short a time period as overnight.

LEAPS and Weeklys

LEAPs and weeklys are both types of options, but they have very different time periods than traditional options. (Weeklys are covered in a bit more detail in Chapter 7.)

For years, option expirations had a range limited from 30 days to 2 years into the future. In recent years, the exchanges have introduced a wide range of new products with different expiration dates. The cleverly named Long-term Equity AnticiPation Securities—or LEAPs (it's a trademark of the CBOE)—have expiration dates from 1 to 5 years into the future. This means they have a large time value relative to the intrinsic value.

Weekly options, on the other hand, are issued on a Monday and expire on Friday of the same week. They have a huge intrinsic value and very little time value when issued, then show a rapid rate of time value (theta decay as the week goes on). Many traders like them as a way to speculate on short-term news events that affect the value of common stock with less of a capital commitment. Because of their fast expiration, they don't make a good stock replacement other than for a day trader.

The Least You Need to Know

- Futures and forwards give holders the obligation to buy or sell an asset at a predetermined price on a predetermined date.
- Swaps give the parties involved the right to trade payments in different currencies or different interest rate structures.
- Credit Default Swaps are insurance contracts against a bond default.
- Newer types of options have longer expirations than other types of options.

CHAPTER 12

Synthetic Securities

Options are contracts based on prices. They aren't securities on an underlying item itself. They are based on the value of the underlying asset. If you have access to the value of the asset, do you need to own the underlying asset, too? This is the question behind options and other derivatives.

If we reduce assets to their payouts, then we can approach them in a different way. We can find ways to replicate the value, possibly at a lower cost.

A *synthetic security* is a package of investments created to have the same payoff as an actual security or asset. They are used to simplify trading and to manage risk. In many cases, they come with a lower cost than the underlying asset they are replicating. On occasion, the market presents an arbitrage opportunity where a synthetic can be used to help generate a profit.

In This Chapter

- Making custom combinations
- Different ways to earn the same pay
- The costs and risks of working with synthetics
- Strategies with synthetics

The advantage of synthetics is they can help you find more ways to make money for the same amount of risk. There are two disadvantages. The first is that the commissions on the trades can reduce or even eliminate profits. The second is if they are not set up correctly, you can take on more risk than you realize and blow up your account. Think of these as advanced strategies.

Setting Up Synthetics

A synthetic security is a combination of two or more financial instruments that have the same risk and the same payoff as a third instrument. It is a way to copy the financial characteristics of a security.

Synthetics can be created to mimic the underlying or the derivatives on it.

When thinking about synthetic securities, think about the payoffs. The handy payoff diagrams shown later in this chapter can be used to show what you're trying to replicate, and then give you clues about what the replication would look like.

A Synthetic Stock

If you own a common stock, then you have a financial asset that makes money if the business increases in value and one that loses money if the business decreases in value. The increased value will come from an increase in the stock price and the payment of a dividend.

Long Synthetic Stock

To have a *long synthetic stock*, you need to:

- Be long a call option
- Be short a put option

The call and put should have the same strike price and expiration. If you have the call and the put, then you have one asset that makes money if the underlying increases in value and one that loses money if the underlying decreases. If both are at-the-money, then the premium should be the same, at least in a perfect world. At any other point, one option will be in the money and one will be out.

Of course, with a long synthetic, you lose the return from any dividend the company might pay.

Here's an example: you buy a 30 January call for $2.97 and sell a 30 January put for $4.15. This is close to, but not precisely, the same as the underlying's price of $29.39, and it generates a net credit position of $1.18.

If you are the shareholder and the underlying asset is at $35 at expiration, then you'd have a profit of $35 − $29.39 = $5.61. If you owned the synthetic, you'd be able to exercise the call for a profit of $35.00 − $30.00 = $5.00, plus the net credit from the premium, for a profit of $6.18. The put holder will let it expire, as it's worthless.

Now, if expiration rolls around and the underlying asset is at $25, the shareholder would lose $29.39 − $25.00 = $4.39. If you were short the put, it would be assigned and you'd have to buy the stock at $30.00, for a loss of $30.00 − $25.00 = $5.00. The call would be worthless. But the premium received would reduce the loss to $5.00 − $1.18 = $3.82.

This example, which uses real numbers for General Motors Company (NYSE: GM) stock and options on the day I wrote this, shows that the synthetic stock gives a return that's mighty similar to the return on the stock. The returns on the long call and short put position are slightly higher, which you would expect because the options position has slightly higher transactions costs. The following graph shows what's going on:

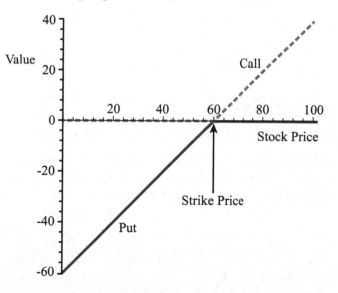

The payoff of a put and a call.

As long as the premiums offset each other, then the money involved in establishing the position goes to 0 and there's a nice, straight line. In theory, a dollar of increase in underlying price leads to a dollar of increase in the position value; in practice, that will be affected by changes in time value and volatility.

That's the same payoff as owning the long stock.

Let's look at being short a stock. In this situation, you have a contract that decreases in value if the stock increases in price. The contract also increases in value if the stock decreases.

Short Synthetic Stock

To have a synthetic short stock, you need to:

- Be short a call option
- Be long a put option

The call and put should have the same strike price and expiration.

What happens if you are short a share of the stock? You make money if the price falls and lose it if the price increases. And what if you have a short call and a long put? You have the same risk (which is substantial, by the way, because there is no theoretical limit on how high a stock can go) and the same return as the short position.

Here's how that looks, using numbers for Facebook (NYSE: FB). You sell a 97.50 September call for $10.15 and buy a 97.50 September put for $12.20. This is close to, but not precisely, the same as the company's price of $97.17, and it costs a net credit position of $10.15 − $12.20 = −$2.05.

If the stock is at $80 at expiration, then you'd have a profit of $97.17 − $80.00 = $17.17 if you had shorted the stock. If you owned the synthetic, you'd exercise the put, buy the stock at $80, then sell it to the put writer at $97.50, for a profit of $797.50 − $80.00 = $17.50. Subtract the $2.05 paid in premium, and your total is $15.45. The call would expire because it is worthless.

Now, if expiration rolls around and the stock is at $125, the short position would lose $125.00 − $97.17 = $27.83. The call holder would exercise, so you would have to buy stock at $125.00 and sell it at $97.50, for a loss of $27.50, less the $2.05 net premium, or $25.45. You'd let the long put expire, as it is way out-of-the-money.

The payoff diagram looks like this:

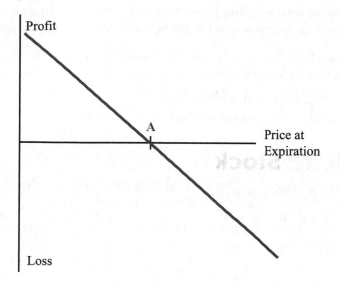

The payoff of the synthetic short stock position.

As with the long position, the premiums should offset each other. A dollar of decrease in underlying price leads to a dollar of increase in the position value.

The payoff of the actual looks the same. For every dollar the underlying price falls, the payoff increases by a dollar.

MARKET MAXIM

Although I mention stocks in many of these examples, the same principle applies to any synthetic options on any underlying asset, including futures contacts.

Synthetic Options

Synthetic options are designed using put-call parity. That's the equation that says:

Stock price = strike price + call premium − put premium

The put-call parity equation can be rearranged like so:

Call premium = put premium + stock price − strike price

Or:

Put premium = strike price − call price + put premium

There are two refinements we need to throw in. The first is the dividend. If the stock pays a dividend, that has to be subtracted from the option holder's return, as the option holder won't receive it. The person who is long the stock will; if it's you, that can reduce your cost of holding.

The second is interest. There is interest lost on cash while the position is being carried, and it costs money to carry positions. If it looks like the synthetic option returns a teensy bit more or less than the authentic position, make adjustments for interest and dividends to see if that's still the case.

A Synthetic Call

Owning a call gives you the right, but not the obligation, to buy the underlying asset at a predetermined price on or before a predetermined date in the future.

But there's another way to think about it. A call is a contract that pays off if the asset increases in price. It does pays nothing if the asset goes down.

Long Synthetic Call

A long synthetic call position involves:

- Purchasing the underlying asset
- Purchasing an at-the-money put option on the underlying

This trade is a version of a married put, and it's a common strategy used to protect a stock position on the downside. Here, I'll discuss it in comparison to a long call so you can understand the payoff structure a little better.

With the long put, you're insuring against the risk of loss on the stock while still retaining the upside potential, as you would with a call. The synthetic long call position pays off if the asset increases in price but pays nothing if the asset goes down. Nifty, huh?

Now, if you want some profit from the asset falling, you'd buy a put that was out-of-the-money. Here, we're looking only at upside.

The following graph shows what's going on:

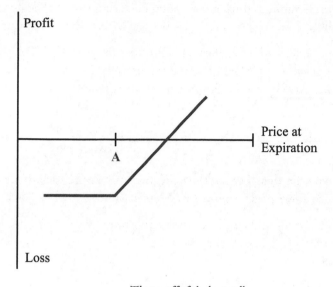

The payoff of the long call.

The purchase of the asset means it will go up a dollar for every dollar increase in price, and the purchase of an at-the-money put means your loss is really limited if the underlying asset goes down in price.

If you remember from Chapter 7, that's the same payoff from being long a call: pure upside, really limited downside.

Short Synthetic Call

A short synthetic call position involves:

- Shorting the underlying asset
- Selling a put on the underlying

With a short call, you collect the premium and then profit if the underlying asset goes down in price. That's exactly what happens here. This is a bearish position.

You can see how it works here:

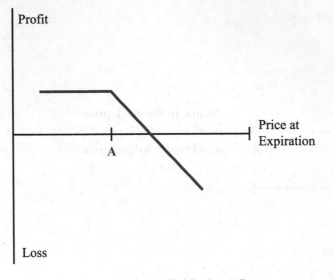

The payoff of the short call.

If the underlying asset falls in price, then the profit will increase accordingly. And if the asset increases, you'll lose money—the same as you would with a short call.

The writer of a call receives the premium; in exchange, she loses money if the asset increases in price, dollar for dollar. That's the same payoff from being short a call: the benefit is all from a decline in underlying price.

> **MARKET MAXIM**
>
> In a synthetic option position, the strike price should be at the money. If not, you won't exactly mimic the risk and return of the traditional position. As a result, there aren't many real-world situations where a synthetic meets or beats the actual.

A Synthetic Put

A put gives you the right, but not the obligation, to sell an underlying asset at a particular price on or before a particular date. The synthetic has the same benefits.

Long Synthetic Put

A long synthetic put consists of:

- A long-call option

- A short-stock position

A put is a position that benefits from a decline in the stock price but does not benefit from price appreciation. A short stock position is one that's really costly if the stock price increases in value. The synthetic put protects against the upside risk while retaining the benefit of a price decline.

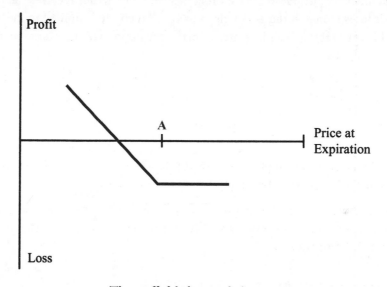

The payoff of the long synthetic put.

If the underlying asset falls in price, then the profit will increase accordingly. Meanwhile, the ownership of the call reduces the potential loss from the asset increasing in price.

With an actual long put, of course, the buyer of the put receives makes money if the asset decreases in price. In theory, this is dollar for dollar. That's why the two charts match. In practice, though, you'll see variations in the rate of price change.

Short Synthetic Put

A short synthetic put looks like this:

- A long stock position

- A short call position

A short put generates income for the writer, and it loses money if the asset falls in price. The upside is limited to the amount of the premium paid.

With the synthetic short put, the same thing happens. The writer receives the premium for the short call. It loses money if the asset falls in price. The upside is limited to the amount of the premium paid because if the asset increases in price, the option will be exercised and the underlying asset will be called away.

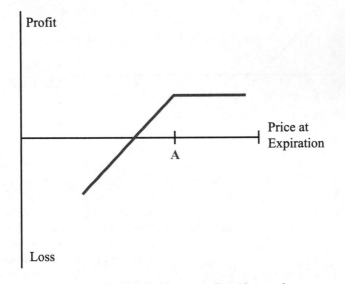

The payoff of the short call and long stock.

If the underlying asset falls in price, the profit will fall accordingly. Meanwhile, the sale of the call means the position's gain will be limited if the asset increases in price.

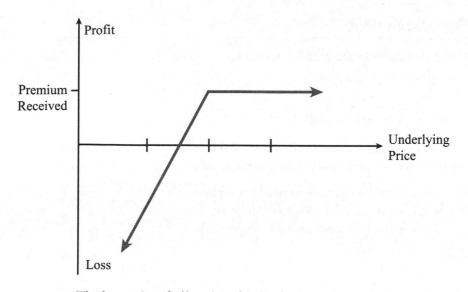

The short put is profitable at the strike price plus the premium received.

As with the long call or regular short put position, the short synthetic put pays off if the underlying asset increases in price.

DID YOU KNOW?

In discussions of synthetics in some options material, you might see references to selling or buying a bond. In academic finance, selling a bond is the same as borrowing money; the entity issuing the bond receives money, and the buyer receives interest and principal over time. Buying a bond or lending money is the same as having money on account to earn interest; someone else is using your money and pays you for that privilege. In the context of synthetics, selling a bond means you are paying interest to cover the costs of being short the underlying or the option. It also means you are giving up interest by having your position. Buying a bond means you have money in your margin account that's earning interest.

The Role of Interest

When comparing the costs of a synthetic versus the costs of the standard position, you have to consider the costs of interest. This comes in three forms:

- The opportunity cost on money committed to the position
- The cost of margin in the options market
- The cost of margin in the underlying market

In many cases, the cost of carrying the underlying asset will be less than the cost of carrying options because options are considered to have more risk than the underlying. The difference in rates will vary at different times, but it might be substantial enough to make the synthetic the better alternative.

A Reminder About Volatility

The discussions in this chapter have looked at the effects of price changes on the synthetic positions. The options prices might not move as expected in the real world because the more volatile the underlying asset, the more opportunities there might be for an option to be exercised. That makes the option on a volatile asset more valuable, and it might affect the decision to go with a synthetic or with the straight option. As a result, the premium received from writing the one type of option might be more valuable than the premium paid to purchase a different option.

Synthetics and Moneyness

For a synthetic stock, the strike and the expiration date of the two options should be the same. As long as that's in place, the position will perform as the stock would—at least in a perfect world. In the real world, options prices will often vary from perfection.

For synthetic options, though, you get to choose the strike price. What should it be? An option that's at-the-money will give the most protection on the underlying, but it will also cost the most. And, the closer an option is to being in the money, the more likely it is to be exercised, thus affecting the position.

Hence, a synthetic should be placed only if you have a good sense of the volatility and other risks of the underlying asset.

What's the Downside?

There are two problems with synthetics. The first is they might not be available because of market conditions. The second is they can be expensive.

In addition to the payoff, you need to consider the costs of carrying the trade, the commissions involved in placing it, and the tax structure that will apply. (See Chapter 18 for more information on taxes.) There are plenty of strategies that look good on paper but don't work in real life, at least not for all traders.

> **DID YOU KNOW?**
>
> The Options Institute, which is the training organization sponsored by the options exchanges, has a position simulator tool that lets you consider interest rates, volatility, and other factors when choosing an option position. You can find it at optionseducation.org/tools/position_simulator.html.

Why and How to Use Synthetics

After making it to this point in the chapter, you might have one big question: why? Why do all this rearranging to create synthetics when the financial markets have done a perfectly good job of creating actual options and other financial instruments? What's the point?

And, in fact, most traders never use synthetics because they have no need to. Others use them only when interest rates make them favorable.

Synthetics come in handy for a few different situations, such as for arbitrage or to manage risks at a lower cost.

Can't Borrow Shares to Short

To sell a stock short, you have to borrow the shares. Brokers do this regularly, but sometimes, there is no stock to borrow—especially if it's the kind of overheated stock that everyone is trying to short. This may be because so much has already been sold short or because many of the shareholders do not allow the shares in their accounts to be loaned.

With a synthetic short stock, a trader can mimic the payoff of a short position without having to borrow the shares. This might have a lower cost and be easier to establish than a traditional short position for a trader who is able to large and manage complex margin requirements. The broker will need to see a large capital position in the account before approving this trade.

No Exchange-Traded Product

The financial markets are a wonder of creativity and disruption. The different participants have the amazing ability to develop new products traders want and need. In almost every situation, the option you want already exists, no synthetic needed.

Every now and again, though, you might want to trade an option on an underlying asset even though the precise option you want has not yet been created. Or maybe the underlying asset doesn't exist in physical form because you're looking at options on a metric rather than an asset.

This doesn't happen often, but sometimes it crops up. In that situation, you can use a synthetic to create the payoff pattern you want. (For an interesting example of this, check out the movie *The Big Short*, or the book of the same title by Michael Lewis, about the 2008 financial crisis. Many traders had reason to believe housing and mortgage markets were overheated, but they had to put a lot of effort into figuring out how to trade on that information.)

Greater Efficiency on Some Hedges

The standard academic valuation discussion of options assumes there are no taxes or transactions costs, and options are infinitely divisible. If you need 15.2 options to hedge a position, then you will be able to buy 15.2 options in this perfect world.

In the real world, options trade in lots of 100. There are commissions, carrying costs, and taxes to consider. When these factors are thrown into the mix, it might turn out that a synthetic is a cheaper, more efficient way to carry out a desired trade. In most cases, however, it will be far more expensive.

The Least You Need to Know

- Options can be thought of as ways to create payoffs rather than contracts to buy or to sell.
- Synthetic securities are ways to replicate the payoffs of options.
- The basis of synthetics is the put-call parity relationship.
- Synthetics have value for certain arbitrage transactions, but most traders never use them.

CHAPTER 13

Arbitrage

By definition, *arbitrage* is a riskless profit. In theory, arbitrage is not possible. It's a useful way to think about how markets work in a classroom, but the real world is very different. When some people talk about arbitrage, they are using the theoretical definition.

In the real world, the word *arbitrage* is used to mean a trade that's similar to theoretical arbitrage, but that has a little bit of risk. This is not the strictest definition of the word. You'll hear the word used in both its strict sense and its more real-world version when you talk to people about trading. It's safe to assume that if an academic tells you arbitrage is impossible, she is talking about arbitrage in the theoretical sense. If a trader tells you it happens all the time, she is talking about the real-word definition of the word.

An understanding of arbitrage will help you understand the options markets and how they work.

All that happens in arbitrage is someone buys cheap in one market and immediately resells the item in another market offering a higher price.

In This Chapter

- The definition of arbitrage
- Theoretical arbitrage and practical arbitrage
- How to use arbitrage strategies
- Waiting for the high-frequency folks

Arbitrage is the key to the functioning of the financial markets. It is the process that forces markets to behave rationally, and so it is the foundation of many options trading strategies for both hedgers and speculators. After all, options draw their value from other securities. That, alone, creates opportunities for arbitrage. On occasion, price discrepancies in other markets can be played with options. For example, if stock prices have not fully responded to the announcement of a merger, an options trade might offer a higher payoff with less risk than working with the stocks.

Here's what that would look like: Company A announces great earnings, and the stock price increases from $23 to $27 in one day, a $4 increase. A call option with a strike price of $23 has a premium of $2.04, despite news of the price increase. You could buy the call option, immediately exercise it to buy stock at $23, then sell those shares in the market at $27. Your profit is the $4 difference in the strike price and the market price, less the $2.04 premium, or $1.96. Nice, huh?

It's so nice you might never see it.

True riskless arbitrage is rare. To the extent that riskless arbitrage exists at all, it is the province of electronic trading systems. The arbitrage strategies used by options traders have very little risk, but the risk is not 0. So why have I included this chapter?

First, arbitrage can happen. Second, many of these arbitrage strategies are available to professional traders, who have access to high-speed trading software and deep pockets. That means these strategies will come up in discussions of the options market.

If you understand what's happening in the market, you'll be in a better position to manage your own, plain-vanilla trades.

The Law of One Price

The law of one price says identical assets should have the same price in every market. For example:

- A share of IBM stock should cost the same in New York as it does in Tokyo.

- The euro/pound exchange rate should be the same in London as it is in Paris.

- An ounce of gold should be valued equally everywhere.

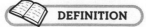 **DEFINITION**

The **law of one price** says that identical assets should have the same price in every market.

If you noticed any of these items were cheaper in one market than another, you would buy in the cheap market and immediately sell in the expensive one. The increased demand in the cheap market and the increased supply in the expensive market would push the prices together, exactly as you learn in any intro to economics class. Until the prices converged, you would collect a profit on the difference with no risk at all.

It doesn't happen often, but when it does, there is money to be made.

Arbitrage and near-arbitrage transactions occur in the options market because of the number of different cash flows that can be replicated.

Arbitrage Strategies

Options are a common part of arbitrage strategies. Even traders who don't normally use options turn to them when arbitrage situations are available.

This section covers some of the most common strategies. Keep in mind most of these involve at least a little risk, so they aren't arbitrage under the strictest definition of the term (which, you may recall, is a riskless profit). The risk relative to the return is less than it would be on a standard trade.

And a better return for a level of risk is a good thing.

Simple Arbitrage

The simplest way to take advantage of arbitrage is to look for situations in which the same asset has a different price in two different markets. Simple, yes?

The concept is simple, but it's very hard to do in real life.

Still, it's not impossible in the options market, in part because there are several exchanges competing for your business. Nearly identical options might trade at slightly different prices on one exchange than on another. If so, buy where it's cheaper and sell where it's more expensive.

These opportunities are rare, especially if you are a retail trader paying relatively high commissions and without a lot of computing power behind you. Still, you might see one someday. You are more likely to see arbitrage opportunities in times of great market stress, because they are not normal.

Option Arbitrage

Another simple arbitrage strategy using options is known as *option arbitrage*. It's a common way stock traders, especially professionals who pay low commissions, include options in their portfolios. It's a form of synthetic trading that allows the trader to buy cheap in one market and sell dear in another.

📖 **DEFINITION**

Option arbitrage is a profit made from identifying a mismatch between option prices and the price of the underlying asset.

For example, let's suppose a stock falls on news, but the prices implied in the option market have not fallen as fast. In that case, the trader buys the underlying asset and a put, then sells a call with the same strike price and expiration date. The strike price is higher than the current stock price. The synthetic short means the trader has bought cheap in the stock market and sold for a profit in the options market, a neat trick that generates a riskless profit.

Scalping

Despite the law of one price, option prices change a little each order placed. Sure, the difference from the right price might be only a few cents, but that's enough of a difference for the scalper.

Scalpers look to profit from changes in an options price, especially in the bid-ask spread. (You might remember from Chapter 2 this is the difference between the price the broker buys the option from a customer and the price at which she sells it to another customer.) There was a time when scalping was a common trade strategy for individual investors, but increased electronic trading has made it very difficult for all but the largest traders. Still, you may hear about it, so you should know what it is.

📖 **DEFINITION**

Scalping is a form of option trade that looks to make small profits from changes in the bid-ask spread.

In normal market conditions, the bid-ask spread for a given option will be steady. As long as supply and demand follow usual patterns, the spread will be the same number of pennies apart. If the spread is a little wider or a little narrower than usual, the scalper swoops in to make a profit.

Here's how it works:

If the spread is wider than usual, that means the ask is higher and/or the bid is lower than it should be. This happens because slightly more people want to buy than want to sell. The scalper views this as a sign to sell the option.

If the spread is narrower than usual, meaning the ask is lower and/or the bid is higher than normal, then slightly more people want to sell than to buy. The scalper views this as a sign to buy the option.

Scalpers must work fast. They make a lot of transactions with very small profits on each of them. There's little risk under normal market conditions. The problem is if supply and demand are starting to change because of some new information coming to the market, the scalper will end up on the wrong side of the market and be crushed. As a result, scalping is sometimes referred to as picking up nickels in front of a steamroller.

In the equity markets, scalpers have been decapitated by high-frequency and electronic trading systems. These identify and close out small price discrepancies so quickly it is almost impossible for an independent trader to keep up. (We're talking fractions of a second here.)

And guess what? The electronic trading systems moved on to the options markets. You might see scalping taking place, but you probably can't participate.

Synthetic Securities

Synthetic securities are a form of arbitrage. The combinations of payoffs are designed to mimic the payoff of options. The reason for doing a synthetic is it is often a cheaper way to achieve the same outcome. A synthetic increases your return for the same level of risk, which means some of your return is in the form of a riskless profit. And that's what you want!

There are enough different patterns that I devote a whole chapter to the topic—Chapter 14. For this discussion, the important points are that options and underlying assets can be thought of as payoffs, and there is more than one way to get the same payoff.

Conversion Arbitrage

Conversion arbitrage is a way to lock in a riskless profit if the price of an at-the-money call is higher than the price of an at-the-money put. You go long a put and short a call (with the same strike price and expiration) on an underlying asset you already own.

If the price of the underlying asset goes above the call before expiration, then the short call will be exercised. That offsets the position in the underlying asset, and the long put expires. The trader's profit is the cost of the put less the premium received for the short call.

If the underlying price falls below the put strike price, the long put can be exercised, and the short call expires unexercised. The profit is the exercise price of the option less the price of the underlying asset, adjusted by the amount of the initial premium position.

Did you see what happened here? As long as the premium received on the put is higher than the premium paid on the call, then the position will have no risk—and a profit is locked in.

The wrinkle is the price paid to acquire the stock. If you end up selling it for a lower price than you paid to buy it, you'll have a loss on the position. Conversion arbitrage can be powerful, but it can't work miracles.

The following tables show the payoff of a conversion on 100 shares of a $45 stock and at-the-money options. The Calculation column shows how the cost was found, and the Cash Inflow (Outflow) column shows the net.

Opening Transaction

Position	Calculation	Cash Inflow (Outflow)
Long $45 put	$1.20 × 100	($120)
Short $45 call	$1.23 × 100	$123
Long $45 stock	margin purchase	$0
Net inflow (outflow)		$3

Closing Transaction If the Stock Falls to $40 at Expiration

Position	Calculation	Cash Inflow (Outflow)
Exercise put	($45 − $40) × 100	$500
Call expires	0	$0
Stock value	($40 − $45) × 100	($500)
Net inflow (outflow)		$0
Profit (opening less closing): $3.00 − $0.00 = $3.00		

Closing Transaction If the Stock Is at $45 at Expiration

Position	Calculation	Cash Inflow (Outflow)
Exercise put	($45 − $45) × 100	$0
Call expires	0	$0
Stock value	($45 − $45) × 100	$0
Net inflow (outflow)		$0
Profit (opening less closing): $3.00 − $0.00 = $3.00		

Closing Transaction If the Stock Is at $50 at Expiration

Position	Calculation	Cash Inflow (Outflow)
Put expires	$0	$0
Call assigned	($45 − $50) × 100	($500)
Stock value	($50 − $45) × 100	$500
Net inflow (outflow)		$0
Profit (opening less closing): $3.00 − $0.00 = $3.00		

Yes, the profit is small. But it also comes with very little risk. In academic theory, all returns are a function of risk, so a return with no risk is, essentially, free money.

Reversal

A *reversal,* also known as a reverse conversion, is another form of option arbitrage. In a reversal, the trader buys the call, sells the put, and sells the stock short. It offers a risk-free profit if the prices of the options are out of alignment relative to the underlying position. This is a rare situation, and it requires plenty of margin in your account. But, if this applies to you, read on!

If the underlying rises above the strike price of the call before expiration, then the call will be exercised. That offsets the position in the underlying asset, and the short put expires. The trader's profit is the put premium less the cost of the long call.

If the underlying price falls below the short-call strike, the call can be exercised, and the long put expires unexercised. The trader's profit is the put premium less the cost of the short call.

As long as the premium received on the put is higher than the premium paid on the call, then the position will have no risk—and a profit is locked in.

The following tables show the reversal on a 100 shares of a $45 stock and at-the-money options.

Opening Transaction

Position	Calculation	Cash Inflow (Outflow)
Long $45 call	$1.20 × 100	($120)
Short $45 put	$1.23 × 100	$123
Short $45 stock	$45 × 100	$4,500
Net inflow (outflow)		$4,503

Closing Transaction If the Stock Falls to $40 at Expiration

Position	Calculation	Cash Inflow (Outflow)
Call expires	0	$0
Put assigned	($45 − $40) × 100	($500)
Stock value	$40 × 100	($4,000)
Net inflow (outflow)		($4,500)
Profit (opening less closing): $4,503.00 − $4,500.00 = $3.00		

Closing Transaction If the Stock Is at $45 at Expiration

Position	Calculation	Cash Inflow (Outflow)
Exercise call	($45 − $45) × 100	$0
Put expires	0	$0
Stock value	$45 × 100	($4,500)
Net inflow (outflow)		($4,500)
Profit (opening less closing): $4,503.00 − $4,500.00 = $3.00		

Closing Transaction If the Stock Is at $50 at Expiration

Position	Calculation	Cash Inflow (Outflow)
Exercise call	($50 − $45) × 100	$500
Put expires	0	
Stock Value	$50 × 100	($5,000)
Net inflow (outflow)		($4,500)
Profit (opening less closing): $4,503.00 − $4,500 = $3.00		

As with the conversion, the reversal is likely to generate a very small profit, but a profit coming with very little risk.

Box Spreads

A *box spread* is also known as a delta-neutral hedge. Delta, of course, is the rate at which an option's price changes as the price of the underlying asset changes. It is a combination of a bull-call spread and a bear-put spread.

A bull-call spread is the purchase of a call with one strike price, then writing a call with a higher strike price. The premium received will be less than the premium paid because the call with the higher strike price will be further out-of-the-money.

The maximum profit on a bull-call spread is the difference in the strike prices, less the net debit position of the premiums paid. The maximum loss is the premium paid.

A bear-put spread involves buying a put with one strike price and then writing a put with a lower strike price. The premium paid on the purchased put will be higher than the premium received on the written put because the purchased put will be closer to the money in value.

The maximum profit on a bear-put spread is the difference in the strike prices minus the net debit position of the premiums involved. The maximum loss is that net debit position—much less than with a naked put.

The bull-call spread posts its maximum profit when the underlying price is greater than the strike price on the short call. The bear-put spread has its largest profit when the underlying price is less than the strike price on the short put.

With a box spread, the profit will be even lower, but the loss is contained. Remember, one of the spreads will lose money, and it's possible both will.

> **DID YOU KNOW?**
>
> The box spread is so called because if you draw a payoff diagram, the range of potential profits looks like a box.

Interest Rate Arbitrage

An interest rate, also known as a yield, is nothing more than the price of money. However, the price of money is a component of the value of many different types of underlying assets. Hence, many traders look to the derivatives markets to speculate or hedge on interest rates. This is known as *interest rate arbitrage*.

> **DEFINITION**
>
> **Interest rate arbitrage** is a trading strategy that looks for differences in interest rates among different types of bonds.

The interest rate itself is driven by three factors:

- The level of opportunity cost in the economy as a whole

- Inflation

- The level of risk for the underlying asset

Differences in interest rates for different types of securities are affected by differences in these specific factors.

For example, the difference in interest rates (known as the spread) between U.S. government bonds and Japanese government bonds is due to differences in inflation and opportunity cost. This is true because these countries are as close to certain to repay their loans as is possible; there is not risk that they will not repay their loans. The difference in interest rates between U.S. government debt and emerging markets debt includes inflation, opportunity cost, and the risk that the loans will not be repaid.

If one of these three factors changes, then the spread must change, too. If the change in the spread is out of alignment with what it should be, then there's an opportunity to buy futures or calls on the bond with the lower-than-expected yield. There's also an opportunity to sell futures or calls on the bond with the higher-than-expected yield.

Sure, a trader could buy and sell the actual bonds, but using futures and calls will be cheaper and easier.

Index Arbitrage

A market index is a collection of stocks used to measure the performance of the stocks in a particular country, industry, or investment strategy. They are used as a performance benchmark and as an investable asset. Traders can use options, futures, and exchange-traded funds to hedge, speculate, and set up *index arbitrage* strategies.

DEFINITION

Index arbitrage is the process of making a profit from price discrepancies between the value of a market index and the value of the securities that are in them.

As a simple matter, the fact that there are different ways to play the same underlying asset means there might be occasional price discrepancies. Price discrepancies are especially likely to occur on days with a high level of market volatility, in which the price of an exchange-traded fund (ETF) on an index might not reflect the price of the stocks in the fund because of the speed and magnitude of the price changes. You could go long an underpriced ETF or short an overpriced ETF and wait for the price to move into alignment before closing out the position.

The problem with using the ETF alone is the market could continue to move—your ETF might be underpriced, but if the market as a whole continues to fall, it will reach the correct price lower than where you bought it.

This is where the multitude of securities comes in. You could buy the underpriced ETF and sell a call on the index. That means you have the premium from the call and protection if the price of the ETF falls. This is very much the province of high-frequency traders. You might see opportunities like this on volatile market days, but as an individual, you will have a hard time executing them.

Merger Arbitrage

News flow creates volatility in the underlying asset. That leads to occasional periods where an asset is not priced properly. And in the options world, volatility adds value.

When two companies announce a merger, there are a lot of details to attend to and a lot of things that can change between the day the merger is announced and the day it closes. For example, changes might affect the price, the currency used to make the acquisition (i.e., cash, debt, or stock), or the date the transaction closes. That assumes that the deal goes through and no other company pops in to make a bid.

In this situation, the options of the buyer and seller company will probably increase in value because volatility will increase until the day the deal closes. That means there might be opportunities to buy in the equity market and to sell in the options market, or vice versa, for a profitable and low-cost trade. There are hedge funds and traders who specialize in these trades, which makes it difficult for individual traders to play in these markets.

DID YOU KNOW?

News flow increases volatility, and volatility, of course, increases option prices. When looking for trades, consider them on underlying assets that are especially volatile.

Commissions, Taxes, and Other Considerations

There's one very big problem with seeking out arbitrage transactions—the costs of putting them into play, including the taxes.

The shorthand is this: if the call price less the put price is greater than the interest expense and commission, less any dividend received, then you should go ahead with the transaction.

Commissions

There's a term in trading called the *alligator spread*. It's a position that looks great based on market prices. However, the profits will be eaten up by the commissions.

You must know what your broker charges, and keep that in mind when you are planning a trade. The more actively you trade, the more important the commission will be to the profitability of your strategy.

Dividends

Those working with single-stock options need to consider the value of the dividend, if the stock pays one. If you are long the stock when the dividend is paid, then you receive it.

Most stocks paying dividends do so once a quarter. The value of the stock falls on the day the dividend is paid. All else being equal, the difference in value between a long call and a short put should be the difference in the dividend before the dividend is paid.

If you have a conversion on a dividend-paying stock when the dividend is paid, then you will receive the dividend. This will reduce the cost of carrying the position.

Interest

If you borrow money to establish a position, then you pay interest. If you use money you already have, then you give up the interest you could have earned if you had kept it on account instead. On the other hand, if you earn a premium from your option, then you have cash you can put in your account to earn interest.

Consider the earlier conversion example. The underlying asset is purchased on margin, so there's no upfront cost. However, there will be interest charged on that position. (If you don't have enough money in your account to meet the margin requirements, the broker isn't even going to let you borrow the additional funding.) On the other hand, there will be interest earned on the premium received for the short put.

A lot of transactions make more sense when interest rates are high then when they are low. When rates are high, the money earned on cash in the account can be enough to help offset other costs.

MARKET MAXIM

Changes in interest rates can turn unprofitable strategies into profitable ones—and vice versa. This is why option traders need to change their strategies often. A trade that works well at one period in time might not work so well in another.

Taxes

Benjamin Franklin said the only two sure things in life are death and taxes. You'll probably owe taxes on your riskless profit, so take that into consideration.

Taxes on options can be tricky. Chapter 18 has tons of information on the tax treatment of options, and that can help you when you plan your trade. More than one trader has been tripped up by a mismatch of long-term losses and short-term gains. Don't be one of them.

Problems and Downsides of Arbitrage

The biggest problem with arbitrage is that profits are very small. The risks are very small, too, but they are rarely exactly 0. That means it doesn't take much to wipe out a lot of hard work finding and placing a trade.

Pin Risk

Many arbitrage strategies call for the purchase of an at-the-money position, under the assumption the price of the underlying asset will be different at the time of expiration. But what happens if the underlying price is exactly equal to the strike price at the time of expiration?

That position loses money. It doesn't happen often, but it does happen.

In trader terms, the underlying price is pinned to the strike price, and a strategy that would be harmed by this is said to have pin risk.

High-Frequency Trading

Professional trading firms know all about arbitrage. They play it by running powerful computer programs with ultrafast connections to find mispriced investments, then buy the cheap and sell the expensive in no time.

How fast? Faster than you can blink your eye.

The problem for traders who are not machines is they can't compete.

High-frequency trading is a significant factor in pretty much all financial markets these days. It has eliminated a lot of the opportunities that day traders had to make money.

The Least You Need to Know

- Arbitrage is the process of making a profit while taking little or no risk.
- The number of different options and options exchanges increase the opportunities for the slight mispricings that make arbitrage work.
- Creating a synthetic might involve different commissions or tax treatments, so they should be considered.
- Many strategies available in the options market, such as scalping, were eliminated in the equity market by high-speed trading.

CHAPTER 14

Technical Analysis

Technical analysis involves looking at the trading history of an underlying asset or a derivative to find trends that might indicate future prices. It often seems like reading tea leaves, but prices contain information about the conviction behind changes in supply and demand. Certain reactions to changes in the outlook of the underlying asset often play out in more or less predictable patterns. Some of these patterns are driven by rational behavior, while some are driven by raw emotion. Either way, these patterns affect prices.

The more conviction, the more information and the more likely a trend is to continue. That's the short answer.

Day trading, especially with common stock, relies heavily on technical analysis. Many day traders work from the charts, with little or no regard for other dynamics influencing prices. Many options traders also work from charts, because most traders close out their positions before expiration. Some find technical analysis to be useful for finding entry and exit points.

In This Chapter

- Understanding technical analysis
- Looking for basic patterns
- Why it's believed to work
- Using technical analysis in trading

Technical analysis is used in other markets, too. It's helpful to have a passing familiarity with some of the major terms and major indicators that you might run across as an options trader. Understanding these indicators both help you see how they affect your own trading, as well as how they affect expectations.

The Basics of Technical Analysis

Technical analysis starts with charts of the performance of an investment. It shows the range of prices over a given time period (usually a day). The charts are designed to show the high, low, and closing prices.

Let's work through an example from a financial website, finance.yahoo.com, using shares of Facebook, which trades under ticker symbol FB.

This is what a bar looks like:

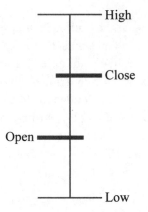

A bar is a straight line showing the range of prices during the trading period. The high for the period is at the top, and the low is at the bottom. Some platforms show the line in red if the price fell over the period and in green if it rose.

Often, the chart will have two parts: a series of bars in the top part and a bottom part showing the volume of contracts or shares. Not every time of underlying asset has a viable volume number (a market index, for example). If a chart includes volume data, though, you can use it to see how much activity is driving changes in price.

A chart with bars and volume looks like this:

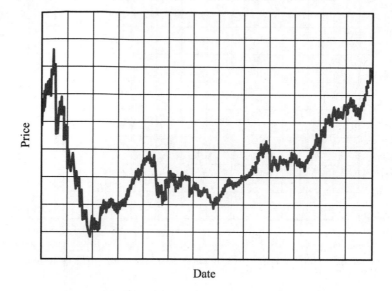

This is a price chart showing a range of bars over a given time period. It might show hourly bars over the course of a day, daily bars over the course of a month, or even annual bars over the course of decades.

These charts are generated automatically by almost every website and brokerage firm that tracks investment prices. They are easy to find and generate. The information shown in these charts is easy to use, too. Without spending too much time or effort, you can see:

- How much the price has changed over time
- Whether that price change has been a smooth ride or really volatile
- How much trading takes place on a typical day
- Whether trading volume changed on days with big price changes

Then, you can overlay the performance of a different market benchmark (discussed in Chapter 19) to show how the price of the underlying asset varies with the price of other market factors. Using this strategy helps you see if the price is moving with the market or against it.

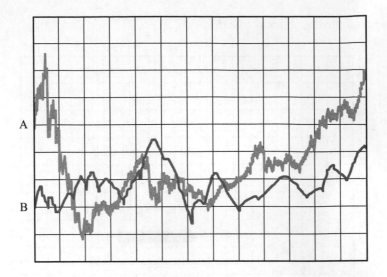

This chart shows the performance of a benchmark index (A) set over a price chart showing an overall market index (B). The benchmark is usually drawn at its closing price for the period.

You've already done some basic technical analysis! Wasn't that easy?

Intermediate Technical Analysis

There are tons of books, seminars, and classes on technical analysis, but a lot of traders are happy with the information gleaned from the basic chart analysis shown earlier. The next level gets into trends, volatility, and reversal.

Trendlines

A trendline is nothing more than a line drawn on a chart, Simple straight lines are shown running through the series of price bars. The following chart shows an example.

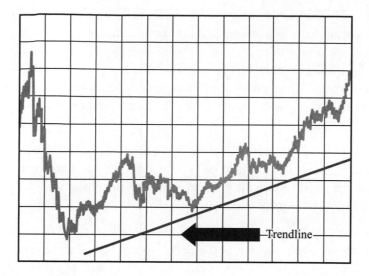

A trendline is simply a line drawn to smooth out the bar chart and show the overall direction of the asset's price.

Trendlines clarify the direction of a trend over different time periods. Some trends play out in a few days over the course of a long-term trend that is moving in a different direction. If the time to expiration of your option position is far out, then long-term trends in the underlying price matter more to you than do short-term deviations from trend.

In addition to the basic trendlines, you'll want to look at support and resistance lines. They look like this:

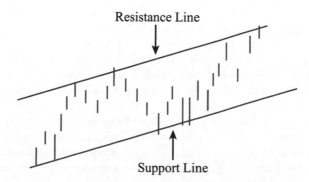

The support line shows the lowest price at which the asset trades in a given trend. The resistance line shows the highest price.

The lines form a channel, with the top line being the maximum price level in the trend, and the bottom line being the minimum price within the trend. This sort of chart is sometimes called the supply zone, because as the price of the underlying asset approaches that price, a growing number of sellers are willing to short. That maximum is the level at which prices resist going much higher. The minimum—or support—level is the price at which lower prices seem to stop. The support level is also known as the demand zone, because at that price, traders are willing to go long the underlying asset.

Traders will buy at the support level, looking at the low line on the channel. The idea is that here, the underlying asset is unlikely to go lower in price, so you'll get the best purchase price here. Then, the trader will watch the price. When it hits the resistance level—top line—the trader will sell because the price is unlikely to go higher.

An option trader might look at the support and resistance levels to manage risk. For example, if you are writing puts, you would want the strike price to be below the support level in order to minimize the risk of the option being exercised. A trader writing calls might want to set the strike above the resistance level.

Of course, trends change, which brings us to the next point.

More precisely, it brings us to the pivot point, which is the formal determination of support and resistance levels. A *pivot point* is the average of the high, low, and close for the day. If the next day's price closes below the pivot point, then the underlying asset has a new support level. If it closes above the pivot point, then there is a new resistance level.

As long as the trend holds, the underlying asset will be relatively expensive when it hits the resistance level and relatively cheap when it hits the resistance line.

TRADING TIP

Resistance levels are used to set prices for collars. You might recall from Chapter 10 a collar is a risk-management tool, which involves buying a put to minimize losses and then selling an out-of-the money call to generate income that covers the cost of the put. (The same effect happens with a long call and short put, so the trader uses whichever options have a price advantage.) By using the support level, the trader can assess the likelihood of downside risk. Meanwhile, the resistance level helps indicate how far out-of-the-money the short call strike price should be to reduce the risk of the underlying asset being called away. The use of support and resistance levels can keep the cost of the collar's insurance reasonable.

Moving Averages

The next step up from drawing a trendline is calculating a moving average. This is the graph of the average closing price for a number of days in the past. It could be 5 days, 30 days, 60 days, or even more. Almost all charting applications will draw these automatically.

Moving averages are useful in and of themselves, but they are also components of other trading indicators:

A *crossover* occurs if the price crosses the moving average line. A crossover above the moving average would indicate the price trend is upward. This means it might be a good time to buy calls or short puts. For example, if the crossover occurred at a price of $30, you could establish a long call position with a strike of $31. Then, you could exercise it if the crossover indicator was correct and then started trading at an even higher price. Or, you could write covered calls with a strike price of $29, under the assumption the indicator held, you would receive the premium, and the option would expire worthless because the underlying asset increased in price. If the crossover cuts below the moving average, then a long put with a strike price below the moving average is more likely to become in-the-money, and a short call with a strike price above the moving average is more likely to expire worthless.

A *convergence* takes place when moving averages calculated over different time periods come together. This is often a sign a trend is ending.

If the moving averages for different periods move apart, then a *divergence* has occurred. This usually means a new trend is beginning.

> **DEFINITION**
>
> A **crossover** is a price that crosses a moving average line and indicates a change in trend. A **convergence** occurs when the moving averages for different time periods (e.g., 5, 10, or 30 days) come together. It often indicates the end of the trend. A **divergence** occurs when the moving averages for different time periods move apart. It often indicates the start of a new trend.

Breakouts

Trends don't hold forever, though. If it changes, then you'll see a channel looks something like this:

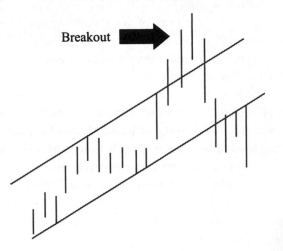

When a price bar crosses the trendline, a breakout has taken place. It signals the start of a new trend.

The *breakout* is the point where the price crosses the trendlines to form a new trend. This new trend has its own support and resistance level.

If a new trend does not start, then the technical analyst would call this a *false breakout*. Hey, technical analysis is not clairvoyance. Instead, it's just one tool among many to help figure out what's happening in the market.

Volatility

Volatility matters to the technical analysis of options for two reasons. The first is that volatility is a key component of an option's price, so using charts as a way to find trends in volatility can improve your understanding of an option's value. The second is that volatility within the options market is a key technical indicator used by investors and traders of all stripes as a way of gauging the sentiment of the market as a whole. If you're trading options, pay attention! (Of course you're trading options! That's why you have this book, right?)

Vega, you might recall from Chapter 4, is how much an option's price changes as the amount of volatility in the underlying asset changes. As the underlying becomes more volatile, the price of the option goes up, and vega tells you how much the price will increase.

A simple way to determine how the volatility implied in the option price compares to a typical level is to graph the implied volatility of the underlying asset and compare that to an historical moving average of actual volatility over a given time period—usually 10, 20, or 30 days. It's hardly perfect, but it does give the trader a good first look at the situation.

By the way, vega doesn't specify if the price of the underlying asset is more volatile on the upside or the downside, only the actual price is likely to vary from the expected price at any given point in time. An option can be volatile even if it goes up a lot in price.

Volatility Cones

A *volatility cone* is a graph showing the amount of realized volatility over different time horizons. The concept was developed by Galen Burghardt and Morton Lane, two futures analysts who published a paper about it in 1990. The cone itself is formed by a plot of the contribution of volatility to the option price as the option gets closer to expiration. In general, the intrinsic value of the underlying asset becomes less important to the price and volatility becomes more important as the option moves closer to expiration.

The chart looks like this:

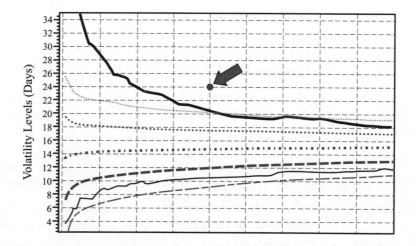

The dot on the chart shows the current implied volatility of the option. The lines show the actual rolling average amount of volatility for the last 30, 60, 90, and 120 days.

The cone itself forms around the historic volatility levels and the implied volatility in the current price.

Volatility cones can be used to compare the amount of implied volatility in the current options price with the actual rolling average amount of volatility for the past 30, 60, 90, or 120 days. That gives you a clue as to whether or not the current option value is fair relative to its historic levels of volatility. If it's underpriced, you buy; if it is overpriced, you write.

> **TRADING TIP**
>
> Volatility cones are useful for determining how much insurance will cost or how wide a butterfly must be for you to profit.

The VIX

The VIX, covered in Chapter 6, is an important measure of the volatility of the options market. Options traders use it to help indicate the market's vega. It is also used as an indicator by people outside of the options market who want a measure of the amount of volatility expected over the next 30 days. After all, the VIX was an important technical indicator before it became a tradeable contract.

Reversals

A reversal is simply a change in trend to the opposite. They are obvious in hindsight, and many chart patterns show where they might happen again in the future.

> **MARKET MAXIM**
>
> Trade what you see, not what you think. Traders have more hard factual information today than they have ever had. Your screen shows you supply, demand, volume, sentiment, direction, price, delta, gamma, theta, vega—everything you need to make a good trading decision. And yet, humans being what we are, we often think we know better than the market. More often than not, we don't.

Basic Chart Patterns

Certain chart patterns are so common—and commonly used—they are almost shorthand for certain market conditions. Most options traders rely heavily on technical analysis, and even those who do not rely on it understand the key indicators. If a head-and-shoulders pattern is identified for a particular contract or underlying asset, then the trader has a measure of the trading range. If the head-and-shoulders pattern completes (discussed shortly), the trader assumes bad things are expected to happen to the price.

Pennants and Flags

Pennants and *flags* are chart patterns showing a short-term deviation from the main trend. These patterns are nothing more than the shape formed by the support and resistance lines of a subtrend.

A flag has parallel lines:

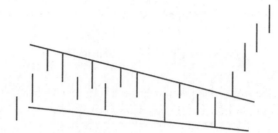

A flag is formed if the support and resistance levels run in parallel.

A pennant has sloping lines, as shown here:

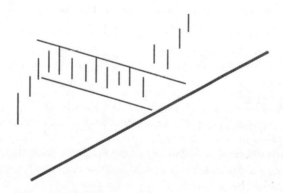

A pennant is formed if the support and resistance levels have different slopes.

Pennants and flags usually show up in the middle of a trend, stick around for two weeks, and then scram. If trading volume falls during this time, it is evidence of *retracement;* when it's over, the main trend will continue. If it increases, you might have a reversal, which is a change in the main trend. A reversal is a good sign of the high or the low for the trend. Given the game is to buy low and sell high, a reversal is great to spot.

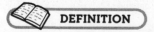 **DEFINITION**

Retracement is the temporary reversal of a trend; a downward movement in a longer upward rent; or an upward phase in a longer downward trend.

Head-and-Shoulders

The *head-and-shoulders* formation is a series of three peaks within a price chart. The one in the middle, known as the head, is greater than the ones to the left and the right (which are, of course, the shoulders). The line separating the head and shoulders from the rest of the chart is known as the neckline. The chart looks like this:

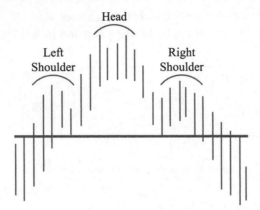

With a head-and-shoulders formation, the price bars arrange themselves into three peaks, with the higher one in the middle.

The specific reason for this pattern is traders are trying to eke out a few more profits at the end of a price trend. There isn't enough demand to keep the trend going, though, and so the price falls.

And, of course, people who see a head-and-shoulders formation tend to respond as though a price decline is imminent, which makes it a bit of a self-fulfilling prophecy in the short term.

At the end of a downtrend, traders will start testing the lows, with the result appearing as a *reverse head-and-shoulders:*

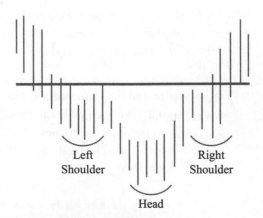

A reverse head-and-shoulders formation has three valleys, with the deeper on in the middle.

A reverse head-and-shoulders formation is as bullish as a regular head-and-shoulders formation is bearish—in other words, very much so.

Cup-and-Handle

Assets fall in price all the time. At some point, the information gets out to all the traders in the market. They reassess the situation and, sometimes, decide it is time to buy again. This activity creates a formation that, if you squint, looks like a cup and its handle.

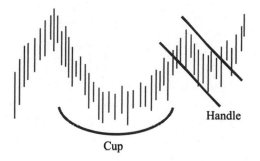

The cup-and-handle formation shows the price bars forming two high peaks, followed by a smaller peak.

The handle is formed by people who bought at the old high and who wait until the price recovers before they cash out. Once they're out, the serious traders who understand the fundamentals will get in and ride the new uptrend.

For example, Idiot Enterprises stock reached a peak of $100 per share in January. Some not-so-smart stock traders decided this was a great time to buy shares because the price increase showed it was a great investment. (This is a really common mistake, by the way, because many traders wait for confirmation of a trend so long they end up buying high and selling low. Oops.) Then, the shares of Idiot Enterprises languish at about $95 for a while until it returns to $100, and the not-so-smart trader decides it's time to sell this disappointing position. The increased number of shares for sale takes the price down to $85. The brilliant trader takes a look at this, and knows Idiot Enterprises has a great outlook for future earnings, and decides to start buying, taking the price back up to $100.

The option trader here would see the potential for an increase in the underlying price as the trend plays out, and take a position to profit. One such position would be a long call with a strike price below $100, which would be likely to move in-the-money. A second position would be to sell puts with a strike price below $85, which would be likely to expire worthless, leaving a net credit position in the trader's account. Nice, huh?

A cup-and-handle tends to cover a long-term trend, with a year or so being common. There will be lots of subtrends taking place over that time. Weeklys won't be affected, but options with long expirations might.

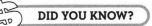

MARKET MAXIM

The trend is your friend until the end. Don't fight trends, but keep in mind they will change. Like Chicago weather, trends will change before you know it—and whether or not you like it.

Gaps

A gap is a break in the price bars. It occurs because of a news event that usually takes place before exchange trading opens, causing a delay as everyone tries to figure out where the price should be. Or traders might be looking at overnight activity in the futures market and bidding the prices on the exchange higher or lower than the previous day's trading range. Sometimes the gap occurs during the trading day. Some exchanges will halt if there is a sudden change in price or volume.

A gap followed by upward trading shows the news was good, which usually indicates an uptrend in the price. A gap on the down side is usually bad.

Theories of Technical Analysis

At its most basic level, technical analysis shows how changes in the supply and demand for a stock have affected price levels over time. It is a way to think about how emotion influences the prices of assets.

Some practitioners of technical analysis have developed more elaborate theories of how financial markets work and of how that activity plays out in technical patterns.

DID YOU KNOW?

The hot area of academic finance is behavioral finance, which looks at how markets are inefficient due to human emotions. Technical analysis was dismissed as voodoo by many academics for many years, but now some think it might show how emotional behavior plays out in market prices.

Fibonacci and Elliott Wave

The *Fibonacci* sequence looks like this:

> 0, 1, 1, 2, 3, 5, 8, 13, 21 . . .

It starts with 0 and 1, the first two whole numbers. Each following number is the sum of the previous two. Hence, $0 + 1 = 1$; $1 + 1 = 2$; $1 + 2 = 3$. It repeats into infinity.

Something else interesting happens when the series reaches double digits and beyond:

> 13, 21, 34, 55, 89, 144, 233 . . .

That is, the ratio of each number to the next on is .618.

Look: $13 \div 21 = .618$. $21 \div 34 = .618$. $55 \div 89 = .618$.

To put it another way, the ratio of the smaller and the larger of two numbers is the same as the ratio of the larger number to the sum of the two numbers. This proportion, 6.18, is also known as the *Golden Ratio* or Golden Proportion. It is the proportion of a perfect spiral and appears frequently in nature. It is also a key proportion used in creating art; one of the first things amateur photographers learn is "the rule of thirds," which is based on this idea.

> **DID YOU KNOW?**
>
> The rule of thirds is a rule explaining how the human eye prefers to look at objects arranged along the Golden Proportion, with is approximately two thirds. Therefore, when taking pictures, you should arrange the items in the frame so the focal point is either one-third or two-thirds of the way from the edge. Your phone's camera app might give you a grid of nine blocks to help you find this point.

The Fibonacci sequence is named for Leonard Fibonacci, the Italian mathematician who discovered it about a thousand years ago. Traders often refer to it as "the Fib" for short.

This is some pretty groovy math, isn't it? And did you think a book about options would get into rules about aesthetics?

All of this gets to trading. Seriously. One trader, Ralph Elliott, became fascinated with the idea of the Fibonacci series. He believed over the long run, the financial markets move in waves fitting Fibonacci's equation, and he developed a system known as the *Elliott Wave*. The basics are these:

- A bull market has three down waves and five up waves.

- Support and resistance levels should be 61.8 percent above lows and below highs.

- Buy any underlying asset down 61.8 percent from its high.

Adherents of the Elliott Wave theory believe these movements can play out in a few hours and over centuries. They tend to look at very long-term price records. There are centuries' worth of data for some underlying assets, such as currencies, commodities, and even stock markets.

Although it might seem nutty, and it's not easy to learn, plenty of traders out there swear by the Fibonacci sequence and the Elliott Wave.

Candlestick Charting

The *candlestick charting* system was developed by Japanese rice traders more than 200 years ago, and it's still used. Because it was developed for a commodities market, it remains popular with traders who deal in agricultural underlying assets. However, there are plenty of stock traders who use it, too.

A candlestick chart is similar to the price bar shown earlier in this chapter, but it has a wider middle section to give you more information:

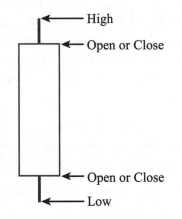

A candlestick is formed to show the open and closing price for each day between the high and the low price, with the length determined by the difference between the opening and closing price for the day.

The rectangle part of the candlestick is known variously as the candle or the body. Its length gives a sense of the volatility the underlying asset. The ends between the open or close and the high and low are known as the wicks (sometimes called the shadows). The candles might be colored in to make trends stand out. Most charting apps set candlesticks to green on up days and red on down days.

Gann

Legend has it, William Gann made $50 million in the stock and commodities markets using a system based on astrology. Some say his secret died with him, while others insist he taught it to a select few. As a result, the precise details of his system are lost in the mist of time, which makes the whole system even more mysterious and more interesting.

There are two things we can say for certain about Gann. Firstly, a money management system attributed to him is popular with traders and gamblers, and it is covered in Chapter 17. Secondly, there is a system in use called *Gann*, which might or might not be his system.

The system currently known as Gann is based on the relationship of price and time. A Gann angle is the number of points traded per time. Hence, an underlying asset moves 2 points in 1 day has a Gann angle of 2 × 1. There are a lot of rules tied to different Gann angles, but the easy one is widely used: if the underlying falls by 50 percent, it is a good time to buy.

Putting It All Together

The value of an option is intrinsic value plus extrinsic value (time value). Time value is a function of both the volatility of the underlying and the amount of time until the option expires. Technical analysis is useful for finding the value of the underlying as well as its volatility.

Technical Indicators and Option Pricing

Factor	Greek	Technical Indicator
Price of the underlying	None	Basic chart pattern
		Trendlines
		Support and resistance
Rate of change in underlying	Delta	Moving average
Volatility	Vega	Volatility cones
		Support and resistance
		Candle length
Time to expiration	Theta	No technical indicator

The Least You Need to Know

- The short-term valuation of many single stocks is tied to technical analysis.
- The price patterns show the how much supply and demand influences changes in market prices.
- Certain patterns are so well known they become their own measures of market sentiment.
- Technical analysis is useful for determining the value of the underlying and the amount of volatility (vega) of an option.

CHAPTER 15

Fundamental Analysis

Fundamental analysis drives a lot of options trading. People take a position believing that something will happen to make their positions pay off. When the evidence backing that belief is strong, the less risky the position will be.

The process is a mixture of global macroeconomic economic analysis and an examination of those factors specific to a particular underlying asset. Someone looking at single-stock equities would track the factors affecting specific companies. A trader in options on agricultural commodities might look at weather trends, and a trader in volatility options would look at movements in the market as a whole.

An option's intrinsic value is tied to the price of the underlying asset. It's time value, or theta, is tied to the calendar, and volatility, or vega, is related to the changes of the underlying. Fundamental analysis can give you a sense of the accuracy of the underlying price's relativity to its value. Also, this analysis can help you understand the factors that might cause the price to change. The greater the time value of an option, the more things can change, and fundamental analysis can give you a sense of whether those changes are likely to move your position into-the-money. It's the next-best thing to clairvoyance.

In This Chapter

- The basics of fundamental analysis
- Determining what drives the underlying asset
- Limitations of fundamental analysis
- Fundamental analysis and options trading

Why Analysis Matters

Because an option's value is derived from the value of something else, and because its value includes the effects of time and volatility, it's easy to forget an option has a relationship to an underlying asset. But it most definitely does.

Here's a common situation: a trader starts writing deep out-of-the-money puts in the equity market to generate income. The logic is that the market has an upward bias anyway, so the option isn't terribly likely to be assigned.

And then, the option is in-the-money, and the trader is stuck with stock she does not want. She is now convinced options are a terrible idea.

In addition, a trader who looks only at the value of the underlying asset might completely over-look the role of volatility, which is huge! Many clues about the amount and sources of volatility can be found through fundamental research. For example, you might be able to discern how much a particular asset is exposed to different market factors. This can lead to greater profits or, at least, fewer unpleasant surprises.

Now, suppose our intrepid trader did research on different stocks and found some she liked as long-term investments but thought they were too expensive to buy now. She wrote deep out-of-the-money puts on the most volatile of them, because greater implied volatility means a higher premium. She collected the income, and then waited. One day, the entire stock market has a break, her options are assigned, and she now has shares of a stock she wants to own, which were acquired at a good price. And, she gets to keep the premium income received from writing the put in the first place. It's a win-win!

Her speculative income strategy fits into her overall investing program. Her research let her use the options market to improve her investment returns.

This is a simple example of how understanding the value of the underlying asset and the amount of volatility it is expected to have can help a trader use options to improve investing. Spend some time learning about how the underlying asset moves before diving into a new market.

Starting with the Macroeconomy

Options are economic assets. Every option is driven by the supply and demand for something in the economy. Even options on something esoteric, such as those on volatility measures, are based on economic factors. In the case of the VIX, which is the CBOE's measure of the expected 30-day volatility of the S&P 500, the supply and demand for options is a function of expectations about the future economy.

Many options traders take a top-down approach and look at the economy of the world as a whole. They are looking for information about growth and volatility as an indicator of how the prices of specific underlying assets might respond to the what's happening in the world.

A general understanding of the state of the world can be gleaned from the regular reading of such major financial publications as *The Wall Street Journal* and *The Economist.* They cover the world's financial markets and look at factors of special interest to investors.

Economic analysts, whose work feeds into the stories you'll see in the financial press, look at the government data. It's easy to find if you want to crunch the numbers or digest the reports yourself.

> **DID YOU KNOW?**
>
> As a general rule, the world's economy and markets are growing. We have more people and more money than ever before. Because of this, most markets will have an upward bias over the long term, but that doesn't mean prices will increase at any particular time. A key part of your research will be looking for reasons why a given underlying asset won't increase in price at the expected pace during your trading period.

U.S. Data Sources

The United States government releases an incredible amount of information about the nation's economy. The main repository can be found at data.gov, which connects you to the different U.S. government agencies that collect data. Here, you can find such information as consumer price indexes, food price outlooks, and international trade data.

Some of the data sources are easier to reach by going through the agency's website directly. The Census Department, census.gov, is a great resource for data about the economy, as is the Bureau of Labor Statistics (bls.gov) and, for commodity markets, the U.S. Department of Agriculture (usda.gov).

For information about interest rates, monetary activity, and the economy as a whole, check out the website for the Board of Governors of the Federal Reserve, federalreserve.gov. Here you'll find definitive information about U.S. interest rates, including expectations for opportunity cost and inflation.

Global Data Sources

The World Bank (data.worldbank.org) collects global economic data, and is a good source of information about trends around the world. The Organization for Economic Cooperation and

Development (data.oecd.org) is a consortium of the world's most economically developed nations, and it tracks an impressive amount of data from member nations as well as other nations.

Of course, the numbers are only as good as the information submitted. Some nations are better at accurate reporting than others.

For economic information about the European Union, the site to see is the European Central Bank, ecb.europa.eu. For Japan, the Bank of Japan's English-language site is boj.or.jp/en. In general, a nation's central bank collects fundamental information about the country's economy. You might not always find what you want in English, though. (Google Translate is useful in these situations to get you to the numbers. The numbers themselves are a universal language.)

> **MARKET MAXIM**
>
> The major financial newspapers, such as *The Wall Street Journal* and the *Financial Times,* publish major data releases and analysis. For most traders, staying up to date with the news is enough.

Analyzing the Underlying Asset

Each type of option is based on a different type of underlying asset. No surprise, the factors driving price changes will be very different for each type of asset. If you're interested in options but don't know where to begin, start by finding an asset that interests you. Then, you can start reading!

Most of these sources are free. Some require registration; some are quite pricey but might be available at your library. And if you're active in an area, it is not only worth your while to pay for research, but also might it be deductible from taxes. Nice, huh?

Single-Stock Options

Single-stock options are based on the value of the underlying stock. Companies are required to submit financial information to the U.S. Securities and Exchange Commission, and many companies release much of other information about their businesses to investors. Although many option traders aren't investors, they will want to look at the same information used by the investor. Meanwhile, many investors use options to augment or protect an equity position or hold LEAPS or other long-term contracts as a stock replacement.

The primary driver of stock price performance is the expected growth rate in earnings per share. Even factors that look like they are not related, such as product announcements or merger activity, ultimately affect earnings per share. After all, earnings are affected by sales growth, investments in products and marketing, and good cost control. They are the source of funds to grow the company and to generate returns for investors.

Investment banks have analysts whose job it is to estimate earnings per share, and they report their numbers to different data service providers. The information is then aggregated and presented by almost all stock quote providers, including such free services as finance.yahoo.com.

The following table offers an example.

Earnings Estimates for Idiot Industries

Earnings Estimate	Current Q	Next Q	Current Year	Next Year
Average	1.19	0.88	4.19	4.74
Number of analysts	27.00	27.00	30.00	28.00
Low estimate	1.14	0.83	4.00	4.50
High estimate	1.26	0.98	4.38	5.08
Year ago EPS	1.09	0.74	3.70	4.18

When you look at analyst estimates, you're looking for two things: the projected growth rate and the range of estimates. In the preceding example, the earnings estimate for the current year is 4.19, right there on the first line. On the last line, we can see the company had earnings of 3.70 for the prior year. That indicates a growth rate of $(4.70 - 3.70) \div 3.70 = 13.24$ percent. The range between the high and the low is $(4.38 - 4.00) \div 4.00 = 9.5$ percent.

If the estimates are in a tight range, then there's less expected volatility. The implied volatility of the option is likely to be small, and the option is likely to increase in value if there's a news event that changes the amount of volatility. If the range of earnings is wide, then the amount of expected volatility is probably large.

Along with the general business and financial news, one great source of unbiased research on companies and exchange-traded funds is Morningstar, morningstar.com. Some of their research is free, and the rest is priced to be accessible to individual investors.

Financial Products

The research on financial products will be similar to top-down research on the economy as a whole, because in essence, that's what you're doing when you're looking at options on market indexes, interest rates, and currencies.

These factors influence the value of these underlying assets. They also influence the value of all options. That's one of the reasons they have proven to be so popular.

A key place to go for information on financial assets is the Federal Reserve Bank's website, federalreserve.gov. Indexes of different economic indicators are prepared by The Conference Board, conference-board.org, and the official arbiter of recessions is the National Bureau of Economic Research, nber.org.

Commodities

Most listed options are for single stocks or financial products, but they are hardly the only ones out there. Depending on your interests and your needs, you might want to look at options on commodities and options on commodities futures. There is a huge range of these derivatives! There also is a huge range of research sources specific to these different markets. Here are a few to check out:

Agricultural products:

- Department of Agriculture Economic Research Service, ers.usda.gov
- World Agriculture Supply and Demand Estimates, usda.gov/oce/commodity/wasde
- Food and Agriculture Organization of the United Nations, fao.org/statistics/en
- American Soybean Association, soygrowers.com
- National Association of Wheat Growers, wheatworld.org
- National Corn Growers Association, ncga.com

Energy commodities:

- The American Petroleum Institute, api.org
- The U.S. Department of Energy, energy.gov/data/open-energy-data
- The International Energy Agency, iea.org
- Energy Intelligence, energyintel.com
- Platts, platts.com

Metals:

- The U.S. Geological Survey: minerals.usgs.gov
- American Metals Market, amm.com

- World Bureau of Metal Statistics, world-bureau.com

- Platts, platts.com

DID YOU KNOW?

You might hear of market events referred to as *black swans*. This term emerged from work by a statistician, Nassim Nicholas Taleb. It refers to a random, unexpected event causing you to reassess your position. The idea is that if you live near a pond where white swans live, you might assume that all of the swans everywhere are white. If, one day, you see a black swan, your assumptions are challenged. At least one swan somewhere is black, and it's possible that the all swans out there are black except for the white ones in your local pond. A lot of fundamental research is involved when trying to determine if an event is a one-off occurrence or a sign of more to come.

Looking at the Calendar

It's obvious, and it's also easy to forget: the time value, also known as theta, is an enormous component of an option's value. The only indicator for it is the number of days left until the option expires. The longer the time to expiration, the greater the time value, because it's more likely some event will occur to bring the option into-the-money. After all, tomorrow will probably be a lot like today, but nine months from now, the world will have new people who do not exist at this moment. (The metaphysics of time is really interesting and freaky stuff. And it applies to options trading!)

Time value is a simple concept that has a huge effect on the price of an option. A very long-term option, such as a LEAP, has its value based almost entirely on time. The time value of a weekly option has very little effect on its price. Everything else is in between. Most brokerage firms publish the time value of an option at a given point in time.

But, like sands through an hourglass, the time value of an option decline as the expiration date draws near. At expiration, it is worth nothing. The writer keeps the premium; the buyer is stuck. The exact rate of decay is the theta, and it varies in part by how much the option is in-the-money or out-of-the-money. There's one binary choice: at expiration, the option will be worth exercising or it won't.

If an option isn't at or near the money a week before expiration, it probably won't be on expiration day. And if it's way out-of-the-money on the day before expiration, it probably won't cross over. If the market is really volatile, it *could* cross over, but remember miracles are few and far between anywhere in the market. It could happen, but it might not.

If you are long an option, you have to decide whether it is better to cut losses by selling an out-of-the money option as it approaches expiration, or to hold on hoping it moves in-the-money instead of expiring worthless. (Hint: it's almost always better to cut your losses and close the position.)

This effect is sometimes known as the option's death spiral: in the days before expiration, the time value of an option declines to 0, and the price of the option falls along with it. The further out-of-the-money the option is, the greater the speed of the price decline.

> **$) DID YOU KNOW?**
>
> On the very first episode of *The Simpsons*, Bart Simpson said, "If TV has taught me anything, it's that miracles always happen to poor kids at Christmas." Miracles make for great TV, but they don't happen often in real life. Could a miracle happen the day before expiration to make bring your out-of-the-money option into major profitability? Sure, it could happen. Will it? Probably not.

Fundamental Analysis in Options Trading

Options valuation is covered back in Chapter 5. There are a few primary factors involved:

- The price of the underlying asset

- The delta, or how much the option's price will change as the underlying's price changes

- The volatility of the underlying asset

- The time value of the option

Other factors, such as gamma (the rate of the rate of change of the price), figure in, but they can't be evaluated without evaluating the basics.

The longer the time to expiration, the more important the time value is to the option price. For an option with a short expiration, the price of the underlying asset is the most important factor.

This is an important point to remember when doing fundamental analysis. Your visibility is limited. That's why there are options in the first place! You can ensure against a different outcome, or you can speculate on it. The key issue over the long run is the amount of volatility. If you understand the issues that make prices change, rather than drive the direction of the change, you'll be ahead of the game.

Although volatility is the often-overlooked component of valuation, the intrinsic value of the option can't be ignored. This is especially true if you're writing short puts settled with the underlying asset and could end up owning it upon assignment.

Naked-short puts on single stocks are risky for this very reason. Likewise, naked-short calls are risky because the underlying asset could have an infinite increase in price—at least in theory—and the writer will have to buy it at the high price if the option is assigned.

If you don't pay attention to the stocks in question, you might end up with a stock you don't want, which continues to fall in price. If you limit your writing to stocks you might want to own, you will be less likely to be suckered. In fact, if you structure your trades so you must buy only the things you are willing to buy, and sell only the things you are willing to sell, you will avoid many of the heartaches of option trading. (Of course, you might avoid some profits, too. It's all a balance between risk and return.)

In theory, markets are perfectly efficient, so fundamental analysis is wasted. In practice, fundamental analysis is a great way to understand your risks and make the markets more efficient. If you don't understand why the market value is what it is, all the efficiency in the world won't protect you from doing something stupid.

> **MARKET MAXIM**
>
> The stock doesn't know you own it. Sometimes, we can get so caught up in a position we forget the stock owes us nothing. Options, futures, stocks, and bonds are things with no emotion and no loyalty.

Putting It All Together

Here's a summary of the role of fundamental analysis in options trading:

- The value of an option can be broken down into intrinsic value plus extrinsic value, also known as time value.

- Intrinsic value is the value of the option relative to the value of the underlying asset when the option is in-the-money.

- An out-of-the-money option has no intrinsic value.

- Time value is a function of both the volatility of the underlying and the amount time until the option expires.

- Fundamental analysis can be used to get more insight on both intrinsic value (for example, by helping the trader understand the potential for price appreciation for the underlying asset) and volatility.

- Time value is the amount of remaining valuation. Is it reasonable?

The following table shows how fundamental factors can help in understanding the Greeks.

Fundamental Analysis and Option Pricing

Factor	Greek	Fundamental Analysis
Price of the underlying		Sources of supply
		Sources of demand
		Prospects for future growth
Volatility	Vega	Factors causing price changes
		Level of expectations
Time to expiration	Theta	Check the calendar!

The Least You Need to Know

- Fundamental analysis is way to understand the value of the underlying asset.
- The analysis process begins with a look at the global economy and how it affects the market for the underlying asset.
- Fundamental analysis includes a look at the factors that are specific to the underlying asset.
- Volatility is one of the fundamental factors in valuing options, but it is often overlooked.

CHAPTER 16

Research Services

There are a lot of people looking to sell services to traders. After you do even the simplest web research on the topic, you will find that ads for different trading systems and services follow you wherever you go online. On any given day, my email has pitches from six different companies offering to give me the secrets to success in the options markets. All I need to do is buy their newsletter with spread trade ideas, or take their online class in the Elliott Wave, or attend their conference on options research, and I'm set.

Some of these offers are worthwhile, but which ones? After all, anyone with a surefire system is too busy sitting on his private beach in Maui and applying sunscreen to have the time to teach you.

The basics of technical and fundamental analysis can be mastered with a little time and practice. Some people want or need more than the basics, though. They need data and research they can't find on their quote screens or in the financial press. They learn better in a classroom than from reading a book. For those who want more, there's plenty out there.

In This Chapter

- Figuring out what you need
- Evaluating the services you see
- Paying without overpaying
- Warnings and scammers

This chapter will help you sort through the different sales pitches so you can find what works for you to trade with more success. This chapter is more of a consumer guide and less of a how-to about research. For that, go back to Chapters 14 and 15.

Determining Your Needs

Before you plunk down your money and commit your time to a paid options service, take some time to figure out what you actually need. This little bit of analysis is critical because many of the service offerings out there are legitimate, but they might not be of use to you.

After you have been trading for a little bit, take a look at your trade diary and your performance numbers to see where you stand. What do you do well, and what could you do better? What do you enjoy, and what causes you pain? And how do you learn best?

When you have a few notes in your trade diary, you'll be in a better position to make a smart purchase.

> **TRADING TIP**
>
> A good starting point, after reading this book, is the Options Industry Council, optionseducation.org. It is a free service sponsored by the options exchanges, and it has a lot of information about different ways to use options in different markets and in different types of accounts.

Your Trading Style

Start by figuring out what kind of trader you are. Are you primarily a hedger or a speculator? Do you use options as a supplement to other trading and investing activities, or is it the primary activity? A long-term equity investor using covered calls for income and puts as stop orders might not need much additional research beyond what she is already doing on the stock market. An active trader with 10 open positions at once, none of which will be in place for more than a week, will have very different needs.

If you're interested in an esoteric approach to technical analysis, such as the Elliott Wave or Gann systems, you'll almost definitely need some assistance. If you are already a proficient investor who is looking to add options to your portfolio, you might not need more than this book.

What Drives Your Market

Are you working with options that are driven by fundamentals? Are they more popular with hedge funds or with retail investors? Are they driven by economy-wide factors or the specifics of their own industry? Do professional traders have access to different data sources than your brokerage firm offers?

Once you find the gap, you can go about trying to fill it.

How You Learn

We are all different people, and that makes the world so very fun and interesting. That goes all the way to how we learn new things. Some people learn best from a book. Others like the discipline of a classroom. And at least a few of us only learn the hard way, through experience.

Think a little bit about how you have learned best in the past. If you are easily distracted on conference calls, then a webinar program is probably not for you. If reading a book puts you to sleep, then look for podcasts and seminars.

This seems obvious, and yet, like so much obvious stuff, we often overlook it.

 **TRADING TIP**

Some people only learn the hard way. They have to make plenty of mistakes on their own before they can even think of taking advice from someone else. Mistakes can be costly, but the cost of silly losses and missed opportunities might be less for some traders than a seminar would be. The key is to keep a trading diary and to review it.

Research Relative to Performance

Performance calculation is covered up ahead in Chapter 19. If you have been trading for a while, you should look at your results to see how you are doing and identify areas of weakness. Then, you can figure out what to do next.

If you don't have much trading history, look at your backtesting and paper trading results to see if there's something that would improve your trading or help you feel more confident. (Skip ahead to Chapter 19 to find out how to do this.)

Types of Research Services

Now that you have a sense of what you need and what will work best with your personality, it's time to think about the different services out there. They fall into four categories:

- Data services

- Research and analytics

- Trade ideas

- Training

Within these categories are a lot of ways of delivering the information: email newsletters, websites, books, seminars, coaching, and podcasts, to name a very few.

By the way, I don't receive any money from any company on the list, nor can I vouch for the services. It is also not exhaustive; there are a ton of great companies—and a ton of bad ones—out there. I have met people at some of the firms listed in this section, but not all. Furthermore, given the number of mergers and acquisitions taking place in the financial industry, who knows if the same people will be at these companies when you're looking. This is all to say: do your research and make your own decisions, using this as a starting point only.

In addition to this list, check out the resources section of the book (Appendix B) for a list of books, publications, and other media that might help your trading.

Data

Data is incredibly valuable to traders. They pay very good money for near-instantaneous feeds of information about prices, orders, technical indicators, and news. Sure, some of this is available for free, but it's not as good as the paid services. (Note that Michael Bloomberg, who designed the leading data terminal used by professional traders, is a billionaire. If information that was just as good was available for free, he would not be so rich.)

There's an excellent chance all of the data you need are available from your broker. Almost all of them offer real-time data on prices, volumes, and implied volatility on single-stock options listed on all the domestic exchanges.

In some cases, you might have to pay extra for data on options on futures, metals, agricultural contracts, or currencies. In most cases, they will integrate with your current trading platform. The definitive list of data services can be found on the OPRA website, opradata.com. OPRA is the Options Price Reporting Authority, and it is a consortium of all of the U.S. options exchanges.

OPRA excludes some of the options traded on the futures exchanges and those traded in international markets. The source for agricultural products is The Progressive Farmer, dtnprogressivefarmer.com. For international data, check out CQG, cqg.com.

> **TRADING TIP**
>
> A good first place to look for data, research, trade ideas, and training is your brokerage firm. Most brokerage firms can help you with most options trades, and they might have services you don't know about—so ask. If you are shopping for a new brokerage, ask about the services offered—this is a key way for firms to differentiate themselves. If you are a hard-core options trader, you might want to use a specialty broker, often operated by the same company. Charles Schwab, for example, has an options trading subsidiary called OptionsXpress, and TD Ameritrade has an active trader service called thinkorswim. The minimums, commissions, and fees might differ, but they should not be your only consideration.

Research and Analytics

Sometimes, you want information that goes far beyond basic price data. You want real research: modeling of different strategies, estimates of future volatility, a detailed analysis of Federal Reserve Bank Policies. You want to learn from someone who has analyzed the underlying and the volatility rather than do it all yourself.

Well, then, you need research and analytics. The difference is that research usually comes in narrative form, while analytics are tools allowing you to spot trends or develop strategies. Once again, the first place to go is your brokerage firm. Many of them offer research, calculators, and other analytic tools that can you use to evaluate trading strategies.

Beyond that, here are a few of the services to check out:

- eSignal, esignal.com
- MarketDelta, marektdelta.com
- MetaStock, metastock.com
- OptionsHawk.com, optionshawk.com
- OptionsPlay.com, optionsplay.com
- OmniTrader, omnitrader.com
- OptionMetrics, optionmetrics.com
- Options Research and Technology Services, orats.com

- RealTick, realtick.com

- REDI, redi.com

- Schaeffer's, schaeffersresearch.com

Trade Ideas

Many research services specialize in offering trade ideas. They do the research and make recommendations you can follow, or not, as the interest strikes you. Some of these have more general market insights and others have more specific trades. In general, the more specific the advice, the more expensive the service. That being said, a more expensive service is not necessarily the best for you.

- Benzinga, benzinga.com

- The Elliott Wave, elliottwave.com

- The Options Insider, theoptionsinsider.com

- Options Monster, optionsmonster.com

- Recognia, recognia.com

- StockTwits, stocktwits.com

- Tradespoon, tradespoon.com

- TradeXchange, thetradeexchange.com

Training

There are a lot of people out there offering educational services for options traders. Some of them are really good. Others? It's questionable. Most of them offer a combination of really basic options information, starting with puts and calls, then get into different strategies you can use. Many of them offer mentoring, in which you will trade alongside one of their traders (usually by phone or webinar connection). Here's a list to start your research.

- The CBOE Options Institute, cboe.com/learncenter/optionsinstitute1.aspx

- Online Trader Central, onlinetradercentral.com

- Online Trading Academy, tradingacademy.com

- Options Trading IQ, optionstradingiq.com

- SMB Options Training, smbtraining.com

- TopStep Trader, topsteptrader.com

- Trading Advantage, tradingadvantage.com

- School of Gann, schoolofgann.com

> **MARKET MAXIM**
>
> Experienced traders control risk. Inexperienced traders chase gains. Speculators take risk in order to generate return. Hedgers are looking to manage risk—but even speculators have to pay attention to ensure they aren't taking risks for which there are negative returns.

Evaluating the Services

As I mentioned before in this chapter, you really have to do your research with all of these different vendors clamoring for your business. Many businesses are perfectly fine but not right for your trading; if your interest is currency and interest rates, it doesn't make sense to sub-scribe to a service covering equity options. If you're mostly writing covered calls for income, you might not need anything special—although there are research services that specialize in ways to improve a buy-write strategy.

Beyond that, you need to find out if a given service will deliver on its promises. Here are a few ideas to help you check up on the businesses that want your hard-earned cash.

Running Some Background Checks

Because the financial industry is highly regulated, you can check on the history of companies and key employees. And you should!

If you do an Internet search, check for comments on message boards and make sure you look beyond the first few pages of results. Be especially wary if the first page or two offer a perfect and shiny picture. Companies don't like bad news on the first page, and they will pay consultants a lot of money to help them with their search-engine optimization to hide bad news. The first result is rarely the helpful one.

Then, turn to the many different regulatory agencies to see if you can find more:

The Commodity Futures Trading Commission, cftc.gov/ConsumerProtection/index.htm, is the primary regulatory organization for the futures markets, so it oversees many businesses covering nonequity options. One of its nifty features is a list of known scams, so you can protect yourself in advance.

FINRA (Financial Industry Regulatory Authority) Broker Check, brokercheck.finra.org, handles registration for people and companies in the equity and equity-options business.

National Futures Association BASIC search, nfa.futures.org/basicnet, handles registration for brokers who deal with futures, also known as Futures Commission Merchants. This can help you research firms dealing with commodity and energy options.

The Securities and Exchange Commission, investor.gov, maintains information on different scams and has a database you can use to research brokers and advisers.

Now, there are a lot of reasons why someone might not show up in these databases. Some types of firms and personnel don't have to register. Still, every now and again, you'll run a search and not only find the person, but also find out some interesting things in his or her past that might affect your decision. For example, maybe the person is barred from the industry for fraud or for stealing money from customer accounts. It happens enough that I strongly recommend you do this.

Are They Running a Service or a Sales Pitch?

A lot of research and trading services are really sales pitches. You sign up for the free or low-priced seminar, then discover there's an additional program costing even more. And at the end of that program, you find out that there's even more information that will help your trading for yet another fee.

Be especially suspicious of anyone offering a free or very-low-priced seminar. (Some exceptions would be free sessions offered by any of the industry organizations, such as the CBOE Options Institute or the Options Industry Council, or a seminar offered by the brokerage firm that you work with already.) These often get you excited, then follow with a pitch for another seminar or a special online training course costing even more money—which, more often than not, will be a pitch for a yet more expensive course.

Ask a few questions before paying any money, such as:

- Do you offer a free trial?

- How much training and support do you offer?

- How long does it take to learn your system?

- What support do you offer?

- If you offer mentoring, who will provide it and how will it be handled?

- How long have you been in business?

- What is the difference between the basic service and any more advanced offerings? How many people subscribe to only the basic service?

- Do you screen people for your trading program?

- Why do people leave your program?

- How are your performance numbers calculated?

- Can I talk to other customers?

> **TRADING TIP**
>
> In many cases, you don't need better research to say in the trading game; you need better money management. Turn to Chapter 17 for ideas.

Using Your Broker

I've mentioned using your broker a few times here, for very good reason. There's a dirty secret in the brokerage business: customer churn is a big problem. That's the rate at which customers close their accounts and have to be replaced with new customers. The most common reason customers close their accounts is they are not successful and decide to do something other than trading options.

One way brokers try to limit churn is to offer customers research and education programs to increase the likelihood of success. If you're having trouble, ask your broker's customer service rep what the firm might offer or what they might recommend. Even if you are not having trouble, ask. You might be surprised at what they offer.

Buyer Beware

The really sad truth is there are some bad actors in the financial industry. You don't have to cover the financial industry long to run into an almost comical array of Ponzi schemes, theft, securities fraud, and bad behavior. Some of these stories make global headlines; others never go much beyond local news stories. I find these stories amusing, but the victims find them painful and ugly.

If it sounds too good to be true, it probably is. There's no magic to trading. Success comes from an understanding of how the markets work, hard work, and a little bit of luck.

There are a lot of great people and great companies out there, but be careful.

The Least You Need to Know

- Some research and trading services can improve your trading.
- You have to know what you don't know to make a research service worthwhile.
- The options exchange has good, free education programs to get you started. Many brokerage firms provide research.
- Caveat emptor, as there are more than a few overpriced, worthless, or outright fraudulent trading services out there.

PART 4

The Business of Trading

Trading for your own account is a business like any other. If you are reading this book as part of your job, this part won't matter much to you. If you are reading it because you want to trade on your own, it might be more important than everything else. Inexperienced traders are often their own worst enemies, and paying attention to the business aspects is the key to sticking around long enough to become an experienced trader.

Chapter 17 looks at trade planning and money management, two keys to success. Chapter 18 covers taxes, a common area of concern, while Chapter 19 discusses performance evaluation. Chapter 20 is all about the emotional pitfalls that take down many traders. Successful trading is as much a mental game as anything. Automation removes some of the human propensity to screw things up, but not all of it.

Armed with this information, you'll be in a better position to make effective trades—and to skip trading entirely if it's not right for you.

CHAPTER 17

Trade Planning

Trade planning is an important discipline for successful trading. After all, trading is as much a mental game as anything. Having a playbook makes it so much easier. Figuring out what to trade and then keeping records will help you trade better and improve over time.

It's not especially complicated, either. Most traders approach the market with an informal plan already. With just a little more work, you can set up a system to help plan and track trades. It really doesn't take a lot of effort to use it, either. Some traders keep spreadsheets; some have notebooks. There's no programming involved!

All you do is plan the trade, trade the plan, and evaluate what happened.

Pick Your Markets

The options industry covers a huge range of underlying assets. You can trade currencies, commodities, stocks, bonds, even market volatility. New types of contracts are invented all the time, with different features. The amount of creativity in the industry is just amazing.

But you can't reasonably trade everything. The more you understand the fundamentals and dynamics in any one market, the more likely you are to have trading success. You'll have better insight on market activity and be better able to place your trades appropriately.

If you have some knowledge of a particular market, start there. If you don't, think about what interests you. Are you fascinated by exchange rates? A stock market junkie? Are you interested in specific companies or the overall economy? Are you stronger at calculus or at accounting? The more something interests you, the more likely you are to want to learn more about it. The research will be more interesting and more useful. That's really important.

> **MARKET MAXIM**
>
> As you go along in your trading, you can add to your markets or change them entirely. Nothing is set in stone here. Find a starting point, plan some trades, and evaluate those trades. Then, figure out what to do next. Maybe you want to stay with a given underlying or strategy and learn more about it, or maybe you want to try something else. One of the reasons for thoughtful trade planning is to evaluate what needs to be changed to improve your trading. That includes the types of options you are working, the types of strategies you use, and the amount of money you commit to each trade.

Pick Your Timeframe

Some of those who trade options are *day traders*. That is, they close out every one of their positions every night. They tend to make a large number of small trades, making performance on high volume of small returns rather than significant changes in any one position.

Swing traders tend to hold on to positions at least overnight and often for several days. Most options traders fall into this category.

Investors are those who hold positions for a very long time. Some investors use options as part of a risk-management or income strategy, but this is not their primary focus when they manage their portfolios.

A key step in planning your trading is to figure out what type of options trader you will be most of the time. If you are going to be a day trader, then you need to arrange your energies and planning around specific days and times. If you are a swing trader, you'll need to figure out how you are going to monitor your positions. If you are an investor who does some option trading, then you have to determine when you will consider options and when you will not.

Set Your Goals

You have to know where you are going in order to see if you are actually getting there! Trading goals are important.

Sure, your goal is to make as much money as possible. But there's more to an effective trading goal than making as much money as you can. Here's a look at some of the considerations:

Are You Beginning or Advanced?

If options trading is your first foray into the financial markets, you should have simpler goals than if you have a lot of market experience but are relatively new to derivatives. The less experience you have, the simpler your goals and trading strategies should be.

The mechanics of researching a trade, placing the order, and then closing it out are complicated enough to trip up any trader. The less experience you have in the market, the more you need to pay attention to the niceties of procedure. Yes, it might be slower and less exciting than you had hoped, but you have to start somewhere.

As you build experience, your trade plans can become more complex.

Are You Speculating or Hedging?

Hedgers and speculators take very different approaches to the market. A speculator's goal is set in terms of profits, while a hedger is looking to minimize losses. Understanding why you are trading will help you set better goals and write stronger trading plans.

Return Targets

A key goal is your expected return. Start by looking at your backtesting information. (Backtesting is covered in Chapter 19.) Are you swinging for the fences or looking for singles? Are you speculating in the hope of making large gains or generating steady income? Or hedging in order to minimize the losses on your account?

Understanding the return potential of your strategy will help you better manage your money.

> **MARKET MAXIM**
>
> There is a tradeoff between risk and return. When you take more risk, you should expect to receive more return. Likewise, when you expect to receive more return, you will have to take on more risk.

The Probability of Ruin

Expected return tells you how much money you can expect to make from your trading. The *probability of ruin* tells you how much money you can lose. That's really important if you want to stay in the game and manage the amount of risk you take. If you're hedging, it's critical to managing your risk.

Here's the equation:

$$R = \left[\frac{(1-A)}{(1+A)} \right]^c$$

R is the probability of ruin. The lower the number, the less risk in your trading strategy.

A is the advantage you have on each trade. This is the difference between the percentage of winning trades you have out of the total number of trades you make. If your trades win 55 percent of the time and lose 45 percent of the time, then your advantage is $55 - 45 = 10$.

C is the number of trades you make.

Let's say you have an advantage of 10 percent and you have five open positions in your account. In that case, your probability of ruin is this:

$$.367 = \left[\frac{(1-.10)}{(1+.10)} \right]^5$$

In other words, if all of your trades can go to zero, you have a 36.7 percent change of losing all your money. To reduce that risk, improve your advantage or make more trades.

An options position can expire worthless. Options are a zero-sum transaction, after all. For every winner, there is a loser. This makes options trading riskier than stock trading, because common stocks rarely lose all of their value.

If your probability of ruin is high and you tend to trade naked options, you need to pay particular attention to risk management.

Risk Limits

If you can lose all of your money on a trade, then it is a very bad idea to put all of it on one trade—no matter how good it seems at the time. The markets do many strange things. That's one reason they are so darn fascinating. There is no such thing as a sure thing.

Let me repeat: there is no such thing as a sure thing.

There are a lot of trades that are really good, though—where the odds are in your favor. If you're more likely than not to make a profit, then you want to take a particular trade. These trades might not be sure things, but they are close. And close makes all the difference to staying in the game for the long term.

> **MARKET MAXIM**
>
> There are old traders, there are bold traders, but there are no old, bold traders. Risk management is the key to trading. It is a combination of protecting your capital and learning discipline that will keep you in the game when the markets are going insane. You might be bold on occasion, but doing it all the time is a recipe for disaster.

The key is the ability to stay in the market. You have to keep some powder dry. If you bet 100 percent on a sure thing that turns out not to be, then you have 0 money to put in the next trade that looks good. By limiting how much money goes into each trade, you will be able to make the next good trade that comes along.

Time and Attention

We all have only so much time and so much energy, which limits the number of trades and amount of trading you can do. It's not a glamorous consideration, but an important one.

Cash Management

The amount of cash you have on hand is a key consideration in your trading strategy. It determines how much open interest you can have at any one time, as well as how large those positions can be. Traders have many different systems for managing their money. Some are ad hoc or intuitive, but there are several with solid statistical research behind them. Some have been used by gamblers for centuries, and others are proprietary, developed by trading firms for internal use.

All cash management systems have the same purpose—to make it highly unlikely that you will ever run out of money to trade. This way, you will always have some money on hand to take advantage of the next great opportunity that comes your way. You have some cash available after a losing trade so you can make another trade to help recover the losses.

Of course, at some point, the account balance might become so small it is not practical to make a trade. If that happens to you, it is your sign to get out of options trading and try something else.

You won't need to pull out your calculator every time you want to figure out your cash management. Some are so simple you can determine the amount to trade in your head. Most trading platforms include money management calculators that do the work for you—and they usually give you a choice from the styles listed below.

Fixed Fractional

The *fixed fractional* method is designed to limit each trade to a predetermined proportion of your total account value. The fractions are almost always between 2 percent and 10 percent of the total account value, with traders using a smaller fraction for riskier trades and a larger fraction for less risky trades. You might make that determination based on something intuitive or by tracking your own trading to see how risky and aggressive your style is.

Once you have that number, which we'll call f, you use it in the following equation to find the number of contracts, N, to trade:

$$N = f\left(\frac{equity\ in\ the\ account}{|trade\ risk|}\right)$$

Trade risk is the amount of money you could lose on your trade. (You can limit it with stop-loss orders—and you probably should.) It should be treated as a positive number, hence the brackets for absolute value. Remember options trading is a zero-sum game—for every winner, there is a loser—and that most contracts expire worthless.

The number will almost definitely be a fraction, so you'll have to round up or round down to determine your trade size.

Fixed Ratio

The *fixed ratio* money management system is popular among options and futures traders. It was developed by Ryan Jones, a trader and author who specializes in the options market. Under this system, you find the number of contracts N you should trade using this equation:

$$N = .5\left(\sqrt{1 + 8\left(\frac{P}{\Delta}\right)} + 1\right)$$

P is the accumulated profit to date, and Δ, delta, is the dollar amount of the minimum trade, usually 100 contracts. (It is not the same as the delta of the option.)

Using this equation, your first trade, with no accumulated profits, would be 1.5 contracts. This system focuses on profits rather than account value, which helps protect your initial capital so you can always stay in the game. As with the fixed fractional system, you will often need to round up or round down.

> **MARKET MAXIM**
>
> Neither the fixed fraction nor the fixed ratio systems are as fixed as they seem. The position sizes generated by the system will change a lot, but no matter the size, they meet the goal of helping you maximize profits while also staying in the trading game.

Gann

The Gann system was developed by William Gann, who developed an esoteric system for trading stocks. The money management system that goes along with it is a piece of cake: divide your money into 10 equal parts, and allocated one part per trade. That's all there is to it.

The Gann money management system is an easy-to-use system for managing risk. There might be systems with more statistical rationale, but it works well enough that many traders use it.

Kelly Criterion

Unlike Gann, the *Kelly Criterion* has solid statistical research behind it. It was a side effect of work done at Bell Laboratories in the 1950s to manage signal-to-noise issues in long distance telephone communications. The researchers noticed their findings could be applied to gambling, and they went to Las Vegas to test it.

In gambling, the odds are against you. The casino is most likely to win, not you. In options trading, the odds are even: for every winner, there is a loser, and the likelihood of being one or the other is randomly distributed. If you have a system that gives you an advantage, so much the better for your trading. All of this means a system that works well for gambling is likely to be even better for options trading.

You need three numbers in order to find the Kelly Criterion:

- The percentage of your trades that are expected to win, known as W
- The average return from a winning trade and loss from a losing trade
- The ratio of the gain from a winning trade to the loss of a losing trade, known as R.

Put these into an equation, like so:

$$Kelly\% = W - \frac{1-W}{R}$$

Then, use the *Kelly %* to determine what percentage of your account you should allocate to any one trade. The Kelly Criterion equation is often known as "edge minus odds" in trading shorthand.

The Kelly Criterion leads to open interest that is concentrated in a few contracts. This maximizes profits but also causes trading accounts to wither quickly when trades go bad. Many traders use half the Kelly percentage in order to prevent rapid reduction in the account.

Martingale

Martingale is another money management system developed for gambling. It was designed for games with even odds, such as a fair roulette wheel. And guess what? Options trading done randomly—with no underlying research system—also has even odds.

Start with a set amount per trade. It should not be all of your capital, and maybe you'll want to use one of the money management systems to determine the size of that initial trade. If the trade succeeds, start over with a new trade of the same size. If it fails, place double the amount on the next trade. If it wins, start over; if it loses, double the amount again for the next trade.

In gambling, this is known as doubling down—the trade that wins will recover your losses on the earlier trades. If you have an infinite amount of money, it will always work. The problem is no one has an infinite amount of money. This is a significant flaw in the martingale system. If you choose to use it, start with a low percentage of capital for your initial trade.

> **DID YOU KNOW?**
>
> In statistics, a martingale is any fair game in which knowledge of the past has no effect on future winnings. It is a random process in which the next value could be any value in the random series.

Value at Risk

Value at risk is a measure of how much money you can lose at a given level of confidence, and it can be used to determine trade size. In fact, this is the risk-management system used by most institutional traders. The program might look at historic returns, variance and covariance, or use a Monte Carlo simulation to calculate risk.

Cost of Carry

The *cost of carry* of an option trade is the amount of money it costs to finance it. Options trades are inherently leveraged. When you write options, you can earn interest on the premium received—how much depends on the terms of your account and the current market rate of interest, of course. When you buy options, you give up interest on the premium paid, at the margin rate charged by your broker.

Cost of carry is higher when the market rate of interest is higher. When that happens, you give up more interest to place a trade and earn more interest on the premium in your account. This changes the return on your position, which is one reason why interest rates are included in the Black-Scholes formula and other options valuation systems.

Plan Your Trade ...

With all this information, it's time to sit down and plan your trade. At first, it will seem almost like an artificial process, but after a while, it will be almost second nature. You won't be able to place a trade without some sort of plan.

You should write down your trade plan, whether in a computer spreadsheet or a bound notebook. It does not have to be fancy, but it has to be done.

By the way, a lot of traders write down their trade ideas and hunches, even if they do not commit money to them. That way, they can go back to see if their ideas were good and whether they should trade them in the future.

How Much Money?

Start by noting the size of the position. What will you be buying or selling? How much margin do you need to commit? (Margin, of course, is the amount of money you are borrowing in your account to establish and maintain your position.) Then, using your money management system, determine how large this trade will be.

Why Trade?

This is the second part of the trade plan. What are you expecting to happen? Why have you placed this trade? What are you looking for in the market to either confirm your trade or tell you it is time to get out?

Setting down the reason for the trade is the most important part of the trade plan. Knowing why you are trading will help you fight off the emotional complications that can interfere with successful trading. It will help you recognize when things are going right—and when they are going wrong—so you can better manage the trade from start to finish.

For How Long?

Are you holding your trade for a day, a week, or until expiration? Will you roll it over at expiration or move on to something else?

Some options traders are day traders. Some are placing long-term hedges. And some do both. Set the target timeframe for your position up front.

> **MARKET MAXIM**
>
> If you don't know where you're going, you won't know when you get there. A trading plan will help you know what you're doing and when so you don't inadvertently take on too much risk or blow through a working position.

... and Trade Your Plan

The trade plan is an active document! You don't write it for the heck of it, but rather to guide your trading. Put it to work.

Order Execution

Your trade plan includes an entry point and an exit point. Paying attention to the market and using limit orders might improve the cost of your position.

A limit order tells the broker to buy or sell a security at a specific price or better. This would be a lower price on a buy order or a higher price on a sell order.

Let's say you are looking to write a call option but want to receive at least $4 for it. You would enter an order to "sell limit 4" using the order entry form on your broker's screen. This is a common type of order. You'll probably see a field reading "order type"; that's where you enter "limit."

"Sell limit 4" means the broker will write your calls as soon as the option price hits $4. Your order will be filled as long as the price is $4 or higher. If the price falls to $3.99, the broker will stop selling calls for you.

If you have a long call position with a price target of $4, you could enter the sell limit $4 order even if the current price were only $2. The order would stay in the broker's system, and then be executed automatically as soon as the $4 limit is hit.

Sticking to Your Limits

If you have set a target for your trade, and the trade hits it, get out. This is especially true on the down side. If a trade is moving against you, you need to get out. The miracle is not going to happen.

Many traders use stop orders to ensure they do not linger too long in a position that is moving away from them.

A *stop order*, also known as a *stop-loss order*, tells the broker to buy or sell as soon as a price is reached in the market. Traders often use these to close out a position automatically when it moves against them. For example, maybe you have a short position on 45 July puts with a premium of $2.35, which was a deep out-of-the money position when you wrote it. You want to limit your risk, so you also enter a stop order to close out the position if the premium were to rise to $5. You tell the broker to buy 45 July puts with a stop of $5: "buy stop 5." You enter that order, and it stays in the system until you cancel it or until the price hits $5.

> **DEFINITION**
>
> A **stop order,** or **stop-loss order,** is an order that tells the broker to stop buying or selling an asset as soon as a specific price level is hit.

The difference between a stop order and a limit order is the stop order will be executed as soon as the price hits $5.00 or more, even if it keeps rising. The limit order will be executed as long as the price is $5.00 or less. Stop orders generally provide more protection for risk management of a current position, while limit orders are good for enforcing entry and exit points when establishing new positions.

There's another type of order, known as a *stop-limit order*, that combines features of the two order types. It tells the broker to execute the order at a specific price or better, but only after it reaches a specific price—but you don't want to chase it. So you could enter "buy 6 limit 7," which would have you buy the option as soon as it hits $6, and you'd keep buying until it hit $7. You'd buy at $5, which would be cheap, but not at $7.50, which might be too expensive.

Stop, limit, and stop-limit orders can help you manage risk and force buy and sell points to improve your trading. They work even if you are away from your trading desk—and even if your emotions are creating the temptation to violate your trade parameters.

Keep a Trade Diary

A trade diary might be part of the trading plan, or it might be kept separately. It is simply a record of the trades placed along with a note about what worked and what did not.

This information is crucial to your long-term trading success.

- Keeping a record holds you accountable, which will help you manage the emotions of trading

- Reviewing your trading diary will help you improve your trading over time by revealing areas of weakness

- The information about risk and reward is a key part of many cash management systems

Managing Your Profits

Part of your overall trading plan includes figuring out what to do with the profits you make from trading. Will you trade it the same way, trade it more aggressively, or pull it out to put into a long-term investment?

Most traders do a combination, but understanding how it works can help you with your trade planning.

Compounding Returns with the Same Strategy

If you keep your profits in your trading account, and use them to trade the same way, you'll keep earning a return on your return. That's great. Compound interest is one of the most powerful forces in finance. It lets your money grow without changing the risk profile of the account.

This is an especially important practice if you are starting with a small account and hope to build it up over time.

Pyramiding

Not to be confused with *pyramid scheme*, which is a type of fraud, *pyramiding* is the process of taking your profits and placing them in riskier trades than are used in the core of the account. You trade the principal value of the account in the usual manner, and then commit the profits to trades with greater potential return—and greater risk.

If the market is moving in the direction of your trades, this will increase the total account value rapidly. If the trades turn against you, then you're left with the core account value.

Traders who favor pyramiding have enough money in their core account to execute their desired trades. They are able to risk their profits but stay in the market with the core of the account. Hence, this is a more advanced strategy.

For stock traders, pyramiding involves leverage. Options trades are inherently leveraged, so there is no change in the order structure to use pyramiding.

Taking Money Off the Table

As trading profits build, it's an excellent idea to move some money into a less risky investment. This doesn't necessarily help your trading, but it does help the rest of your life.

And that's good, because it will help you manage the emotion of your trades.

If you speculate in options, then the options account is probably the riskiest part of your portfolio. You can reduce your portfolio risk by diversifying into other assets. As your profits build, pull some money out and place it into government bonds, real estate, or even bank CDs. Sure, the returns will be much lower, but the risk will be much lower, too.

> **MARKET MAXIM**
>
> Money management is one form of portfolio diversification. Each system forces you to have more a combination of positions and cash as a way to reduce your overall risk. Taking money out of your trading account is another way to diversify your overall portfolio.

The Least You Need to Know

- Plan your trade and trade your plan.
- Determine what options you want to trade and how you want to trade them.
- Have a money management system, and use it.
- Keep track of your trades in a trading diary.

CHAPTER 18

Taxes

Taxes are charges imposed by the government to raise money to pay for such things as roads and defense. People can (and do) debate all night and all day about the levels of taxation and the appropriateness of some types of government spending, but you know what? The debate only matters on Election Day.

The rest of the time, you're stuck with the laws as they are in place right now. As with so many other things, trading is a taxable activity. How it is taxed depends on what sort of trade you make, how much time it covers, and your status with the IRS. An individual is treated differently from someone who qualifies as a pattern day trader or who is hedging as part of a trade or business.

A bit of a warning: I'm not a tax expert. I've done a lot of reading and talked to a lot of people, but I can't promise this is accurate. Tax laws are complicated, and they change all the time. Treat this chapter as a general guide to use when talking about your situation with a tax professional.

A second warning: sometimes, traders find themselves in situations in which losses are disallowed so they end up owing more in taxes than they earned in cash. This is not good.

In This Chapter

- The form of your profits and taxation
- Keeping track of deductions
- Paying what you owe
- Tax advisers for traders

A third warning: tax laws change, so what's in this book might not be accurate when you sit down to do your taxes. I'm sure you're a nice person and all, but I'm not going to go with you to an audit or plead your case in tax court.

In fact, you will probably need a professional to help you with your taxes if you are trading options. Taxes are barely a do-it-yourself proposition for anyone these days, traders least of all.

Income and Capital Gains

Before you can determine your taxes, you need to determine the form of your gains and losses from trading. "Money" is not the right answer. The Internal Revenue Service puts money into detailed categories, which determine the amount of losses you are allowed to take against gains as well as the rate of taxes you pay.

Depending on your trading strategies, you might have a combination of the following:

Dividends   These are payments companies make to shareholders from profits. Option holders generally don't receive these, but stockholders might.

Interest   This is money earned from loaning out money to someone else. A bond is a loan to the issuer. A bank account is a loan to the bank. You probably won't have interest income from an option, but you might earn it from other investments or from the cash balance in your trading account.

Long-term capital gains   When you sell a financial instrument, the difference between the sales price and the price you paid to buy it is a capital gain (if positive) or a capital loss (if negative). Under current U.S. tax law, a capital gain or loss is usually considered to be long term if it is held for one year or more. The gain or loss is recognized only if the position is closed out; otherwise, any gains or losses exist only on paper.

Short-term capital gains   A short-term capital gain, or loss, is exactly like a long-term capital gain (or loss), with one difference. Under current U.S. tax law, it is a gain or a loss on a position held for less than one year.

Earned income   If you receive money for trading as your job, it is considered earned income. If you are trading for a prop trading firm (a company in the business of trading for its proprietary account), you might be receiving earned income. It will be reported to you at the end of the year on an IRS Form W4 (for employment income) or 1099 (for miscellaneous self-employment income).

Know what's what, or you'll pay too much. Holding on to a stock position an extra few days can lead to big savings at tax time. And who doesn't want that?

Your tax bracket is based on the amount of income you have and your marital status. It is applied to any additional income you make, not all of the income you earn. When planning, look at the highest rate for which you'll qualify. You can find it in the instructions to IRS Form 1040. The relatively different handling of long-term and short-term capital gains at different rates is shown in the following table.

U.S. Tax Rates for 2015

Bracket	Long-Term Capital Gain	Short-Term Capital Gain
10%	0%	10%
15%	0%	15%
25%	15%	25%
28%	15%	28%
33%	18.80%	33%
35%	18.80%	35%
39.60%	23.80%	39.60%

Proceeds and Basis

The difference between income and capital gains is the first big cut in understanding taxes. The next two you need to know are *proceeds* and *basis:*

- Proceeds are the funds received from the sale of a financial asset.

- Basis is the price paid to establish a position.

In most cases, commissions and premiums paid are used to increase the basis rather than reduce the proceeds.

Consider these examples:

- You bought 100 shares of ABC at $10 and sold 8 months later at $20, but you paid a commission of $20 to buy and $20 to sell.

    Long-term gain = (100 × $20) − (100 × $10) − $40 commission fees = $960

- You bought 500 shares of e-Gizmo at $9 and sold at $6 3 weeks later when it tanked. You paid the same commission of $20 per trade.

    Short-term loss = (500 × $6) − (500 × $9) − $40 commission fees = −$1,460

How Options Affect the Tax Basics

The basic rules about income and capital gains apply to options, but with several significant exceptions. Some of these apply to how options are treated, and others involve options as they affect other positions in your portfolio. Finally, some of the rules could stand a little more explanation than is given in the preceding section. Are you ready for some fun? Let's get started.

> **WARNING**
>
> The Alternative Minimum Tax (AMT) was established in 1969 to ensure wealthy people could not use deductions to get out of paying taxes. For the 2014 tax year, the AMT calculation applied to adjusted gross income of $305,050 for married couples filing jointly. At that point, you have to do the AMT calculation and pay either your regular tax or the AMT, whichever is higher. If you are subject to the AMT, many deductions will be disallowed, including investment expenses and capital losses. If you're close, be careful with your trading income. If you're reading this book because you have employee stock options, pay special attention to AMT issues. Some types of these options will trigger the AMT, regardless of income.

The Tax Rates, Applied

This section has a long and detailed overview of how tax obligations are calculated and how tax rates apply to all the forms of money that comes in and goes out for an options trader. It will give you some guidance on how your trades might be affected.

Dividends

You might have dividends from stock positions in your account backing covered calls or that you received from put option assignment. Dividends are generally taxed at the same rate as long-term capital gains. To receive the lower dividend rate, you must hold the stock for 60 days of a 121-day period, beginning 60 days before the ex-dividend date of the payment (the ex-dividend date being the date the stock trades without the value of the dividend). Got that?

Here's the catch—any days the stock position is hedged don't count toward the 60-day required holding period.

Also, dividends are not treated as investment income when subtracting investment expenses.

Capital Gains

Remember, a capital gain is the profit made from buying low and selling high. If you buy high and sell low, then you have a capital loss. The gain or loss is only recognized when the position is closed out; until then, it exists only on paper and is not taxed.

If the gain (or loss) is on a position held for less than 12 months, it is considered short term. Otherwise, it is a long term gain (or loss).

Within each category, losses can be used to offset gains when calculating taxes, because you do not have to pay taxes on losses! First you take your long-term gains and subtract your long-term losses. Next, take your short-term gains and subtract your short-term losses. The numbers then go on your tax return.

And yes, there is a catch: you can only take a loss of $3,000 over and above any capital gains on any one year's taxes.

> **DID YOU KNOW?**
>
> The original policy idea behind separating capital gains into short term and long term was to encourage long-term investments in the economy and to discourage speculation on price changes. However, the time periods used to determine short term and long term have changed over time and might change again.

Capital Gains and Short Sales

A short sale isn't exactly comparable to a transaction triggering the capital gain and loss rules because you don't own the asset you sold. So what do you do?

The IRS generally holds that the gain recognized when a short sale is closed is a short-term capital gain, no matter how long the short position was opened. The exception is if the trader uses an underlying asset held elsewhere, and owned it for 12 months or more, to close the sale.

Here's an example:

You borrowed 500 shares of e-Idiot.com and sold them at $15 per share. Eighteen months later, your suspicions about the company's faulty accounting practices turned out to be true, and you sold the shares at $2 each. You paid a commission of $20 per trade and annual interest of 10 percent.

> Short-term gain = (500 × $15) − (500 × $2) − $40 commission fees − $1,125 interest on original loan value = $5,585 short-term gain

This can be reduced by short-term losses only.

Capital Gains and Puts

Because of the relationship between puts and shorting an asset, the IRS considers gains and losses on put trades to be short-term gains and losses, no matter how long they were in place.

The exception involves a married put position, which consists of having a long position on a put written on an underlying asset you already own. In this case, the profit and loss is based on the time period the underlying was owned.

Here are two examples:

You write puts on 100 shares of e-Idiot.com and receive a premium of $3.75 each. The expiration is 15 months away. The options expire worthless, so you are able to keep the premium. You paid a commission of $10 on the trade.

> Short-term gain = (100 × $3.75) − $20 commission fees = $375 short-term gain

Ten years ago, you bought 200 shares of BigPharmaCo for $5 each. The stock is now trading at $30. You buy put options on 200 shares at $0.46, a strike price of $29.50, and an expiration date a month away. At expiration, you exercise the option. You paid a $0.20 per share commission when you bought the stock and a $20 flat fee commission when you bought the puts.

> Long-term gain = (200 × $29.50) − (200 × $5) − (200 × 0.46) − (200 × $ 0.20) − $20 = $4,748

Wash Sale Rules

You might have come up with a brilliant idea while reading the above paragraphs: why not sell a stock that has declined in value, receives the tax benefit of the capital loss, and then buy the stock back so you can profit when it goes up in value? Then, you could have your cake and eat it, too! Right? Sort of. But here's the thing: you aren't the first person to think of this strategy. Hence, the IRS has what it calls the *wash sale* rule. It will disallow any losses taken if the trader repurchases "substantially identical" securities within 30 days of the loss.

You can still keep the original purchase price as your basis, and use the later sale price as your proceeds. The loss is used to reduce your basis.

The IRS has also ruled that selling an in-the-money put option is the same as buying a "substantially identical" security to the underlying asset. So if you sell your stock and replace it with an in-the-money put, your gain or loss cannot be recognized until the option is expired. You can spend the cash in the meantime, though.

Here's how it works: to raise cash, you sell 100 shares of IdiotBook at $36.50. Two months ago, you had purchased these shares at $15.25. You still like the stock, though, so you write in-the-money puts on 100 shares with a strike price of $37 and receive a premium of $1.35 each. The option is assigned, so you receive the shares and sell them a week later at $37.50. The initial profit is added to the proceeds of the transaction.

Short-term gain = (100 × $37) + (100 × $37.50) + (100 × 1.35) − (100 × $15.25) − (100 × $37) − $80 commissions = $2,330

On the gain side, of course, the effect is mostly cosmetic. With losses, you'll have to wait to recognize them until you are out of the game for at least 30 days.

You like day trading that oh-so-volatile IdiotBook stock. And you get stuck. You purchased 100 shares at $35 and then the company reports disastrous earnings per share. Plus, you have a $2,330 gain to offset, so you sell them at $25 per share. Still, you want to stay in the stock because you've heard they have some great new products coming out, so you write in-the-money puts on 100 shares with a strike price of $24 and receive a premium of $1.18 each. The option is assigned, so you receive the shares and sell them a week later at $26.

Short-term loss = (100 × $25) − (100 × $35) + (100 × 1.18) + (100 × $26) − (100 × $24) − $80 commissions = $762

The loss is reduced by the subsequent transaction. It can't offset the earlier gain unless it happens in the same calendar year.

DID YOU KNOW?

One way around the wash sale rule is to qualify as a *pattern day trader* with the IRS. This means you trade enough that it could be considered to be a business, even if you are the only employee and customer. The details are covered later in this chapter, and they are important if you plan on trading options or other securities a lot.

Capital Gains and Calls

To the IRS, being long a call is the same as being long the same amount of stock. If you hold the position for less than 12 months, it's considered to be a short-term position. Longer than that, it would be a long-term position.

You bought calls on 100 shares of iDiot at $3 each and sold 15 later at $3.56, but you paid a commission of $20 to buy and $20 to sell.

Long-term gain = (100 × $3.56) − (100 × $3) − $40 commission fees = $16

You bought calls on 100 shares of iDiot at $3.56 and held them to expiration, 3 months later. You paid a commission of $20 to buy them. There was no commission at expiration.

Short-term loss = (100 × $0) − (100 × $3.56) − $20 commission fees = −$336

Capital Gains and Options on Stock Market Indexes and on Nonequity Underlying Assets

The income tax rules for options on single-stock equities follow the rules for common stocks themselves. Options on other underlying assets, including on stock market indexes, are handled differently. For these, the trader has to mark to market at the end of the year (meaning, calculate the difference between the value of the contract at the beginning of the year and its value at the end of the year), then take 60 percent of the difference as a long-term capital gain or loss and the other 40 percent as a short-term capital gain or loss. The ending value then becomes the new starting value for the next year.

Premium Income and Capital Gains

Remember back at the beginning, when I noted that the IRS had distinct categories for different sorts of cash inflows? Well, many people write options, both puts and calls, for the income generated by the premiums. The IRS considers this to be a short-term capital gain, not investment income and not income earned from work. You don't have to recognize the capital gain from premium income until the position is closed out.

This is important to note because many people use covered calls as a way to generate income from stock issued by a company that does not pay a dividend. It's a popular technique, but it has tax consequences.

Interest Income

Any interest income earned from an option trade, such as interest income earned on cash received from premiums, is reported annually by the brokerage firm and taxed at ordinary income rates. (Okay, brokers pay little to no interest on cash balances these days, but that could change as interest rates increase.) This is one straightforward aspect of options and taxes.

The following table breaks down the tax effects of your option account.

Summary of Options Tax Rules

Transaction	Time Period	Rate
Dividends received	Any	Long-term cap gains
Asset sale	Less than 1 year	Ordinary income
	More than 1 year	Long-term cap gains
Short sale	Any	Ordinary income
Long equity put	Any	Ordinary income
Married put	Any	Rate on holding period of underlying

Transaction	Time Period	Rate
Wash sale	30 days	Based on total time in underlying
Long equity calls	Less than 1 year	Ordinary income
	More than 1 year	Long-term cap gains
Index options	Mark to market	60 percent long term, 40 percent short term
Premium income	Any	Ordinary income
Interest income	Any	Ordinary Income

Closing an Option Position

One of three things can happen to an option: it will be closed out with an offsetting transaction; be in-the-money and exercised; or allowed to expire worthless.

Each one of these transactions results in a different tax situation.

Using an Offsetting Position

If an option is closed out with the purchase or sale of an identical option, then the transaction is treated as a short-term capital gain (or loss), no matter how long the initial position was held.

Assignment or Exercise: Call Edition

Whether you choose to exercise or exercise chooses you (via assignment), the option writer uses the strike price plus the premium received as the relevant sale price of the underlying asset. Whether this is a sale or loss, short term or long term, depends on the price of the underlying asset and the length of time it was owned.

Assignment or Exercise: Put Edition

The writer of a put option must buy the asset at the time of exercise. For tax purposes, the basis of the transaction is the strike price plus any commissions. The sale proceeds of that asset would include the premium. As with a call, the length of the position for tax treatment will depend on how long the total position is in place.

Worthless Expiration

If the option expires worthless, the writer recognizes a short-term capital gain equal to the amount of the premium. The buyer has a short-term capital loss.

Straddles

In trading, a long straddle is a combination of a long call and long put, with the same strike price and expiration. A short straddle is a short call and short put, with the same strike and expiration. This position will increase in value whether the stock goes up or down in price. It's a way to profit from extreme volatility.

Antistraddle Rules

Under the tax law, a straddle isn't a straddle; it's a transaction involving offsetting positions. The results at tax time aren't pretty:

- The holding period is suspended during the period of offset.

- The wash-sale rule applies.

- No deduction for losses is allowed to the extent of the unrecognized gain at the end of any offsetting unrecognized gain at the end of such year and not otherwise deferred under the wash sale rule.

- A successor position is one which is on the same side of the market as was the original position, which replaces a loss position and is entered into during a period beginning 30 days prior to the date of the disposition of the loss side and ending 30 days after the disposition. However, a position entered into after all positions of the straddle have been disposed of will not be considered a successor position.

- All carrying charges and interest expenses, including margin, are added to the basis of the long position. The basis is reduced by the dividends received on the stock included in the straddle.

The Explanation

But what does this antistraddle limitation mean? I've wrestled with this, and I've dreamed of teaching tax accountants how to write. Trust me, there are few things in life less fun than reading tax law.

It means this: if you have an offsetting position, you can only deduct the loss to the extent that it matches the gain on this particular position. You can't carry it over to reduce other gains you have on other positions. In no case can you have a gain that is free from taxation because of a paper loss.

Furthermore, you can't use your offsetting position to turn a short-term gain into a long-term one.

Right now, you're probably confused. That's why options traders should find tax advisers who understand how these things work.

Antistraddle and Offset Rule Exemptions

There are some exceptions to these antistraddle rules, and they are important for an options trader.

Married Puts

A married put, which is a long put held against a long position in the stock, is exempt from the offsetting position rules as long as the put was acquired on the same day as the stock, and the shares in question are identified as those that will be delivered if the put is exercised. If the put expires, then the price of it is added to the basis of the stock.

Qualified Covered Calls

A covered call is a call option written on a stock you already own. To be qualified for exemption from the offsetting position rule, a covered call must be written with more than 30 days to expiration and a strike price not less than the strike price below the closing price of the stock on the day the option was written. In other words, the call must be out-of-the-money when it is written.

There's a reason for the determination of qualification. If you have a short-term gain in the underlying security, you could use an in-the-money call option to receive cash now while extending the holding period just enough to turn the gain into a long-term gain. Like magic, an 11-month gain and a 60-day option turn into cash today and a lower tax bill. This is the sort of thing that makes IRS lawyers sad, and sad IRS lawyers write regulations pushing their sorrow onto you.

Who Are You, Anyway?

The IRS has specifications to help answer this most basic question of existence. You have to know who you are to understand the key aspects of your tax treatment.

Investors

To the IRS, investors are people who buy and sell securities in order to generate income from dividends, interest, or capital gains. That sounds like just about everyone in the financial markets, yes? And it pretty much does include everyone who is trading who is not doing it in the process of conducting a trader or business.

If the IRS considers you to be an investor, the following tax considerations apply:

- Capital gains and losses must be segregated into short term and long term, then netted against each other. Only $3,000 in losses in excess of gains might be deducted.

- The wash sale rule applies.

- Certain expenses are deductible if they exceed 2 percent of adjusted gross income.

- Interest might be deducted if it is incurred to buy or carry investment property that produces taxable income, but the expense cannot exceed net investment income.

Dealers

Dealers purchase, hold, and sell securities to customers in the ordinary course of business. It is highly unlikely an individual who is trading options would fall into the dealer category. However, if you are reading this book because of a business, or if you have customers, then you need to keep records clearly specifying which securities are held for your own account and which are reported for the business. Furthermore, gains and losses on holdings in the business account are handled using *mark-to-market accounting.*

> **DEFINITION**
>
> **Mark-to-market accounting** means the value of the assets held in inventory are valued at the current market price, not the price at which they were acquired. Capital gains and losses are not recognized, but gains and losses on inventory are recorded every year based on the year-end market price. The mark-to-market election simplifies trade accounting, but it brings its own nuances into play.

Traders

Mark to market simplifies a lot of the rules for handling capital gains and losses. Instead of having to track gains and losses per trade, you track them on the value of the account as a whole and carry them over into income.

The IRS allows individual traders to take the mark-to-market election if they qualify as pattern day traders. To do this:

- You need to show your primary investment activity is trading to profit from changes in security prices rather than dividends, interest, or capital gains

- Your trading activity is "substantial" in terms of the frequency and dollar amount of the trades and the amount of time spent on them

- You must carry out the activity of trading with continuity and regularity

- You make money for at least 3 out of every 5 years

As an added bonus, those qualifying as traders can deduct all their expenses; they are not subject to the same limitations as investors.

You'll almost definitely need a tax professional to help with this. I discuss that more at the end of the chapter.

Options in Retirement Accounts

One way to solve the tax issues surrounding options is to trade them in your individual retirement account. There are two main types:

- In a traditional IRA, the contributions are tax deductible and the withdrawals in retirement are taxed as ordinary income.

- In a Roth IRA, the contributions are not tax deductible, but the gains are not taxes, either.

In either type of account, you don't have to worry about straddle rules, 60/40 breakdowns, and other rules. There's one catch, though: you can't trade on margin in a retirement account. As a result, you cannot write a call unless it is covered with a position in the underlying asset in the same account. You cannot write a put unless you have enough cash in your account to buy the underlying asset if it is assigned to you. This means many combo and spread strategies are off-limits.

On the other hand, you are free to trade long calls and long puts in your retirement account. You can also use covered calls and protective puts. These can go a lot way toward managing risk and generating additional return.

> ⌇ **WARNING**
>
> At the time this book is being written, the U.S. Department of Labor (which oversees pension and retirement accounts) was considering a ban on all options trading in IRA accounts. Check out the situation with your brokerage firm before you place a trade.

Deducting Investment Expenses

Recognizing that making money with options takes effort, study, and skill, the IRS allows people to deduct certain expenses used in their trading and investing activities.

There are limits, though. You can't deduct more than the value of your trading capital—so beware if you trade a lot of naked positions. And, if you are not a trader, you can only deduct investment expenses if those plus your other miscellaneous itemized deductions exceed 2 percent of your adjusted gross income.

Research and Advice

The IRS allows you to deduct the following costs:

- Accounting fees
- Any legal expenses you might incur
- Clerical help, if you need it
- Investment advice
- Magazines, newspapers, subscription websites, and other research services
- Office expenses
- Safe deposit box rental
- The price of this book!

How to Handle Commissions

Commissions are not listed with investment expenses, because those are included when calculating capital gains or losses. You can't take them until the position is closed out, though, whether you hold it for hours or decades.

Investment Interest

If any part of your strategy involves borrowed money, and it might, you can deduct the interest paid as long as you didn't borrow money against your house. (Real estate interest is a different category of expense.)

The One Expense You Can't Deduct

You can't deduct travel. You can't buy an option on the euro and then deduct your honeymoon in Paris as research on your investment. You can't buy a call on Disney stock and deduct a trip to the Magic Kingdom as a way to check out the potential volatility. And you can't deduct the cost of travel for investment seminars unless they qualify as investment advice. An options training seminar given by one of the exchanges probably counts; a lecture on retirement planning given on a cruise ship definitely does not.

Your tax adviser can give you more advice on this.

> **TRADING TIP**
>
> When dealing with the taxes, the general rule is if you think you have found a clever way to get a write-off, someone else probably tried it already and the IRS shut it down back then.

Hiring a Tax Adviser

Because taxes can complicate an options position, you really need the help of a tax expert. This person will help you figure out what you owe and advise you on ways to manage your strategies in order to reduce your tax burden. You want to pay what you owe, no more and no less.

Types of Tax Advisers

There are several types of professionals who are authorized to represent taxpayers before the IRS. They have different backgrounds but often overlapping functions. These are the people who do the bulk of tax preparation and who usually have the deepest knowledge of the regulations.

Certified public accountants handle most tax issues. These are people who studied accounting in college and passed an exam. They have to maintain professional standards and take continuing education courses. Many of them specialize in tax preparation, and these are generally the best resource for a trader.

An enrolled agent is a person who has passed a rigorous IRS exam on income tax topics. They know taxes inside and out. Many of them also have an industry specialty. An enrolled agent who also knows trading could add a lot of value to your trading plans. One who specializes in work with artists? Not too much.

Tax attorneys can prepare taxes and represent tax payers, but their expertise is generally beyond what most traders need. They are the people who will research proposed trading strategies and argue them before the IRS. Brokerage firms and major trading firms rely on them, but you probably don't need one.

Special Considerations for Traders

In addition to the people listed earlier, plenty of other people can prepare taxes. You could do it yourself or have your niece who is studying accounting in college do it, though chances are good the nuances of options will trip you up. The same goes for using a storefront service or a tax preparation volunteer. Sure, your local senior center might offer to do your taxes for free, but the volunteers are assuming most of those people who show up will have a pension and maybe a little interest income from a CD, not a printout of trade confirms involving multileg option positions.

Tax preparation software can help, but again, it probably doesn't go into enough detail for an active trader. A professional can get it done fast and well, and that alone is worth the money.

MARKET MAXIM

Be sure any adviser you use knows how to handle taxes on trading. I can't say this enough.

State Taxes

Every state has its own philosophy about income taxes, and in some states, that includes taxes on investment income. The rules usually follow the IRS rules, but not always. Your tax adviser can help you with this, too.

The Least You Need to Know

- Taxes are a key consideration for options traders.
- The IRS classifies trade proceeds and losses as either income or capital gains, and as either short term or long term.
- Losses offset gains only if they are in the same category.
- Most traders will benefit from hiring a tax adviser who understands trading.

CHAPTER 19

Evaluating Performance

At some point, a friend or family member is going to ask how you are doing, and as a matter of fact, it's an important question you ought to be asking yourself independent of your nosy relatives. Are you some sort of financial genius, or should you fall back on the age-old advice, "Don't quit your day job"? Basically, you need some sort of metric to judge how much money you are making, and how that stacks up relative to the time, money, effort, and sleepless nights you have invested in your strategy.

In This Chapter

- Pretrade testing
- Planning the trade
- Midtrading tracking
- Post-trade evaluation

To get a better handle on your answer, we need to better define what we are asking:

- How are you doing overall?

- How are you doing relative to the market and relative to your peers?

- How does your return on trading options compare to a money market account?

- How does your return on trading options compare to an index fund?

- Do you want to look at it for individual trades, or in aggregate?

- How do you account for options that haven't been exercised yet?

These questions fall under the umbrella of performance evaluation. The simplest answer is to compare what you have now to what you had when you started. If you're ahead, it's all good, right? Not so quick; you need to evaluate whether the net difference is fair compensation for your time and risk. A careful, quantitative analysis can help you fine-tune your strategy to improve your performance over time.

This section will discuss a trial run (simulating how you will do without actually doing it), record keeping, and a few methods to quantitatively evaluate your performance.

Learn About Options, Not Strategies

It might seem like options trading is about learning a lot of complicated strategies with strange names. The options business has always seemed like something apart from regular stocks and bonds. The lore of the trading pits and the role of options trading in the media reinforce the idea of options as something different and difficult, and many new options traders think they need to learn the complicated stuff first.

In fact, it's the opposite. Start with the basics: what a put is, what a call is, what it means to write and to buy, and how the prices change. If you understand the basics, you'll be able to think about the payoffs as you put together trades. Simulation trading helps. Focus on this before worrying about butterflies, condors, and Christmas trees. The simple stuff will carry you through.

Testing Before You Trade

Performance evaluation starts before you trade. If you're speculating, you want some idea of how your strategy will work. If you're hedging, you'll need a sense of what your potential downside is and what it will cost to buy protection.

Start by watching the markets. Create a few trades—or a full-on strategy—and see how they play out before you commit actual money. How did that work out?

This process is known as simulated trading. You can start by simply making a note on a piece of paper on in a spreadsheet about your trade idea, then checking to see how it would work. Some questions to ask include the following:

- If you want to write covered calls, what is the premium you would receive?

- How does that compare to the risk of the underlying asset being called?

- If you wrote a covered call today, how likely is it you would want to close the trade in the next day? Week? Month?

- What would it cost you?

Think of this as watching the waves before swimming in the ocean. It's better to identify the undertow before you get caught in it.

Keeping notes of trade ideas will get you started, but most brokerage firms and many of the exchanges offer simulated trading systems. One to try is the CBOE's virtual trade tool, which you can find online.

Simulated trading lets you try out your ideas and see how they work with play money. It gives you a really clear idea of what you do and do not understand about options trading, and it lets you test new trade strategies without risking actual cash.

Keep in mind that with play money, you might not have the emotional attachments that undo traders. Some people do really well with play money, then panic when they deal with the real thing.

Assuming you're happy with the results, you can move on trading small amounts of real money. If not, go back to the drawing board and think of some new trades.

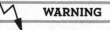 **WARNING**

Don't assume you are a trading genius if your first few real or fake trades work out. The markets regularly humble even the best traders.

Backtesting

If you're planning to be a frequent options trader, especially a day trader, you might want to see how your strategy would have worked in the past. That's why many brokers offer backtesting services. You can run your trading system with historic data to see how it would have performed in times past.

Backtesting is especially useful for seeing how your trading would work under different market conditions than you see right now. It can help you evaluate whether to change your strategies if current market conditions change, and it can give you a sense of the amount of risk you are taking.

When you set up a backtest, you specify the types of trades you would make, and the time they would run. One of the things you are looking for is the number of opportunities that come your way given your strategy. Nothing works in all markets, all the time, and some profitable situations might not appear often enough to be worth your while.

And don't worry, the markets will change. As traders like to say, the four most dangerous words in the English language are "this time is different." History repeats itself in the options market as it does anywhere in life.

Simulation

Sometimes called paper trading, simulation is similar to backtesting in that it lets you run a strategy without committing any money. The difference is simulation works in current market conditions rather than with past data.

With most simulated trading systems, you can either trade in real time, placing buy and write orders, or you can specify the parameters of automated trades and watch them play out. You might be looking for specific signals to buy and to sell; you would enter those to see how they work.

Both backtesting and simulation have the same problem, which is that you're not trading with real money. That means you might not be affected by emotions the same as you will be when trading in real time with real money. That's okay; they both give you a starting point. If your trading system does not work in a simulated environment, it isn't likely to work in the real world, either.

By ruling out a less-than-ideal strategy, you can concentrate on those that have a greater chance for success. That's all you're doing here.

> **MARKET MAXIM**
>
> Don't make perfect the enemy of the good. Your trading system needs to be good enough. It will need constant refinement, but it will never be perfect. That's okay.

Tracking Trades

If you are satisfied with your backtesting and simulation performance, either using historic data or real-time markets, you can move on to trading with real dollars. When that happens, it is critical that you track your trades so you can evaluate your performance.

The good news? It's not hard to do.

A Simple Trading Diary

A trading diary is a record of each trade you placed, why you placed it, how it worked out, and why it did or did not work out. This can be maintained along with a trading spreadsheet or kept separately.

A trading diary does not have to be fancy. Plenty of traders use old wire-bound notebooks they keep next to their computers. Others make a form they copy and keep in a loose-leaf binder. The important thing is having notes in real time, rather than waiting until a day or a week later when the passage of time and the color of emotion might influence your recollections about why you traded and how it worked for you.

Here's what each diary entry should include:

- Date and time the position was opened
- The name, option, strike, and expiration
- Number of options purchased
- Premium paid or received
- Reason for making the trade
- Date and time the position was closed
- Price at which the position was closed
- Reason for closing the trade
- The realized gain or loss (Track it now to make your life easy at tax time.)
- A brief explanation of the trade and note of any lessons learned

If you keep track of your trades as you open and close them, you'll be able to see what you did and why it worked (or didn't), free from the haze of memory and emotion.

Spreadsheet

Many brokerage firms provide trade tracking services. They collect the data in a format that can either be analyzed on their platform or downloaded into a spreadsheet so you can analyze it yourself.

Setting Up a P&L

P&L stands for "profit and loss," and it's the record of what you're making from your trading. This is an extension of the trading log. If you keep your trading diary in electronic format, you can calculate your P&L there.

It's pretty simple: how much did you start with, how much did you end up with, and what is the percentage change? If you trade daily, set it up daily. If you're less active, check less often.

If you are trading on a regular basis, it might make sense to see what your hourly wage is as well. If your week's profit is $100 and you spent an hour trading, you're doing okay. If you spent 40 hours trading, maybe not.

Calculating Overall Performance

Finding your basic profit and loss is a simple process. Other measures of performance are strangely complicated. It seems simple—how much money you have at the end compared to how much money you have at the beginning. The problems ensue if you add money to your account, take money out, or want to figure out what your return is for different time periods. You might not care about this information, or it might be useful when comparing your performance to that of professional managers.

The absolute amount of money you make from trading only tells you part of what you need to know. The other part is determining how you perform relative to the amount of risk you take and relative to other things you could be doing with your time and money.

Types of Return

When people in the financial markets talk about return, they are thinking about a few different forms of calculations. There are a few different calculations that have different uses in performance analysis. You might only care about very basic return info, or you might want more detailed statistics. You might also want to understand what a research service is talking about when it makes claims for its performance. No matter the reason, this section will help you out.

TRADING TIP

If you're looking at different newsletter and signaling programs, you might want to look at their performance claims and how they were calculated. The fact of the matter is that the different methods generate slightly different return numbers, so you want to be sure you are making comparisons using the same types of returns.

Compound Average Rate of Return

The *compound average rate of return* starts with a simple percentage change equation. It is used for a single time period in which no money was added or withdrawn. If you wanted to compare how much money you had at the end of the period (EOP) with how much you had at the beginning of the period (BOP), the equation you use is:

$$EOP \div BOP - 1$$

That's simple.

The compound average rate of return for one time period is probably given on your brokerage account statement. If you're looking at more time periods, the math gets a bit trickier. You're now looking for the compound average growth rate (CAGR), which is also known the geometric mean. Mathematically, it is the nth root of n numbers multiplied together. The equation looks like this:

$$\sqrt[n]{\frac{EOP}{BOP}} - 1$$

The easier way to solve this is to use the GEOMEAN function in Excel. This metric evaluates what your returns would have to be over a period of time to achieve the same net result, and it allows you to smooth out the ups and downs to come up with an overall average. If you earn 10 percent return on each of three years and lose 20 percent during a fourth, then your geometric mean return is 13.5 percent.

Time-Weighted Return

A true *time-weighted return* is a bit of a mess to calculate to hand, but it gives you the clearest information about how an investment did with money coming in and coming out. The good news is your brokerage firm might calculate it for you.

Here's what goes into the calculation. First, you find the compound average growth rate for each time period before an addition or withdrawal of money is made. Then, you do another CAGR starting the day of the deposit or withdrawal, then taking it out until right before the next deposit or withdrawal, and then so on. The time period is usually the number of days. Then, all of the CAGRs are multiplied together to get you the return for the year.

If you are looking at different money managers or commodity trading advisers to handle your options investing, you'll want to see their time-weighted return information. That will give you a good idea of how they handle investments with money coming in and coming out.

Modified Dietz Method

The problem with the compound average rate of return is it does not handle additions and withdrawals of money. If you want to see how you are doing relative to professional traders, or to compare your results to a fund's results, that's an important number to know.

Here's what the Modified Dietz Method looks like:

$$(EOP - BOP - deposits + withdrawals) \div (BOP + deposits - withdrawals)$$

The only problem with this is that it doesn't consider when the money came in. In this calculation, a deposit in January would have the same effect as a deposit in December, even though in reality, the effects on performance would be very different. Still, it helps break out an increase in account value between an increase from investment returns and an increase from new deposits.

> **TRADING TIP**
>
> Many people in our culture use money as a way to keep score. As a result, they often lie about how their investments are doing, or do the calculations incorrectly, or talk about the winners and not the losers. Don't ever let a braggart at a cocktail party make you feel bad about how your investments are doing or how much money you have, because those who talk often aren't doing the walk.

Dollar-Weighted Return

Also known as internal rate of return (IRR), the *dollar-weighted return* is the rate of return that makes the present value of a stream of numbers equal to zero. It has a lot of value for calculating the returns in which all of the numbers are positive, and so you see it often in calculating returns on bonds and venture capital. It has less value for options, where you'll almost definitely have a few losing trades.

But, if you come across it, here's the information on calculation. You either use the IRR function in Excel or in a financial calculator.

Arithmetic Average

An *arithmetic average* of profit (or loss) on trades is a number you want to know to help improve your trading. It is nothing more than calculating the individual return for each period, summing them all up, and dividing by the number of periods. (This is the calculation that the AVERAGE function in Excel does.) If you double your investment for two years and lose it all during the third, on average, you increased your money by one third each year, which isn't a particularly good measure for how you did in any given year, or how you did overall.

This number is not so useful finding out the return on your money, but it is helpful in risk calculations, covered in the next section. Knowing it puts you way ahead of traders who figure they are doing all right because they still have money in their accounts.

Risk Calculation

Return gets you to one point of information. The other point is the rate of return relative to the amount of risk you take—*risk calculation*. After all, a big return earned on very little risk is a lot better than a big return for an even bigger level of risk.

Return is a function of risk, by the way. You don't get a big return without taking a big risk. That's another reason not to trust braggarts at cocktail parties.

Batting Average

A lot of traders look at their *batting average*—the percentage of their trades that make money to the percentage that lose money. Also known as their win-loss percentage or win ratio, it gives you a sense of how effective your trading strategy is. It is also useful in many money management systems covered in Chapter 17.

If you are dependent upon a few huge wins to offset a typical losing trade, your strategy has a lot more risk than if a larger number of trades win, even if they generate a smaller amount of return.

Standard Deviation

Standard deviation is one of the numbers your P&L spreadsheet can generate for you. The math looks at how much each particular trade's return deviated from the average trade. In fact, it's the same equation used to describe the volatility of an underlying asset.

The higher the standard deviation, the greater the volatility of your returns and the greater the risk you are taking in your portfolio.

Sharpe Ratio

Once you have the standard deviation, you can find the *Sharpe ratio*, which is nothing more than the return divided by the standard deviation. The higher the Sharpe ratio, the greater the return relative to the risk taken.

Benchmarking Performance

If I said I earned 10 percent on my money last year, would that be a good return? Suppose I said I lost 5 percent, would that be good?

Obviously, it depends! And what it depends on is the return available elsewhere in the market, the return for the amount of time committed to trading, and the amount of risk taken.

This section will look at the factors you need to compare to your trading in order to determine how you are doing.

Relative to a Market Index

The alternative to trading options is to invest directly into a market index fund, commodity trading account, bond, or currency. One way to see how options are affecting your return is to compare it to an appropriate index.

You can use the relevant underlying index to see if you are getting benefits over and above investing in the underlying asset directly. This is especially useful if you are using options to hedge.

In addition, the Chicago Board Options Exchange publishes a buy-write index that can give you a sense of how a covered-call strategy should perform. If your primary interest is covered calls, this is a good way to track your performance.

Relative to the Time Committed

Trading takes up time. You might be doing it full-time as a form of employment or part-time as an activity designed to make money, as a productive hobby. Whatever the reason, you're putting time and energy that could be put to a different endeavor into the trading.

And so, a very simple but important calculation is to take the amount of money earned from trading, after costs, after subtracting out the initial investment, and dividing it by the number of hours spent.

One Final Note

As every investment industry disclosure says, past performance does not indicate future results. Go forth and trade, but remember tomorrow might not be like today.

The Least You Need to Know

- Performance analysis starts before you trade.
- Backtesting and simulation can help you evaluate strategy performance in a variety of market conditions.
- Keep track of your trades to see how you do.
- There are several ways to calculate percentage gains, depending on what you want to show.

CHAPTER 20

Training Your Brain

Trading is as much mental as anything. There are plenty of people who are good at market analysis, but they can't pull the trigger or manage risk effectively.

If you are planning to trade options regularly in order to speculate on changes in the market, you need to consider the mental aspects of trading. For that matter, all investors need to understand the separation between the market and their very real and rich lives.

The options market is neutral, both morally and economically. It is about matching the interests of hedgers and speculators. Many people approach it as nothing more than a marketplace for financial tools. But some, especially those who trade full-time, can be caught up.

In This Chapter

- Controlling emotions
- Planning your trading
- Knowing when to walk away
- Finding alternatives

Controlling Your Emotions

Every trader knows the big ugly emotions that can turn trading from risky to treacherous. They affect everyone at one time or another, and some of us have felt more than one at once, and more often than once in a while.

Although I offer a few tidbits of advice about how to avoid falling into these emotional traps, emotions are so complex and so deep-seated that simple tips probably won't be enough to overcome them. The information presented here will help you be aware of what's going on. If you have a small tendency toward a particular behavior, the tips might help keep it in check or get you back on track.

If you have a large tendency to overreact to your emotions, the discussion might help you figure out big ways to manage your emotions so they don't control your trading. Traders have been known to take up therapy, meditation, or athletics to help manage emotions. This is far better than, say, alcohol, cocaine, and financial ruin.

Or, the discussion of emotion might cause you to choose to do something else, which is fine by me. If I keep people who would be bad at trading from taking it up, then I have done a valuable service.

Doubt

Doubt creeps in whenever trading isn't going exactly as you wanted it to. Maybe you should get out now? Heck, even if it is working out, you might start doubting the trade size. Should you have doubled up? Closed out a few points ago? Placed a hedge on the position?

What are you doing trading anyway?

All of a sudden, you are busy rethinking everything you have ever done. In your entire life.

Self-assessment and self-awareness are good things. Both will help you improve your trading. But wait until after the trading day! Write a trading plan. Stick to the plan. Assess how it worked out after you close the trade. Then, determine if you could have done something else to improve on it.

The more you trust your plan, the less doubt you'll have when you're trading. You'll have more confidence and become a better trader.

> **MARKET MAXIM**
>
> When in doubt, palms out. Floor traders relied on hand signals to place buy and sell orders. Holding your hands up with the palms facing toward you meant you wanted to buy—you wanted to bring the option to you. If your palms were out, you wanted to sell—to push the option away from you and to another trader. The idea here is if you don't know what to do, close out your position and move on to another one.

Fear

Derivatives markets are a zero-sum game. For every winner, there is a loser. It can be frightening to be on the losing side, too. It is hard to watch your money disappear.

And it's easy to turn every loss into a catastrophe. So easy. And so dangerous.

A little fear is okay. It can keep you from behaving recklessly, from placing trades without regard to what the market is telling you. Too much fear will keep you from taking appropriate risk in placing trades as well as hold you back from closing out positions when it is time to close them out.

The best ways to avoid fear? Test your system, plan your trades, and have money to fall back on.

Greed

Speculators trade in order to make money. That's what they do. Therefore, greed is a good thing, right? Wrong.

Money itself is neutral, but greed is not. Greed is the desire for more money for its own sake. A trader in the throes of greed will take too much risk, cut corners, wait too long to close out a trade, and question all of his decisions. He will not be satisfied with his trading, and in the push to get more—and more, and more—he will be ruined.

> **MARKET MAXIM**
>
> Pigs get fat, hogs get slaughtered. People speculate in options to make money. That's a given. But the drive to make money can cloud common sense. There is a point where enough is enough; trying to make more can lead to sloppy trading and excess risk. You want to be fat and happy, not out of the game.

The way to avoid greed is to realize the size of your trading account is not the same as the value of your life. Some people report that giving money to charity helps them keep perspective by helping those who have less. Others work to keep a life outside of their trading so they really have more than their account to value.

Overconfidence

You know that saying about pride goeth before a fall? It is true in life and true in trading. Confidence is good. Overconfidence is lethal.

The moment you think you have it all figured out, something will happen to trip you up. I have no idea what will happen, only that it will.

But many traders come to think they cannot go wrong, and so they take too much risk. They get sloppy: they stop planning and tracking trades; they break their risk limits. They brag about how they doing.

When the inevitable happens, it's harder to take than it would be otherwise because of the over-confident behavior.

The way to avoid this is strict discipline. Set limits. Stick to them. It's not always fun, but it works.

> **MARKET MAXIM**
>
> The worst thing that can happen to a new trader is making money on your first trade. Trading isn't easy. Successful traders have a mathematical mindset, stay calm under pressure, and do the work of planning their trades. Yes, sometimes they make money because of sheer, dumb luck, too. If your first trade is a winning trade, you might start to believe you can do well without doing the work.

Anxiety

The ruthlessness of the market can lead to almost nonstop second-guessing. Should you place a trade? Now, or wait? What strike should you use? What expiration? What if it doesn't would out?

There are about a million questions you can ask about every single trade. If you ask them, you'll never have time to place an order. Anxiety forces traders to question everything to the point where they can do nothing.

The way around anxiety is to have systems for trading and money management that you trust. This means you have to test your trading plan, track your trades, and evaluate the results. The more automatic it becomes, the less likely anxiety is to undo your hard work.

Many brokerage firms offer trade testing services, or you can do it yourself. The process is simple: first, you figure out how you want to trade. Are you interested in writing puts? Looking for momentum signals on charts? Whatever it is, first you identify what you want to trade. Write it down. Then, see how that trade works out. What was the return? Compare the results to an appropriate market index. (The exchanges have data on different strategies that can help.) Repeat. If your broker has a database of historic prices, you can see how your strategy would have performed over long periods of time with actual data. Testing isn't difficult, and it is important.

It helps to have money outside of your trading account so you don't come to see every trade as a make-or-break proposition. If anxiety is crippling, therapy or medication might help.

Boredom

Some elements of trading are less than interesting. For a part-time or sporadic trader, it's easy to walk away for a while. If you're trading full-time, though, there's a temptation to take chances to make things exciting that actually make your trading position worse.

In the days of floor trading, traders would sometimes horse around and play games with prices to alleviate boredom. It was much harder to get bored in such a stimulating environment, and when the market was not making things interesting, there were plenty of people who would.

The modern trader, working off of a computer screen, is likely to feel boredom more often than his floor predecessor ever did. The temptations for alleviating boredom are many, making it worse.

Cat videos won't improve your trading.

One of the best things you can do when you are bored is to learn a new aspect of trading. This might be time to learn some new strategies, research options on different markets, or study different trading techniques.

Many brokers offer mobile apps so you can trade from your smart phone. These are generally not a great idea, except as a backup. First of all, speeds are generally less reliable than those from a full-fledged computer. I live near a major league ball park, and my mobile service is terrible on game days. Secondly, if you are always tied to the market by your phone, you won't get the breaks you need to keep your perspective on both the market and life.

Depression

Depression is a real illness. It interferes with many aspects of life, and trading is one of them.

If everything seems hopeless to you, you are less likely to take appropriate risks and to follow through on your trading plan. You'll just sit, and be sad, and do only the work you need to do to trade.

Some forms of depression clear up with time, but not all. Many people need therapy or medication to help them, and that goes for traders.

And if trading is really bringing you down, walk away. No one says you have to do this.

Importance of a Trading Plan

A trading plan can help keep the emotions of trading in check. When situations get complicated, go back to the plan. It will help you build trust in your trading system, develop confidence in your skills as a trader, help you manage your money, and force you to address limits. All of these things will help you trade with less emotion, and that's good.

Trading as a Thoughtful Endeavor

It's not for nothing that so much trading has moved to electronic systems. It takes a lot of the emotion out of the game. A computer does not feel, and it thinks only as much as it is told to do.

The programs computers use are designed by people. Electronic trading combines the best of being a human with the best of being a machine.

You're all human, no machine. So you have to use that to your advantage. Approach your trading with some logic. What do you want to do, and why? That's a trading plan! It's really that simple.

With a plan in place, you're better able to apply your perspective and knowledge to a roiling market with less emotional interference.

Evaluate Your Plan

A trading plan is not set in stone. It is a process, not a set of rules. That means if your approach to trading isn't working, you can change it.

In fact, you should change it, as market conditions change all the time. Trades that make no sense when interest rates are low are a great idea when rates are high. Hedging is more important—and more valuable—in a volatile market than in a stable one. What works once might not work again, or it might not work again for a while.

If you find that emotion is getting you undone, work your anxiety out in planning your trades and your strategy, not in executing it. Do you need to change what you're doing? Try a different market, a different strategy, do more research? What's different, and what's the same?

Careful evaluation of the plan, away from the market, is a lot better than second-guessing it while you're working with real money in real time.

Learning, Without Emotion

The reality of life is most of us only learn the hard way. No matter how much we know about how to do things, no matter what cautionary tales we hear or who we know or what we read, we end up doing stupid things.

But those stupid things teach us lessons. If you track your trades, you can get a better sense of where you're screwing up and why. You can make that evaluation away from the market.

Go, sit in a café with a warm beverage and a sweet treat, take a look at your trading diary, and look for places where you can improve. You might find you're doing better than you would have thought in the press of the market.

MARKET MAXIM

If you don't know who you are, the market is an expensive place to find out. The pressure of the markets will put your emotions and your personality into sharp focus. The difference between success and failure is as much one of personality as anything. Trading is great for some people and terrible for others. The better you know yourself, the less likely you are to suffer unnecessary losses. And you will have losses, no matter how good of a trader you are.

Having an Outlet

Do you love to trade? Excellent.

Good traders like what they do and spend a lot of time and energy researching, planning, and evaluating trades. They also know when to quit.

In the olden days, it was easy. The options market was open from 8:30 A.M. until 3 P.M. Chicago time. When it closed, trading was done for the day. The folks in Chicago did their paperwork and retired to Ceres or Cactus for drinks before taking the train home. Everyone else enjoyed the quiet after the phones stopped ringing.

And now? People can trade almost all the time. Some contracts have extended trading hours. Thanks to electronic trading, people can place trades in markets in any time zone in the world. Currency markets are open 6 days a week, 24 hours a day. It's hard to stop for the day.

And that's not good.

Balancing Life

I've been self-employed for 17 years. In that time, I've noticed that successful self-employed people all seem to have either dogs or children to force them onto a schedule and away from their desks, at least for a few hours a day.

Whether your interest in options is to supplement your other personal investing activities or to be a full-time trader, you need to spend some time and energy away from the market. You can trade all the time, on your phone and in the middle of the night, but you should not.

If you need to schedule a vacation, go for a walk with your phone at home, or go to dinner and a movie with people you care about, do it.

The combination of money, emotion, and adrenalin in the financial markets can destroy you, if you let it.

A Walk-Away Fund

It's so much easier to heed limits and take breaks from trading if you don't need the money. No matter what your endeavor in life, you'll have more freedom and less stress if you can accumulate a walk-away fund (sometimes known by other, more colorful, terms).

It's simple:

- Don't trade all your money.

- On a regular basis, take some money out of your trading account and put it into other investments.

- Keep an emergency fund with enough money to cover 3 to 6 months of expenses in a federally insured bank account. The return is lousy, but the money will be there when you need it.

- Trading is risky, so your nontrading assets should be in less-risky, even boring, assets.

These strategies mean you can afford to stop trading for as long as it takes to get your head together and refresh your perspectives. You can pay your bills even if your trading isn't cooperating this month. And, you can enjoy the fruits of your labors in the markets.

If You Have a Problem

Having lived in Chicago during the heyday of people-intensive open outcry pit trading, I've seen a lot of people do well with trading. They worked at something they loved, made decent money, provided for their families, and contributed to their communities.

I've also seen a lot of people crash and burn. As in: divorce, alcoholism, cocaine abuse, and bankruptcy. Or worse. One futures trader of my acquaintance is spending the rest of his life in prison for financial fraud, committed with the help of an arson that led to the death of his mother.

There are bad people in every profession; trading is no different. Unfortunately, the money available in trading tends to attract some bad people, and the stress causes some good people to become undone.

> **WARNING**
>
> One of the realities of trading is many traders aren't trading, they are gambling. The options business is as much about insurance as speculation, and most of those who speculate are taking an appropriate level of risk for the return they expect to receive. However, a few traders cross the line. Trading, to them, is a respectable casino. They take improper levels of risk and live for the rush of the win. If you think you might be confusing the two, check out Gamblers Anonymous, gamblersanonymous.org.

The Least You Need to Know

- Trading is a great occupation for some people. Success is as much mental as anything.
- Traders can be undone by doubt, fear, greed, overconfidence, and other emotions.
- A disciplined approach to trading and money management helps control emotion.
- Traders need something happening beyond trading, and they should be aware of the emotional damages some traders have suffered.

Glossary

all or none   An order for options or other securities that tells the broker to fill it only if it can be filled in full.

alligator spread   Trader jargon for a position idea that looks great based on market conditions except for the fact that brokerage commissions will eat all the profits.

alpha   The Greek letter used in many asset pricing models to represent investment performance that did not come from market risk but rather from the investment manager's skill.

American option   An option that can be executed at any time between its purchase date and its expiration date.

arbitrage   Literally means "riskless profit"; used to take advantage of a mispricing in the market by buying the underpriced asset and simultaneously selling the overpriced asset.

arithmetic average   The mean of a series of numbers, found by adding all the numbers and then dividing by the number of items in the series.

ask   The price at which the broker sells an option to you. It is the higher of the two numbers in the bid-ask spread.

assignment   The process that the exchange uses to determine which of the many option writers will be responsible for the exercise of a particular option.

at-the-money   The term used to describe an option if the strike price is equal to the current price of the underlying.

back spread   A position in which a trader has more long options than short options on a given underlying asset.

batting average   The ratio of the number of winning trades to the number of losing trades.

beta   The Greek letter used in many asset pricing models to represent exposure to market risk. The market as a whole has a beta of 1; assets with more risk have a beta of more than 1, and those with less risk have a beta of less than 1.

bid   The price at which a broker buys an asset from a customer.

bid-ask spread   In price quotes for options and other assets, the bid-ask spread is the difference between the price that the broker pays to acquire an asset and the price at which she sells. The difference is the broker's profit.

binary options   A type of option that specifies an event, such as an asset hitting a certain price, and pays out only if that event happens. These are risky and often unregulated.

binomial model   An asset pricing model that looks at the likelihood of two different outcomes, then the likelihood of two outcomes for each of those. It is a way to think about option prices.

Black-Scholes   An option pricing model that considers interest rates, volatility, price of the underlying asset, and time to expiration.

black swan   A term used to describe the risk of an unusual event. The question the event raises is whether it is a one-time happening or the first of many.

box spread   So-called because the payoff diagram forms a box. It involves a long call and short put at one strike price, along with a short call and a long put at another strike price.

breakout   In technical analysis, the point where the price of a financial asset crosses the trendline.

butterfly spread   A combination of a bear spread and a bull spread, using puts or calls, designed to take advantage of extreme volatility.

buy-limit order   An order to buy a financial asset that includes instructions to the broker to execute the order only if the asset is at or below a predetermined price.

buy-to-close   An option purchase order used to end a short position.

buy-to-open   An option purchase order used to establish a long position.

buy-write   A basic but effective option strategy involving writing calls on underlying assets that are already in your account. Also known as *covered calls*.

calendar spread   Buying a call with one expiration date and then selling a call on the same underlying asset with the same strike price but a different expiration date.

call   An option that gives the right, but not the obligation, to buy an underlying asset at a predetermined price on or before a predetermined date.

candlestick charting   A technical analysis system that combines information about price and volume in the same chart entry.

cash settlement   At expiration, the option holder receives (or pays, for a put) the cash value of the underlying asset rather than the underlying asset itself.

clearinghouse   The organization that ensures the purchases or sales of options take place and that the cash or underlying asset is transferred properly when an option is exercised.

collar   Also known as a *fence,* this strategy involves having a long call and a short put, or a short call and long put, at different strike prices above and below the price of an underlying asset.

collateralized debt obligation   A security formed by combining a large pool of bonds and then selling off parts of it.

commodity   A raw material or agricultural product, such as metals, fuels, or grains.

compound average rate of return   Also known as the *geometric average* or the *time-weighted return,* this involves multiplying all the numbers in a series together and then taking it by the root of the number of items in the series. This is used to consider compounding.

condor   A strategy similar to a butterfly but with a range of strike prices. It is used to benefit from volatility.

confidence index   The yield on high-yield bonds divided by the yield on intermediate-quality bonds. The greater the relative return people demand for intermediate-quality bonds, the more concerned they are about the economy. This measure was first developed at *Barron's,* the financial newspaper.

contingent order   An order to buy or sell an asset that depends on a certain price being reached.

convergence   A convergence takes place when moving averages calculated over different time periods come together. This is often a sign a trend is ending.

conversion   An arbitrage strategy used when the price of an at-the-money call is higher than the price of an at-the-money put. You go long a put and short a call (with the same strike price and expiration) on an underlying asset you already own.

cost of carry   The interest rate charged on money or securities borrowed for a trade.

covered call   Also known as a *buy-write strategy,* this is a basic but effective option strategy involving writing calls on underlying assets already in your account.

covered option   An option and the asset needed if the option is exercised. This includes writing a call on shares of stock you already own, or writing a put with enough cash in your account to buy the underlying if the option is exercised.

credit default swap   A derivative contract that is a form of insurance on a collateralized debt obligation. It pays off if the collateralized debt obligation goes bankrupt.

crossover   In technical analysis, a *crossover* occurs if the price crosses the moving average line. It is often used as a signal to make an options trade.

cup-and-handle   A technical analysis formation that shows how less-informed traders react, creating an opportunity for those who have better information.

day order   An order to buy or sell a security that is good only on the day that it is entered.

day trader   Someone who wants to profit in the financial markets by making a large volume of small trades that are closed out at the end of each trading day.

delta   The rate at which an option price changes, given a change in the price of the underlying asset.

derivative   A financial contract that draws its value from the value of another asset.

divergence   In technical analysis, the point where the moving averages for different periods move apart. This usually means a new trend is beginning.

dividend   A payment that a company makes to its shareholders from its profits.

dollar-weighted return   An investment performance calculation that looks at the changes in the total dollar value of a portfolio.

"edge minus odds"   A money management system used by traders that is based on the percentage of winning trades you make relative to the total number of trades. Also known as the *Kelly criterion*.

Elliott Wave   A theory of technical analysis based on cycles of market activity that are decades or even centuries long.

equity option   An option that trades on the value of individual stocks.

European option   An option that can be exercised only on the expiration date.

exchange-traded fund (ETF)   A type of mutual fund that trades on an exchange like a share of stock. These are commonly issued on different market indexes and often used in different option strategies.

exercise   The process of using the option to buy or sell the underlying security.

exercise price   The price at which an option can be exercised. Also known as the *strike price*.

exotic   An option written on an unusual underlying asset or with unusual features. These are often individually negotiated, not standardized.

expiration   The date and time at which the option must be exercised or it becomes worthless.

expiration cycle   The set of expiration dates that apply to a particular option.

extrinsic value   The difference between an option's premium and the amount by which it is in the money. Also known as *time value*.

fence   A strategy that involves having a long call and a short put, or a short call and long put, at different strike prices above and below the price of an underlying asset. Also known as a *collar*.

Fibonacci sequence   A series of numbers found in nature and mathematics that is the basis of some technical analysis systems. It is equal to the sum of two numbers in a series, as follows: 0, 1, 1, 2, 3, 5, 8, 13, 21 …. *See also* Golden Ratio.

first derivative   In calculus, the term for the rate of change. In options trading, this is known as the delta.

fixed fractional   A money management system for traders that is based on trading a predetermined percentage of the account, adjusted for the amount of risk on the trade.

fixed ratio   A money management system for traders that is based on the amount of profit that is expected for a given position size.

flag   A chart pattern in technical analysis that shows a short-term deviation from a trend.

forward contract   An agreement to buy an underlying asset at a predetermined date in the future at a price agreed upon today. This is usually a customized contract.

fungible   Items that are interchangeable. For example, one dollar bill is as useful as another, so dollar bills are fungible items.

futures commission merchant   The regulatory term for a broker who is licensed to deal in futures contracts.

futures contract   A derivative contract that gives you the obligation to buy or sell an asset at a specified future date for a specified price.

gamma   The rate at which the delta of an option changes as the price of the underlying asset changes.

Gann   A complicated theory of technical analysis based in part on money management.

gearing   The word used in UK English for leverage, which is the use of borrowed money to increase risk and, it is hoped, return.

Golden Ratio   A series of numbers found in nature and mathematics that is the basis of some technical analysis systems. It is equal to the sum of two numbers in a series, as follows: 0, 1, 1, 2, 3, 5, 8, 13, 21 …. Also known as the *Golden Proportion*. *See also* Fibonacci sequence.

good 'til cancelled (GTC) order   An order to buy or sell something that is in place until the person who places the order requests otherwise.

good 'til date (GTD) order   An order to buy or sell something that is in place until a prespecified date.

Greeks   The slang term for the Greek letters used in options valuation. *See also* alpha; beta; delta; gamma; rho; theta; vega.

head-and-shoulders   A technical chart formation of three peaks in a row, which is considered an indicator of a price decline.

hedge ratio   Also known as *delta;* the ratio between the change in an option's value relative to the change in the value of the underlying asset.

hedging   Using derivatives to ensure against unfavorable price changes in the underlying asset.

implied volatility   The portion of an option's price that is not attributed to the price of the underlying, the time to expiration, the strike price, or interest rates. It is a measure of how volatile the market expects the underlying asset to be.

in-the-money   A term used to describe options that are profitable to be exercised.

index arbitrage   A trade that looks to make a profit on the difference between the value of a market index and the value of the assets that make up the index.

index option   An option based on the value of an underlying financial market index, such as the S&P 500 or the Financial Times Stock Exchange Index.

interest rate arbitrage   A trade that looks to make a profit from the differences in interest rates among different types of bonds, such as the difference between government bonds and high-grade corporate bonds.

interest rate option   An option that is based on the value of debt securities such as U.S. government bonds.

internal rate of return (IRR)   The discount rate that makes the current value of an investment equal to its purchase price.

intrinsic value   The portion of an option's price that is attributed to the price of the underlying asset.

investor   Someone who looks to make a profit from holding financial instruments for a long period of time.

iron butterfly   A trade similar to a regular butterfly except it involves selling the mid-strike straddle and buying the surrounding strangle.

iron condor   A trade similar to a regular condor except it involves selling the mid-strike straddle and buying the surrounding strangle.

Kelly criterion   A money management system used by traders that is based on the percentage of winning trades you make relative to the total number of trades. Also known as *edge minus odds.*

law of one price   Says that identical assets should have the same price in every market.

leverage   Using borrowed money to increase the risk on a trade in the hopes of increasing the return.

limit order   An order to trade an item that kicks in only when a specified price is reached.

long   A synonym for owning an asset.

long straddle   The purchase of a call and put with the same strike price. It pays off if the price of the underlying asset increases or decreases significantly. *See also* straddle; short straddle.

long strangle   The purchase of a call with one strike price and a put with a higher strike price. It pays off if the price of the underlying asset increases or decreases significantly. *See also* strangle; short strangle.

long synthetic stock   An option position that mimics the payoff of a share of common stock. It consists of a long call and a short put on the same underlying asset.

Long-term Equity AnticiPation Securities (LEAPS)   A type of option that expires in 2 to 5 years rather than the shorter time periods of most exchange-traded options.

margin   The amount of cash or securities that must be on account with a brokerage firm in order to borrow money or to take a leveraged position, such as an option trade.

margin agreement   The contract a customer signs with a brokerage firm which states that he or she understands the risks and costs involved with margin.

margin call   A notification that a broker sends to a customer if the customer's margin falls below the minimum required for the positions in the account. If the customer does not deposit more cash or securities, the broker will close out the customer's position.

mark to market   The process of updating the value of trading accounts at the end of the day to reflect the official closing price for the day.

market maker   A trader who is in the business of ensuring that there are buyers and sellers for a particular option. If no orders come from the public, the market maker will take the trade. Most market makers then hedge their positions.

market order   An order to buy or sell an asset at whatever the current price might be.

market sentiment   The overall mood of the market. Is the average trader feeling confident or fearful?

married call   An options trade that involves shorting the underlying asset and buying calls to protect against a price increase in the underlying asset.

married put   An options trade that involves buying the underlying asset and buying puts to protect against a price decrease in the underlying asset.

martingale   A money management system popular with gamblers and traders that calls for starting with a small initial position. If the position loses, then the next trade should be made with twice the amount of money. The trader should keep doubling the size of the position until a trade wins. Then, he or she should start over.

merger arbitrage   A trading strategy designed to take advantage of price changes in underlying assets that result from a merger announcement.

mini   Futures contracts that are sized for individual investors.

Modified Dietz Method   An investment performance calculation that considers the effect of cash deposits on the investment account.

moneyness   The catch-all term for describing how the underlying price of an asset is relative to the exercise price. Is it in-the-money, at-the-money, or out-of-the-money?

Monte Carlo simulation   A statistical technique used in the valuation of options and other assets that looks at the value under a range of distributions of the variables that affect the price.

moving average   A series of averages derived from successive segments (typically of constant size and overlapping) of a series of values. In trading, this may mean looking at results for 5-, 15-, or 30-day periods.

multiple-listed option   An exchange-traded option that can be traded on several different exchanges.

naked option   A short option position in which you do not own the underlying (for a call) or the means to buy it (for a put), so you have greater financial exposure if the option is assigned.

net credit   A positive balance in your trading account.

net debit   A negative balance in your trading account.

one cancels other (OCO) order   A contingent order to purchase or sell an asset that, if executed, will cancel a different order.

one triggers other (OTO) order   A contingent order to purchase or sell an asset that, if executed, will cause a different order to be executed.

open arbitrage   A trade that seeks to profit from price volatility at the very start of market trading for the day.

open interest Contracts in an options or futures market that are available for potential exercise because they have not been closed out, exercised, or allowed to expire.

open outcry A style of trading that involves human beings on the floor of the exchange who match buy and sell orders. This style of trading is mostly obsolete, having been phased out in favor of electronic trading, but it is still used to trade certain options.

option A contract that gives the holder the right, but not the obligation, to buy or sell an asset at a predetermined price on or before a predetermined date in the future.

option repair An option strategy designed to minimize a losing stock position with the purchase of a call option near the current price and the sale of an option near the original purchase price.

options agreement A contract that a customer signs with a brokerage firm in which the customer acknowledges receiving a guide to options from the broker and understands the risks and fees involves with trading options.

options chain A list of all the options available on a given security.

Options Clearing Corporation (OCC) The organization that guarantees the clearance and exercise of options on financial contracts in the United States.

options cycle The cycle of months in which options on a given underlying asset expire. Typical cycles are January, April, July, and October (JAJO); February, May, August, and November (FMAN); and March, June, September, and December (MJSD).

Options Industry Council (OIC) An organization sponsored by the U.S. options exchanges to provide educational services to options traders.

options on futures Options that trade on the underlying value of futures contracts, especially futures on commodities and currencies. This is often the only way to trade options on certain commodities.

options series Puts or calls on the same underlying asset that have the same exercise price and expiration date.

out-of-the-money An option price that is not profitable to execute.

over-the-counter (OTC) option An option that does not trade on an organized exchange. These are often customized by a broker to meet a particular customer's needs.

parity The point at which an option is in the money and has no time value, which usually occurs immediately before expiration.

partial fill An order to buy or sell an option that cannot be executed in its entire amount, so only a part of the order is completed.

pattern day trader   A brokerage customer who executes four or more day trades within 5 business days, provided that the number of day trades represents more than 6 percent of the customer's total trades in the margin account for that same 5-business-day period.

pennant   A chart pattern in technical analysis that shows a short-term deviation from a trend.

physical delivery   In the futures market, the practice of delivering the underlying asset instead of the cash value at expiration.

pin risk   The risk to the writer of an option that the price of the underlying asset will be at or near the option's strike price at the time of expiration.

pivot point   The average of the high, low, and closing prices from the previous trading period, used in technical analysis to measure an overall trend.

position limit   The maximum number of contracts that any one account holder can have in the same underlying asset. May be set by either the exchange or the brokerage firm.

premium   The price of the derivative.

price improvement   The ability of a broker to help a customer buy at a lower price or sell at a higher price than at the time the order was placed.

probability of ruin   A key concept in trading money management that measures the likelihood of a single trade wiping out an account.

protective put   A put option purchased by the owner of the underlying asset as insurance against a price decline.

put   An option that gives the holder the right, but not the obligation, to sell a security to someone else at a predetermined price on a predetermined date.

put-call parity   The normal situation in the market, in which the underlying asset price is the same as the price of a long call plus a short put, assuming the same strike price and expiration.

put-call ratio   The number of put options divided by the number of call options written on a particular underlying asset. The more puts that are being purchased, the more people are betting that the market is going to fall.

pyramid scheme   An investment scheme in which the people at the top are paid by those at the bottom. It's not relevant to options trading at all, except as a reminder that frauds abound in finance to take advantage of people who expect something for nothing.

pyramiding   A system of money management in which you borrow against profits to try to increase the amount of gains from trading.

repurchase agreement   An agreement to sell an asset and then buy it back at a predetermined (and usually higher) price at a predetermined date in the future.

retracement   A temporary price change within a longer trend.

reversal   A change in the direction of a price trend. Also known as a *reverse conversion.*

reverse head-and-shoulders   A technical chart formation of three valleys in a row, which is considered an indicator of a price increase.

rho   The Greek letter used for the sensitivity of options to a change in interest rates.

risk-free rate of interest   The interest rate on an investment that will be repaid with certainty. The U.S. government bond rate is usually used at the risk-free rate.

roll   A trade that involves closing out an open option position while at the same time establishing a new one at a different strike price.

sale contingency   An option included in some real estate sales that gives the potential buyer the right to pay money to walk away from the sale if their current house does not sell in a given period of time.

scalping   A trading strategy that looks to make a large number of short-term trades with small profits based mostly on volatility of the bid-ask spread.

sell-limit order   A sell order placed with the broker for a financial asset with instructions to execute it only if a predetermined price is met or exceeded.

sell-to-close   An order to that tells a broker to sell an option in order to close out an existing position.

sell-to-open   An order that tells a broker to sell an option in order to establish a new option position.

sentiment indicator   A metric used to help options traders and other market observers discern whether prices will be going up or going down.

settlement price   The price at which a trade is finalized.

Sharpe ratio   A measure of investment performance that shows the risk-adjusted rate of return.

short sell   A trade that involves borrowing an asset, selling it on the market, and then repaying it with more of the asset purchased later. If the future price is lower, the short seller keeps the profit between the price of the sale and the price of the repurchase made to cover the position.

short straddle   The sale of a call and a put with the same strike price. It pays off if the price of the underlying asset increases or decreases significantly. *See also* straddle; long straddle.

short strangle   The sale of a call with one strike price and a put with a lower strike price. It pays off if the price of the underlying asset increases or decreases significantly. *See also* strangle; long strangle.

short   The trading term used to designate selling a position.

single-stock option   An option on shares of a particular stock.

slope   The amount a line varies from being perfectly vertical or perfectly horizontal; used to measure the rate of change.

speculator   A trader who looks to take risk to make a profit.

spot price   The price of an asset as it is currently quoted in the market.

standard deviation   A statistical measure of how much a given return on investment differs from the average return, used as a way to measure volatility.

stop order   An order that tells the broker to stop buying or selling an asset as soon as a specific price level is hit. Also known as a *stop-loss order.*

stop-limit order   An order that tells the broker to start executing at a given price or better and then stop the execution as soon as another price level is hit.

straddle   An options trade that involves buying a call and a put with the same strike price. It is a play on volatility. *See also* long straddle; short straddle.

strangle   An options trade that involves buying a call with one strike price and a put with a lower strike price. It is a play on volatility. *See also* long strangle; short strangle.

strap   A risk-management transaction used by institutional options traders. It involves two long calls and one long put.

strike price   The price at which an option can be exercised. Also known as the *exercise price.*

strip   A risk-management transaction used by institutional options traders. It involves two long puts and one long call.

swap   A transaction that involves trading a series of payments, such as trading fixed-rate interest payments for floating-rate interest payments.

swaption   An option on a swap.

swing trader   A trader who holds positions for more than a day but usually for only a few days or weeks.

synthetic security   An option position that mimics the payoff of the underlying asset.

theta   The rate at which an option's price changes relative to the passage of time.

time value   The amount of an option's price that is related to the amount of time left to expiration. The longer the amount of time remaining, the more valuable the option.

time-weighted return   Also known as the *compound average annual growth rate,* this involves multiplying all the numbers in a series together and then taking it by the root of the number of items in the series. This is used to consider compounding.

underlying asset   The asset on which an option's value is drawn. It may a common stock, a market index, a commodity future, or even a characteristic of the market such as volatility.

underlying price   The price of the asset on which an option is written, and a key component in the price of an option.

value at risk   A statistical measure of the amount of money that could be lost on a given trade, used to track option trading risk as well as design hedging positions.

vega   The Greek term used to show the sensitivity of an option price to a change in the volatility of the option's underlying asset. It is denoted by the Greek letter nu.

VIX   The Chicago Board Options Exchange's index on the volatility of options on the Standard & Poor's 500 Index. It is used as a measure of expected volatility in the financial markets, and there are options that trade on the VIX itself.

volatility   How much the price of an underlying asset is likely to change, often measured by standard deviation.

volatility cone   A technical indicator used in options trading. It looks at the amount of implied volatility in an option's price over different time periods.

wash sale   The sale of an asset and the repurchase of a substantially similar one within 30 days.

weekly   An option that expires each Friday. Weekly options have very little time value.

wheel trade   The use of a short put option to establish a position in an underlying asset and the use of a short call to sell it.

writer   The trader who sells an option.

Resources

As much as I and the editors of this book would love for it to be comprehensive, there's only so much we can do. Options trading is complex, and you might find you need more information. These are some great resources for you.

Books

There are so many great books and other publications written about the financial industry and used by people in it that this is only a sampling. It includes books that I used in writing this book, that I especially liked, or that will give you more information about critical topics.

Barron's Dictionary of Finance and Investment Terms
by John Downes and Jordan Elliott Goodman
This dictionary is not published by the same company as *Barron's* weekly newspaper, but it is an indispensible resource for investors. The dictionary is a useful guide to technical terms and jargon that you will come across while trading, and it gives precise technical definitions of terms that are often thrown around with the assumption that the reader already knows what they mean.

The Black Swan: The Impact of the Highly Improbable, Second Edition
by Nassim Nicholas Taleb
This is a bestseller with a lot of insight into volatility. He discusses the effects of what he calls "Black Swan" events, unpredictable events with low probability and profound effects on financial markets. Examples include 9/11, earthquakes, and asteroid impacts. Taleb asserts that change occurs in spurts, not along a gradual continuum, and demonstrates this notion with lively writing and entertaining examples. His basic thesis is that the world is dominated by essentially random unpredictable events, and our efforts to predict the future based on the past are a fool's errand.

Chicago Board of Trade Handbook of Futures and Options
Chicago Board of Trade
This is an old but useful guide to futures and options trading written by the folks who have been doing it since 1848. It describes the history of derivative products and explores some of the unprecedented changes that electronic trading has brought to the marketplace. Helpful to beginners and more seasoned professionals alike, the guide gives a good overview of the basics and also discusses more complex and sophisticated strategies. Look for it at your library.

Calculus Made Easy
by Silvanus Thompson
Even though this book was published so long ago, it remains superior to every book on calculus published after it. The key options variables—delta, gamma, vega, theta—all come from calculus. You don't need to know calculus to trade options, but this book will give you a little more insight into the meaning of price movements. At a minimum, it will explain what you never quite grasped back in high school math class.

Fortune's Formula: The Untold Story of the Scientific Betting System That Beat the Casinos and Wall Street
by William Poundstone
This book tells the story of Bell Lab scientists and a gaming theory professor at MIT who developed numerical methods such as counting cards and strategies for gambling on roulette to game the gaming industry and then turned their sights on Wall Street to amass personal fortunes. The Kelly criterion system of money management is one result of their efforts. The book is not a rigorous treatment of the theoretical merits of the criterion, but more an enthusiastic recounting of true stories about a colorful cast of characters who applied the formula to an assortment of enterprises with varying degrees of success.

The Handbook of Portfolio Mathematics: Formulas for Optimal Allocation and Leverage
by Ralph Vince
Vince is a programmer who worked for some hedge funds and then put together this mathematical treatment of trading techniques. He's written a few different books; this one distills the essential elements of his earlier books on application of mathematics to portfolio management and risk management. It also presents various trading models and means to create other models. Vince especially emphasizes money management. This is a great guide for those looking to develop their own trading systems.

Investments, Tenth Edition
by Zvi Bodie, Alex Kane, and Alan J. Marcus
A solid standard text, this basic guide to investment fundamentals is used in many college MBA classes. The book focuses more deeply on options, futures, and other complex security derivatives than its peers. It is probably more theoretical and detailed than any options trader needs, but I used it as a reference in writing this book.

IRS Publication 550, "Investment Income and Expenses"
All you need to know about options and income taxes, in excruciating detail, updated for each tax year. This is complicated, and it may not answer your question, but it will provide the guidance you and your tax adviser need to keep you on the level with the feds.

Options as a Strategic Investment, Sixth Edition
by Lawrence McMillan
This is a good, thorough, theoretical overview of options trading. It's a good next step after reading this book, as it targets experienced and advanced options traders. The book includes many proven techniques and detailed guidance for options trading in a variety of market environments. The latest edition has an expanded section on market volatility.

Options: Essential Concepts and Trading Strategies, Third Edition
The Options Institute
This authoritative reference manual is produced by the Options Institute, the educational branch of the Chicago Board Options Exchange, and gives a comprehensive description of the options marketplace. This manual covers the territory from basic to advanced trading strategies, discusses pricing and risk, and includes the different perspectives of individual investors and institutional investors.

The Options Playbook
by Brian Overby and TradeKing
The Options Playbook is a lovely, spiral-bound book that sets out the basics of options trading. In particular, it has clear payoff diagrams for just about every strategy you could ever use, along with a clear description of how it works. It's a practical guide to putting together a position, and especially good for those who will be trading options frequently.

Taxes and Investing: A Guide for the Individual Investor
The Options Industry Council
This guide was prepared by the staff of Ernst and Young, now known as EY, and it is available on the Chicago Board Options Exchange website. It is a detailed guide to the tax liabilities and preferences generated by different investment transactions, especially those involving options.

The Trading Game: Playing by the Numbers to Make Millions
by Ryan Jones
Money management is a key aspect of successful trading, and this book sets out the details of money management and risk management to help traders improve. It's a great guide for those who want to learn more about the topic and reduce some of their trading risks.

The W. D. Gann Master Commodity Course: Original Commodity Market Trading Course
by W. D. Gann
The commodity trading course presents W. D. Gann's methods of commodity trading using a variety of geometric, charting, and trend analysis techniques, which he developed from the 1920s through the 1950s. Gann was a Freemason, and his many forecasting methods include astronomical and astrological systems which remain controversial, though potentially useful. Some traders swear by them; many other use his money management system and ignore the rest.

Zero Sum Game: The Risk of the World's Largest Derivatives Exchange
by Erika S. Olson
Olson worked at the Chicago Board of Trade during its merger with the Chicago Mercantile Exchange. This was a major transaction in the world of derivatives, and it included a bidding war and lots of political intrigue. If you're interested in the industry and its history, this is a fun read about a pivotal event.

Movies and Television

This is a small section, yes, but it's not empty! Here's the cable channel and the movie that illuminate the world of trading.

CNBC
CNBC.com
CNBC is a cable and online news network that is a long staple of traders. Some of the programming is sensational, but other aspects of it are really useful. And, a lot of traders like having up-to-the-minute financial news reporting on in the background while they work.

Trading Places (1983)
This movie, starring Dan Aykroyd and Eddie Murphy, has one of the best depictions of open outcry trading anywhere. This is a comedy about two rich brothers who own a commodity trading firm and mess with the lives of Aykroyd's and Murphy's characters as part of a bet. The aggrieved men get their revenge by manipulating the market for frozen orange juice contracts. This is a lot of fun, and a little bit educational. Even though open outcry is mostly obsolete, it still takes place, and it still influences the trading culture.

Newspapers and Other Publications

The news industry and the financial industry are close, because traders need good news. (Several major market indexes, such as the Dow Jones Industrial Average, were invented by publishing companies to sell newspapers.) Here are a few to check out.

Barron's

barrons.com

Barron's is a financial newspaper focused almost exclusively on financial markets. The paper is published weekly, but *Barron's* also has a website with more current information. The paper includes weekly discussions of the previous week's events and a roundtable discussion surveying the opinions and predictions of various financial gurus, along with book reviews, opinion pieces, and profiles of financial instruments and finance professionals. Its annual review of online brokers is a must-read if you're shopping for a new broker.

Bloomberg

bloomberg.com

Bloomberg's website is full of detailed news about business and finance. It's a great source for breaking financial news. The company sells high-end terminals to traders, and it also has a huge news service to go with it.

The Economist

economist.com

The Economist is a London-based weekly newsmagazine that provides some of the best reporting on financial issues and emerging markets anywhere. It covers the news from an economic perspective, and it offers regular analysis and opinion on economic indicators. It is owned in part by the Rothschild family of banking fame. The magazine (and website) covers world events and politics in addition to economic news, but nevertheless remains a useful source of economic information and metrics.

Financial Times

ft.com

Financial Times is a London-based daily newspaper printed on pink-ish paper. It also operates a website that focuses on economic and financial news. It is a competitor to *The Wall Street Journal* and largely serves the same niche, though with a more Eurocentric slant.

Investor's Business Daily

investors.com

Investor's Business Daily is a financial newspaper that has a special focus on stock trading. It was founded by William O'Neil, who developed a system of technical analysis for stock trading. This will be of most interest to traders who work in single-stock options.

Reuters

reuters.com

Reuters operates a business newswire, and many brokerage firm trading platforms collect stories from it. It also has a good website with global business news. This is a place for almost real-time facts and press releases to keep you up to date on what's happening as it happens.

Traders Magazine

tradersmagazine.com

This magazine and website cover news specific to traders. It's less about strategies and more about the structure of the market. Given how fast the markets are changing, that makes it really useful for serious traders.

The Wall Street Journal

wsj.com

I almost wasn't sure if I needed to mention the *Journal* here. It's ubiquitous in the financial world because it's good; in addition to its U.S. business coverage, it has strong English-language coverage of Asian markets.

Websites

Benzinga

benzinga.com

Benzinga is a website aimed at traders. It includes podcasts, internet radio, news stories, and columns covering market issues and trading ideas. It's a good way to see what other traders are thinking, which can help guide your trading and give you insights beyond what you get from your own trade diary.

CBOE Options Institute

cboe.com/learncenter

The Chicago Board Options Exchange has an extensive selection of information about options trading for people at just about every level with just about every need. Most of the programs are free, too. The website has articles, webinars, news updates, and other information to help you learn and refine trading.

Investopedia

investopedia.com

Investopedia is a broad, web-based resource focused on all aspects of investing. The website includes tutorials, a financial dictionary, test prep services, trading simulation software, quotes, and articles. It is a tremendous resource whether you know what you are looking for or are just interested in poking around.

Khan Academy

khanacademy.org

The Khan Academy is a nonprofit educational 501(c)(3) organization with the mission to provide educational materials about math and science on a web platform for free. The Finance and Capital Markets section of the Khan Academy website has an entire section with some 40+

short college lecture-style YouTube videos about options, futures, and other derivatives. Like a college course, the lectures start with the basics and become increasingly more complex and sophisticated.

The Options Insider

theoptionsinsider.com

This website offers news, analysis, and podcasts on everything related to options trading. It has a lot of really good and current news and information to help you adapt your trading to the current state of the markets.

Options Industry Council

optionseducation.org

Funded by all of the options exchanges, the Option Industry Council's education programs are extensive, and they are free. The goal is to train people to use options successfully so they keep trading. It has a lot of good, free online classes and information that will fill in the gaps for all but the most sophisticated traders.

The Root of All

therootofall.com

This is my own blog. The love of money may be the root of all evil, but money has a huge role in our lives. It covers all sorts of money-related topics, including some news and analysis on options trading.

SeekingAlpha

seekingalpha.com

This website for traders and investors features contributions from industry professionals about trade ideas and current market news. The bias is toward the stock market, but those working in other markets will find usable information, too.

TradeXchange

thetradeXchange.com

TradeXchange is mostly a paid website for serious options traders, although there are some free blog posts and videos. The paid website includes a forum for traders to discuss the markets, free of a lot of the trolling and touting that takes place on a lot of free trading forums.

Index